University Access and Success

The challenge of widening access and participation in higher education in a manner that ensures students are successful in their studies is a major issue globally and a significant research-focus within higher education studies and higher education policy. Similarly, the challenge of under-preparedness of students entering higher education has become increasingly pertinent as universities in both developed and developing countries struggle to improve their throughput rates in a context in which schooling no longer seems to provide sufficient preparation for entering university.

In this book Merridy Wilson-Strydom applies the capabilities approach to better understand university access and participation and draws on a rich case study from South Africa to critically and innovatively explore the complex and contradictory terrain of access with success. The book integrates quantitative and qualitative research with theory and practical application to provide a new framework for considering and improving the transition from school to university.

University Access and Success will appeal to academics and researchers in the field of higher education internationally. The book also contributes to the growing body of international and comparative scholarship on the capabilities approach in higher education and will therefore be of value to higher education practitioners, such as those working in the promotion of teaching and learning, higher education quality assurance, institutional research and student affairs.

Merridy Wilson-Strydom is Senior Research Fellow in the Centre for Research on Higher Education and Development at the University of the Free State in Bloemfontein, South Africa.

University Access and Success

Capabilities, diversity and social justice

Merridy Wilson-Strydom

LONDON AND NEW YORK

First published 2015
by Routledge
2 Park Square, Milton Park, Abingdon, Oxon OX14 4RN

and by Routledge
711 Third Avenue, New York, NY 10017

Routledge is an imprint of the Taylor & Francis Group, an informa business

© 2015 Merridy Wilson-Strydom

British Library Cataloguing in Publication Data
A catalogue record for this book is available from the British Library

Library of Congress Cataloging in Publication Data
A catalog record for this book has been requested

ISBN: 978-1-138-01777-1 (hbk)
ISBN: 978-1-315-78021-4 (ebk)

Typeset in Baskerville
by RefineCatch Limited, Bungay, Suffolk

For Liam and Matthew – may you be conscious of the injustices around you and work for change where you can.

Contents

8 University access for success 150

Illustrations

Acknowledgements

The research on which this book draws was conducted between 2009 and early 2014. There are thus many people who participated in and contributed to the research, both directly and indirectly. First of all, I would like to express my sincerest gratitude to all the high school learners, first-year students, school principals and teachers, and university lecturers for participating with such enthusiasm and willingness. For funding that supported elements of the study, I am grateful to the Ford Foundation and the Council for the Development of Social Science in Africa (CODESRIA). Research assistance was provided by Evelyn Siyoko, Laura Drennan, Evodia Motsokobi, Sikelewa (Skye) Ntsokota, and Lisa Drennan. Thank you too to Merlene Esau and Anneline Keet for inviting me to work with the first-year social work students.

Driekie Hay has been a constant pillar of support for my work in higher education over many years, and I am ever grateful for her guidance and friendship. To all my friends and colleagues from the Directorate for Institutional Research and Academic Planning (DIRAP) who have helped and supported me in so many different ways, I thank you. The following deserve special mention: Anneri Meintjes, Beate Gadinger and Pearl Mogatle. Lis Lange provided helpful and astute commenting on early versions of this work. Since 2013, I have been fortunate to participate in the Vice Chancellor's Prestige Scholar Programme (PSP). Thanks are due to Jonathan Jansen, Jackie du Toit, Neil Roos and Corli Witthuhn for their encouragement with the project of writing this book. The PSP writing retreats provided a wonderfully productive space for writing, and for receiving helpful comments.

I first encountered the capabilities approach and human development ideas in 1999 when I was an MPhil student in the Oxford Department of International Development. I am grateful for this early introduction and for the foundational concepts that I learnt at that time. Now, fifteen years later, I find myself in the enviable position of working in the newly formed Centre for Research on Higher Education and Development (CRHED) at the University of the Free State, South Africa. CRHED was founded and is led by Melanie Walker. The intellectual environment that Melanie has created at CRHED is phenomenal and has had an immense impact on my thinking. Through CRHED activities, I have had the opportunity to discuss ideas and questions with several key scholars in the fields of capabilities and higher education research. I am particularly grateful for the insightful inputs Monica McLean made to this research, and to Sandra Boni for helpful discussions about participatory research and visual methods. To all the postgraduate students and post-doctoral fellows in CRHED with whom I have been privileged to share such interesting and thought-provoking discussions, in particular Talita Calitz, Mikateko Höppener, Oliver Mutanga, Sam Fongwa, Sonja Loots and Thandi Lewin – thank you. I would like to make special note of my gratitude to Melanie Walker for being such an inspiring role model and mentor, and for welcoming me to CRHED. Melanie has supported and commented on this work from early drafts and actively encouraged me to write this book.

Special recognition and thanks are due to my parents, Mike and Gill Wilson, for always encouraging me to do and be the best I can and for setting such a good example of what hard work and self-discipline mean. My parents-in-law, Kalie and Alida Strydom, have also supported me in various ways. Even though we do not always agree on the details, Kalie Strydom's knowledge of and passion for higher education has been an important inspiration for me over the years. Special thanks are due to my husband, Francois, for being a constructively critical sounding board for my ideas, for his fabulous support and contribution in our home and for always believing that I could write this book, even when I felt doubtful. To my two lively little boys – Liam and Matthew – thank you for your unconditional love, boundless energy and enthusiasm for life and especially for asking difficult, but very pertinent questions, such as 'But why do you even want to write a book Mommy?' I hope the dedication answers this question.

Abbreviations

ACT	America College Test
AP	Advanced Placement
CAPS	Curriculum Assessment Policy Statement
CHE	Council on Higher Education
DHET	Department of Higher Education and Training
GNP	Gross National Product
HDI	Human Development Index
HDR	Human Development Report
HSC	Higher socioeconomic context
LSC	Lower socioeconomic context
MoE	Ministry of Education
NACAC	National Association for College Admissions Counselling
NBTs	National Benchmark Tests
NCHEMS	National Centre for Higher Education Management Systems
NSC	National Senior Certificate
NSFAS	National Student Financial Aid Scheme
OBE	Outcomes-based Education
OECD	Organisation for Economic Co-operation and Development
SA	South Africa
SAT	Scholastic Aptitude Test
SPSS	Statistical Package for the Social Sciences
SRC	Student Representative Council
UC	University of California
UCT	University of Cape Town
UK	United Kingdom
US	United States

1 Introduction

[T]he world in which we live is not only unjust, it is, arguably, extraordinarily unjust.

(Sen 2006, 237–238)

In September 2010, as part of the multi-year study that this book draws on, I asked first-year students enrolled at a South African university to draw a picture of their experience of coming to university. These drawings visually highlighted the diversity of experiences and powerfully expressed the injustices faced by many students. Consider the following two drawings as illustrative examples:

Can c the whole world
before me – A new one
to experience

Drawing 1.1 The world before me

(white, female, first-year student, Health Sciences)

Drawing 1.2 Up against a brick wall

(black, male, first-year student, Economic and Management Sciences)

These two drawings place in stark contrast the capabilities of two young people entering the same university. For one student, a world of opportunities are visible and await, for the other, a brick wall hides any vision of what might be in the future, and stands between the student and possible success. As such, these two drawings highlight major differences in the quality of life or well-being of these two students. How are we to interpret this from a social justice point of view? And, even more importantly, what can be done to break down the brick walls that limit some students' chances of success? Situated within an overarching commitment to fair and just education, and particularly higher education, in this book I attempt to answer these perplexing questions. This has been done by focusing on the transition from school to university, through the lens of the capabilities approach as developed by Amartya Sen and Martha Nussbaum (Nussbaum 2000, 2011; Sen 1993, 1999). The capabilities approach provides a framework for seeking to understand what young people entering universities are able to be and to do and what limits their being and doing, and so requires us to develop a more nuanced understanding of the agency and well-being of students admitted to university.

This has been an ambitious project, since my starting assumption was that it is not possible to fully understand access to university – and more specifically, the experience of the transition from school to university – by researching only one of either the schooling or university sectors. As such, this book draws on empirical research that has encompassed an exploration of the school to university transition from the perspective of high school and university students, a unique contribution in the access literature. The outcome of the research is the formulation of a capabilities-based social justice framework for the transition to university. Drawing on this framework, universities and schools can identity targeted interventions for working towards better preparing prospective students while they are at school, through a focus on building transition to university capabilities.

This book contributes to the fields of higher education and the capabilities approach in at least four ways, by (1) sharing the perspectives of high school learners and first-year university students on the transition from school to university; (2) expanding the capabilities and higher education literatures with a specific focus on access (widening participation) and the transition from school to university; (3) demonstrating how the theoretical concepts of the capabilities approach can be operationalised and empirically applied in a specific higher education context; and (4) providing a framework that schools and universities could use/adapt to support students making the transition to university.

Dilemmas of access

The universities in which we work, located as they are within an 'extraordinarily unjust' (Sen 2006, 238) world, are themselves 'extraordinarily unjust'. Arguably, broadening access without meaningfully providing conditions for success is one way in which this injustice is manifest. This section is headed 'Dilemmas of access' to highlight the fact that, despite decades of research on access related issues, this terrain remains deeply problematic, and unjust, within most university systems across the world. Researchers and practitioners have yet to identify ways to break down the brick walls many students face when entering university (see Drawing 1.2), despite the progress that has been made. It is thus necessary to find new ways of thinking about these access dilemmas, and I propose that the capabilities approach provides one means of doing so. Although university access in South Africa provides the empirical and contextual foundation on which my argument is constructed, the dilemmas of access are certainly not unique to South Africa. Increasing access to higher education and improving students' chances of success in their university studies have been, and continue to be, an important research focus within higher education studies and higher education policy in South Africa and beyond. In the past decade, South Africans have witnessed how the challenge of under-preparedness of students entering higher education has increasingly dominated public and academic discourses, as universities struggle to improve their throughput rates in a context in which schooling no longer provides sufficient preparation for entering university. This challenge has also been gaining prominence in higher education literature globally. These international and national trends, as well as student performance at the case study university itself, highlight the importance of understanding how levels of preparedness impact on success at university and efforts towards building a more just system. Current debates, and the extensive literatures on access issues, can be usefully grouped into four main thematic areas, namely: access and success/graduation, access and socioeconomic contexts, access and schooling, and access and readiness. In the following sections, I provide a brief overview of each thematic area in the international and South African contexts, as a means of setting the scene for the arguments that follow in the rest of the book.

Access and success/graduation

Student success and retention is a challenge experienced by universities globally, and much has been written on the topic of retention. Although it is not my intention to cover the broad field of student retention and success, it is useful to consider the extent of the challenges faced, to put the present study into context. The National Centre for Higher Education Management Systems (NCHEMS) reports that, of the 2009 cohort of freshman (first-year college students) in the North American higher education system, between 64.4 per cent and 82.7 per cent continue on to their second year of study.[1] The average three-year graduation rate[2] across all states in the United States (US) was 29.2 per cent in 2009, and the six-year graduation rate[3] was 55.5 per cent.[4] For students in the United Kingdom (UK) (both mature and young entrants), the Higher Education Statistics Agency reports that the non-completion rate from first-year to second year was 12.9 per cent for the 2011/2012 entrants.[5] The graduation rate in the UK was 38.7 per cent in 2007 (OECD 2010). In the European context, Denmark is the most successful with about 80 per cent completion, while Italy, Hungary and Poland have the lowest completion rates (e.g. 46 per cent for Italy) (Quinn 2013). In the South African context, the retention rate from first to second year is about 70 per cent, only 44 per cent of students complete a three-year degree after five years of study, and an estimated 15,000 students from the 2000/2001 cohort of first-year students were 'lost' to the system, i.e. were no longer enrolled at university and did not graduate (Scott 2008, 2010). The graduation rate for South African universities averages at about 17 per cent (CHE 2012). Further interrogation of the South African data highlights the diversity-related injustices that continue to plague the higher education system, even though the country is 20 years into democracy. Three national cohort studies conducted since 2000 have shown the ongoing and major disparities in both access and success based on race. So great are the inequities that only about 5 per cent of black youth in South Africa are currently succeeding in any form of higher education (CHE 2013). The impact of learning in environments, embedded within a complex history of unjust social structures and institutional cultures which still remain divided across a multitude of social dimensions, is clear.

Access and socioeconomic context

Access and success is also greatly influenced by class or socioeconomic context divisions. There is much evidence to support this claim from studies conducted in different countries and contexts. Notable examples from the UK include the work of Furlong and Cartmel (2009) and Archer et al.'s (2003) edited book, focused on social class and higher education. Quinn (2013) has tackled similar issues in the

European context and Marginson (2011) in the Australian context. Across all of these studies, we see that students from poorer socioeconomic backgrounds are most likely to drop out of university, or to perform relatively poorly compared to those from wealthier socioeconomic contexts.

Similar patterns are seen in South Africa. In many cases, the students making up the cohort of the unsuccessful within South African universities are those from poor backgrounds who then find themselves in debt and without a qualification. For example, the 2010 review of the National Student Financial Aid Scheme (NSFAS) reported a 72 per cent dropout rate for students with NSFAS support (DHET 2010, xiv). When the NSFAS review was carried out, there were more than 10,000 NSFAS borrowers who were blacklisted by credit agencies, although there have been moves afoot more recently to remove students from credit bureau listings (DHET 2010, xviii). Sen warns that 'the power to do good almost always goes with the possibility to do the opposite' (Sen 1999, xiii). In many respects, widening participation without putting in place mechanisms to support success is doing just this – increasing access to university for those previously excluded but also creating a generation of unsuccessful and further indebted young people.

Access and schooling

Although student success is a complex phenomenon with many influencing factors, one of the key issues highlighted by decades of research globally is that of pre-university preparation or quality of schooling (Conley 2005; Kuh et al. 2007; Pascarella and Terenzini 2005). The state of schooling in South Africa has been the focus of much attention and critique for several years, and the schooling sector continues to deal with the difficulties of transforming a deeply divided and unequally resourced education landscape. Challenges of an inappropriate curriculum, poor levels of teacher preparation, lack of resources in schools, the absence of a culture of teaching and learning, and questionable leadership within schools and district structures have been widely documented in academic publications and popular articles. Obviously problems in the South African schooling system influence the levels of preparation of students entering higher education in the country and the effects of poor schooling are evident at many levels, yet, this is not a South African-specific phenomenon as tends to be portrayed in media reports, even though the unique historical background of the South African context creates a certain distinctiveness. The Standards for Success project that was started in 2000 in the North American context focused on identifying the specific knowledge and skills needed for success. The study showed that, in many instances, schools were preparing prospective students to meet admission criteria for college or university, but not necessarily to be successful once admitted (Conley 2005, 2008). Conley refers to this as the gap between being *eligible* and being *ready* for successful higher education study (Conley 2005, 2008). Understanding this gap and how to bridge it are critical for more socially just higher education systems.

Access and readiness

Research has pointed to a range of reasons for the gap between eligibility and readiness. This includes the extent to which students have developed important cognitive strategies for effective learning, have covered sufficient content knowledge, have acquired academic behaviours necessary for success and have the contextual skills and knowledge to understand how higher education works (Conley 2008). These factors are related to research on epistemological access which emphasises the importance of understanding disciplinary conventions that underpin what counts as knowledge and informs how knowledge is constructed (Morrow 2009a). Morrow states that 'epistemological access is learning how to become a successful participant in an academic practice' (Morrow 2009b, 78; see also Bernstein 2000). Research on epistemological access emphasises the role of personal and social histories and contextual embeddedness in the learning process. As was alluded to earlier, several authors have also highlighted the impact that demographics such as race, socioeconomic background, gender and the family's level of education have on readiness for higher education. These types of factors commonly define the contexts from which students come and within which they are functioning, and so must be understood when considering access and readiness and interventions to improve readiness (Hurtado 2010; Kuh et al. 2005, 2007; Mushi 2003; Tinto and Pusser 2006).

Several influential theories of student development and performance at university include student background and pre-university academic and social experiences as factors in their models, but less attention is directed to how universities might work with schools to improve student readiness prior to entry. Many studies focus on measurable performance, such as standardised admissions tests, or school marks (grades) and the extent to which these predict university level success (for some examples, see Bowen et al. 2009; Pascarella and Terenzini 2005). Less research has focused specifically on the interface between school and university, particularly in terms of the capabilities that entering students need to improve their chances of success, and the educationally purposeful activities required at school level for the development of students' capabilities to learn effectively and to cope with the cognitive demands of higher education. Conley summarises this challenge well when he states that 'a key problem is that the current measures of college preparation are limited in their ability to communicate to students and educators the true range of what students must do [and be] to be fully ready to succeed in college' (Conley 2008, 3).

Drawing on rich empirical data collected from high school learners and students, in this book an argument for a capabilities-informed theorisation of university access is presented, to respond to the many complexities inherent in the access domain at global and local levels. In the coming sections I briefly introduce the South African higher education context and the empirical work on which this book is based.

South African higher education in brief

South Africa's persistent patterns of political exclusion, race and class discrimination and inequality have their roots in colonialism, the emergence of the mining sector and resultant need for cheap labour. Racial discrimination was later formalised and legalised through the apartheid system of governance (Dison et al. 2008; Ross 1999). This complex history has had major implications for how the purpose of education, and higher education more specifically, were and are understood, particularly as part of state governing mechanisms. The education sector was integral to apartheid ideology and practice. Universities were defined as 'creatures of the state' and assigned specific purposes in support of the state ideology (Bunting 2002). All levels of education were differentiated on the basis of race and ethnicity. Eight different government departments controlled education institutions which resulted in even further fragmentation of the national education system. By 1994 when the new democratically elected government came into power, the country had 36 higher education institutions serving different race and ethnic groups and also offering either theoretical qualifications (universities) or vocationally oriented programmes (technikons). Through a comprehensive restructuring process, these 36 institutions were merged to form 23 institutions – eleven universities, five universities of technology and six comprehensive universities (CHE 2004, 59). Cloete (2002) describes the first two years after 1994 as 'a massive, participatory drive towards policy formation'. The culmination of the policy formation phase was the report of the National Commission on Higher Education released in 1996. The next phase included the development of the White Paper 3 – A Programme for Higher Education Transformation. Released in 1997, it was followed by the Higher Education Act 101 promulgated in the same year. From the late 1990s the focus turned to implementation of this new policy and legislative environment (Cloete 2002, 87–88; CHE 2004). The White Paper 3 specified four purposes for South African higher education (MoE 1997, 7–8):

1. To meet the learning needs and aspirations of individuals through the development of their intellectual abilities and aptitudes throughout their lives. Higher education equips individuals to make the best use of their talents and of the opportunities offered by society for self-fulfilment. It is thus a key allocator of life chances and an important vehicle for achieving equity in the distribution of opportunity and achievement among South African citizens.
2. To address the development needs of society and provide the labour market, in a knowledge driven and knowledge dependent society, with the ever-changing high-level competencies and expertise necessary for the growth and prosperity of a modern economy. Higher education teaches and trains people to fulfil specialised social functions, enter the learned professions, or pursue vocations in administration, trade, industry, science and technology and the arts.
3. To contribute to the socialisation of enlightened, responsible and constructively critical citizens. Higher education encourages the development of a reflective

capacity and a willingness to review and renew prevailing ideas, policies and practices based on a commitment to the common good.

4. To contribute to the creation, sharing and evaluation of knowledge. Higher education engages in the pursuit of academic scholarship and intellectual inquiry in all fields of human understanding, through research, learning and teaching.

In February 2001 the National Plan for Higher Education (NPHE) in South Africa was released. The NPHE outlined the framework and mechanisms through which the policy goals and transformation imperatives of the White Paper and Higher Education Act could be implemented (MoE 2001). Among others, the NPHE established indicative targets for the size and shape of the higher education system. Of particular relevance is the recommendation that the participation rate in higher education should increase from 15 per cent to 20 per cent and the strong focus on equity issues (MoE 2001). This policy environment has translated into many visible changes in the sector. For example, in terms of increasing access (massification), the system in 2010 enrolled 892,943 students, compared with 525,000 in 1994 and 394,700 in 1990 (CHE 2004, 61, 2009, 19, 2012, 1). Thus, the headcount enrolment in higher education more than doubled between 1994 and 2010. Yet, nationally, the participation rate in higher education remains at 16.3 per cent which is below the national target of 20 per cent (CHE 2010, 3). Although not yet legislated, South African higher education is currently in the midst of further policy development, this time with a broader focus on higher education and training. The White Paper for Post-School Education and Training released in late 2013 again gives central place to social justice in education, which has been positioned as one of the central policy goals (DHET 2013, 4). With respect to university access, the new White Paper calls for further growth to a participation rate of 25 per cent by 2030. Although the purposes of universities specified in the new White Paper are broadly aligned to those of the 1997 White Paper, there are some important differences of emphasis. Drawing on the country's National Development Plan (NPC 2011), the following three purposes of universities are specified:

*   Universities educate and provide people with high level skills for the labour market;
*   Universities are the dominant producers of new knowledge, they assess and find applications for existing knowledge, and they validate knowledge and values through their curricula; and
*   Universities provide opportunities for social mobility and strengthen social justice and democracy, thus helping to overcome the inequalities inherited from our apartheid past.

(DHET 2013, 27)

On paper then, South Africa defines the purpose of higher education in what we might call a socially progressive manner that positions higher education as a public good. However, in practice, there is a complex tension between the goals of the country's dominant model of neoliberal economic development and those related to social equity and redress (Badat 2007; Dison et al. 2008; Fataar 2003; Waghid 2009). Arguably, the neoliberal human capital formation role of higher education has been given greatest emphasis in South African higher education practice at national and institutional levels, although a public good discourse remains evident. In this light, the change in ordering of the core purposes of universities from the 1997 to the 2013 White Paper, to place skills development for the labour market upfront, is telling. This neoliberal approach to university education, even when placed within a broader social justice agenda, has had critical consequences for access to university, as outlined in greater detail in Chapter 2.

South African schooling in brief

The growing disintegration of quality schooling in South Africa (except for a small number of independent and semi-independent ex-Model C[6] schools serving a tiny minority of learners) has been well documented. Further, much has been written about the history of South Africa's education system and the transition process since the fall of apartheid (for some examples, see Bloch 2009; Christie 2008, 2004; Fiske and Ladd 2004; Taylor et al. 2003; Vanderyar and Jansen 2008). Like higher education, the school system, up until the early 1990s, had been firmly designed along racial and ethnic lines, with an explicitly ideological approach to curriculum. Christian Nationalist Education was for white South Africans, premised on 'a practice of racial domination, obedience to authority and education as preparation for rule' (Bloch 2009, 44), and Bantu Education was for black South Africans where 'education was for obedience in a divided society and economy that seemed to feed blacks only the morsels of what South Africa had to offer' (Bloch 2009, 44). The management of schooling was fragmented into 18 different departments, formed, administered and funded on a racial basis. Spending on the education of white children was approximately ten times the spending on education for black children (Fiske and Ladd 2004). As a result, schools designated for black children were severely underfunded, poorly resourced, overcrowded and with a teaching staff who were poorly trained (Chisholm 2004). These deeply problematic schooling environments become further complicated as education itself became a site of anti-apartheid struggle. In particular, educational resistance centred on the vastly unequal schooling system, ideologically bound approach to curriculum and pedagogy, and being forced to learn in Afrikaans, all within the context of growing resistance to the overarching apartheid apparatus.

From 1994, the schooling landscape was drastically reformed. This included the restructuring of the 18 racially-divided education departments into nine provincially-based departments, a completely revised approach to budgeting designed to support the achievement of equitable educational outcomes. There was a decentralisation of educational control and all educational institutions were opened up to all race groups. In the schooling context, these changes were specified in the South African Schools Act of 1996 (Republic of South Africa 1996). The preamble states that:

> this country requires a new national system for schools which will redress past injustices in educational provision, provide an education of progressively high quality for all learners and in so doing lay a strong foundation for the development of all our people's talents and capabilities, advance the democratic transformation of society, combat racism and sexism and all other forms of unfair discrimination and intolerance, contribute to the eradication of poverty and the economic well-being of society, protect and advance our diverse cultures and languages, uphold the rights of all learners, parents and educators, and promote their acceptance of responsibility for the organisation, governance and funding of schools in partnership with the State.
>
> (Republic of South Africa 1996, 1)

The various policy and curricula changes that have followed, have in one way or another, sought to contribute to the achievement of this ideal, although in practice often the opposite has resulted. One particularly contested area has been that of the school curriculum. Harley and Wedekind (2004) note that the scale and extent of curriculum change seen in South African schooling is likely to be unparalleled in the history of curriculum change. One of the major problems with the newly introduced curriculum was the focus on outcome statements (outcomes based education) without any specification of content or pedagogy. The result was that the better resourced and better trained teachers were able to engage with the curriculum in more meaningful ways (or in some cases continue teaching as they always had) than more poorly resourced and poorly trained teachers could. As a result, this change contributed to growing educational inequality rather than working to undermine it (Christie 2008; Fiske and Ladd 2004). Further curriculum revisions were released in 2002, and this has formed the basis of the school curriculum being implemented during the time of data collection for this study. After 12 years of schooling, learners write the National Senior Certificate (NSC) on the basis of which admission is granted to higher education for those meeting the entry criteria. [7]

This complex historical legacy, both during and post-apartheid, has given rise to what van der Berg et al. (2011, 8) refer to as the double burden faced by poor learners in the country. While internationally there is much evidence to show that poor children attending poorer schools tend to underperform compared to their peers in better resourced schools, in South Africa this is compounded by our past. In addition to the current burden of poverty, there is also the burden of attending a school 'that still bears the scars of neglect and underfunding under the apartheid dispensation' (van der Berg et al. 2011, 8; see also, South African Institute of Race Relations 2010). Although significant expansion of the schooling system and a lengthening of the average years of education of successive age cohorts has been achieved since the early 1990s, the performance of learners has grown increasingly problematic (Simkins and Paterson 2005; van der Berg et al. 2011). Further compounding the curriculum, school resourcing, major inequalities and poor performance of learners in South African schools has been the performance of teachers and the increasingly dominant role of teacher unions in the education sector. A general lack of professionalism among many teachers, principals and education officials, particularly in poorer contexts, has been documented (for example, Bloch 2009; Colditz et al. 2009).

While it is tempting for universities to argue that addressing the myriad problems in the schooling sector is not the work of a university, this is somewhat short sighted. Obviously resolving these deep running problems in South African schools is going to require major changes across various levels of society, from individual learners and teachers, to families and communities, government, private sector and trade unions. Nonetheless, this does not mean higher education has no role to play. Work on the transition to university must be located within this highly unequal and relatively low performing school sector. At the least, this requires that universities consider their own readiness to provide access to students leaving a poor quality schooling sector, as well as identify innovative ways to work with schools to better prepare learners for university by building capabilities for a successful transition, and, perhaps then, in a small way at least, also potentially contribute to school improvement.

Introducing the study

This book draws on empirical data collected during a multi-year study that took place between May 2009 and February 2014. Against the background of the many socially unjust outcomes of widening access sketched earlier (and elaborated on in Chapter 2), the study was guided by four research questions:

1. How do first-year university students experience the transition to university?
2. How do high school learners in their last three years of high school experience the process of preparation for and access to university?
3. How can these experiences of the interface of school and university be theorised using a capabilities-based social justice framework?
4. What interventions might support efforts towards a more socially just transition to university?

The study focused on one university in South Africa and a sample of 20 local high schools, selected in partnership with the provincial Department of Education. Situated within a pragmatist research paradigm, the study made use of an integrated, parallel mixed methods research design (Teddlie and Tashakkori 2009). A total of 2,816 high school learners in their final three years of schooling completed a largely quantitative survey focused on educational practices at school. The survey included Likert-scale items about types of educational practices emphasised at schools, time spent on various activities both within and outside of school, opportunities for interactions with diverse peers and with teachers, and a series of demographic questions including details of parental/guardian's levels of education (Wilson-Strydom and Hay 2010; Wilson-Strydom 2014). Selected from this large quantitative sample, a group of 33 high school learners participated in a week-long holiday programme that focused on preparing for university. During this holiday programme, a wide range of qualitative data was collected, including learners' written responses about their university knowledge and expectations of university (Wilson-Strydom 2014).

At the university level, I worked with first-year students in 2009 and 2010, using focus group discussions as well as visual methodologies (Wilson-Strydom 2014). In 2009, ten focus group discussions took place, each of approximately one hour duration. The discussions were focused on exploring students' experiences of coming to university, as well as the extent to which students felt that their schools prepared them for university. The data collection process in 2010 made use of visual methods to delve deeper into students' transition experiences. After completing a short demographic questionnaire, students were asked to write a paragraph describing how they experienced their first month at university. Working on a blank A3 page, students were then asked to draw a picture of their experience of coming to university. Wax crayons and coloured pens were provided. These drawing activities were done in groups, similar in composition to the 2009 focus groups. In all groups, participation was voluntary and anonymous. In order to better understand the emerging student results, a series of individual interviews were conducted with a total of 14 university lecturers who teach first-year students. These interviews provided a broader appreciation of how university readiness is understood by lecturers and what this means for approaches to teaching and learning

Drawing on all of this empirical data, a capabilities-based social justice framework for the transition to university was developed (see Chapters 6 and 7). A key part of the framework is the formulation of a list of seven capabilities that are needed for making a successful transition to university. In February 2014, these capabilities for success at university were work-shopped with the new class of first-year social work students at the case study university. This provided an additional opportunity to gather empirical data enabling further reflection on and verification of the list. The range of empirical data informing the argument presented here is summarised in Table 1.1, together with an outline of the sample size for each data collection activity, the research instruments used, and the sample demographics (see also, Wilson-Strydom 2014).

Conducting quality mixed methods research requires careful management of the range of data collected, based on the protocols of each method. In all cases, the data collection followed standard ethical procedures of voluntary participation, freedom to withdraw from the study at any time, confidentiality and anonymity. At the time of volunteering, participants were informed of how their contributions would be used in the data analysis and resultant publications. No student or high school learner names were recorded on the research instruments, so ensuring anonymity. Permission for the research was granted by the case study university and the Provincial Department of Education that has responsibility for schools in the province. Permission was requested from the school principals of the

Table 1.1 Summary of empirical data

Level of study	Type of data	Sample size	Research instruments used	Sample demographics
School level	Quantitative (Likert scale)	2,816 high school students	• South African High School Survey of Learner Engagement	• Grade 10 (37.8%), Grade 11 (32.8%), Grade 12 (29.4%) • Female (54.3%), male (45.7%) • Black (71.9%), white (24.5%), other/no response (3.6%)
	Qualitative	33 high school students (nested sampling)	• Written reflections on schooling experience and plans to attend university • 'University knowledge' questionnaire (open-ended questions)	• Grade 11 (66.7%), Grade 12 (33.3%) • Female (58.0%), male (4.2.0%) • Black (97%), white (3%)
University level	Qualitative	128 first-year university students	• Focus group interview schedule and form for demographic details	• Female (61.7%), male (38.3%) • Black (75.8%), white (24.2%) • Living in university housing (66.4%)
		142 first-year university students	• Students experience of the transition to university response sheet and A3 page for drawing	• Female (61.4%), male (38.6%) • Black (58.4%), white (38.7%), other/no response (2.9%) • Living in university housing (70.7%)
		14 lecturers teaching first-year students	• Semi-structured interview schedule	• Female (43%), male (57%) • Black (43%), white (57%) • Ten different disciplines
		23 first-year social work students	• Workshop – including group discussion of seven capabilities, and individual qualitative comments on each capability	• Female (91%), male (9%) • Black (87%), white (13%) • Living in university housing (35%)

20 participating schools and data collection took place at time that best suited each school. Each school received its own report of the data collected from the specific school for planning purposes. In all other reports and publications, including the overall report submitted to the Provincial Department of Education, no school names were used. Instead, each school was assigned a number.

The quantitative data was collected using optical scanning forms, scanned and then imported in the Statistical Package for the Social Sciences (SPSS) for cleaning and analysis. The quantitative analyses were done across all 20 schools, as well as by school type and taking high school students' demographics into account. For the purposes of this book, the quantitative data is used descriptively as a means of understanding readiness and experiences related to the transition to university. Differences across school type and by demographic grouping were explored as this was an important part of understanding the conversion factors that impacted on the transition to university (reported on in Chapter 7). The large volume of qualitative data was managed using NVivo software. All interviews and focus groups were transcribed verbatim. I conducted several rounds of qualitative coding, starting with open coding which allowed themes to emerge from the data and so ensured that I stayed as true as possible to the voices of the high school learners and university students. Following the open coding, two additional rounds of coding were done, one focused on dimensions of university readiness and the other on the capabilities framework. All qualitative data sources were analysed using the same codes, and were carefully checked and cross checked to ensure consistency and accuracy. This allowed for an integrated exploration of the responses of the high school learners and university students across the various qualitative sources.

Personal positioning

As researcher, I see myself as a participant in a research process that seeks to construct knowledge and understanding that can be of value in practice, aiming to advance social justice in higher education. When I began this study and when most of the data was collected, I was working at the case study university in the area of university access and admissions testing. During the course of the research I moved into the university's institutional research directorate where my focus was largely on access and undergraduate education. I was thus immersed in access and social justice issues. From both a personal and professional perspective, I am deeply committed to the cause of students entering university under-prepared and often with little chance of success within current university environments. I regard this as a situation of injustice. It is my commitment to a more just higher education system that provided the inspiration for this research, as I believe that workable solutions to this complex transition can be found, particularly if schools and universities can work together towards this common goal. High school learners and university students have a range of often contested perspectives; this study listens to these voices, to understand, and then present them, making an important contribution to wider awareness and policy development. The agency of each of these groups of actors is critical in working to facilitate the transition from school to university. I find that the capability approach provides a particularly powerful framework for understanding learner and student agency and, importantly, the limits placed on it by educational institutions and the broader social context. In recognition of the central importance of individual agency, I have intentionally sought to present the voices of these agents in the form of quotations and extracts from focus group discussions, students' written contributions and drawings. I trust that the voices and agency of the participating students speak out strongly through this text. My reasons for writing this book are neatly summed up by Hart, who drew substantially on the capabilities approach in her study of widening participation in higher education in England:

> [I]n terms of educational policy and pedagogy there is a possibility of simply upholding existing structures of inequality and maintaining the false image of a meritocratic society based on qualifications and credentials. Alternatively there is a possibility of emancipatory practice which attempts to expand young people's capabilities and develop opportunities for them to pursue a life they have reason to value. This requires listening to students about the constraints they identify to their well-being and agency freedoms as well as assisting them in identifying unseen barriers and constraints. It is about preparing them for the inequalities and injustices they may face and helping to equip them as far as possible to negotiate such circumstances to their best advantage.
>
> (Hart 2009, 401)

It is my aim that the research and theorisation presented here contributes, in a small way at least, to the quest for 'emancipatory practice' in the area of access to university.

Terminology

Capabilities

At the broadest level, 'capabilities' refers to opportunities people have to live the kind of life they have reason to value; in other words, opportunities for well-being (Nussbaum 2000; Sen 1999). While Sen tends to use the singular notion of 'capability' in his writing, Nussbaum explicitly uses the plural 'capabilities' to emphasise that the elements making up people's quality of life are plural and qualitatively distinct. She argues that these different elements cannot be combined into one notion, or metric, of capability (Nussbaum 2011, 18). Following this line of reasoning, and to avoid confusion, I use the term capabilities throughout. We will return to consider the meaning of capabilities and the capabilities approach in greater depth in Chapter 3; however, it is important at the outset to consider Nussbaum's distinction between internal and combined capabilities. *Combined capabilities* are the various opportunities available to a person and *internal capabilities* are the fluid and dynamic characteristics, abilities, or traits of a person. Internal capabilities are not a person's 'innate equipment' (Nussbaum 2011, 21), rather, they refer to characteristics and capacities that can be developed. Further, internal capabilities develop within familial, social, political and economic contexts which may support or undermine their development. In this sense, internal capabilities can be seen as a type of *personal power* needed to be able to function, given supportive external and social conditions (Crocker 1995, 161). This is the sense in which I am using the concept of capabilities here; as personal powers which includes skills, abilities and opportunities.

Learner/student

The distinction between learner and student, which is peculiar to the South African context, can create confusion when discussing international literature where it is common to find reference to high school students. In the South African education environment, post 1994, the term 'learner' is used to refer to those in the schooling system and the term 'student' to those learning in environments other than schools. Thus, in this book I consistently use the term learner when I am writing about schooling and student when writing about higher education, irrespective of national context.

Race

While I do not subscribe to racial classification, the extent of injustice remaining following the long legacy of racial classification in the country demands that these categories be used (with care) when arguing for a more socially just higher education system. Rather than using the problematic, and somewhat arbitrary, apartheid-based categorisation of African, Coloured, Indian and White, I make use of the terms 'black' and 'white' only. When used in this manner, the concept of black includes all who do not fall into the historically privileged group known as white.

Social justice

Falling within the intersecting realms of philosophy, politics and legal theory, social justice is a topic that has received attention from various perspectives. Miller (1999) provides a useful definition as a starting point for sketching a theoretical landscape of social justice in relation to higher education:

> When we talk and argue about social justice, what exactly are we talking and arguing about? Very crudely, I think, we are discussing how the good and bad things in life should be distributed among the members of a human society. When, more concretely, we attack some policy or some state of affairs as (being) socially unjust, we are claiming that a person, or more usually a category of persons, enjoys fewer advantages than that person or group of

persons ought to enjoy (or bears more of the burdens than they ought to bear), given how other members of the society in question are faring.

(Miller 1999, 1)

Drawing on Miller's definition, social justice is here understood as interrogating how different individuals or groups are faring in comparison with others in a specific context (such as a university) or more broadly in society.

A note on how this book can be read

Since this book seeks to enter into conversation with higher educationists as well as those working with the ideas of the capabilities approach more broadly, I have sought to present the chapters in a manner that allows the reader to focus on the areas of most interest for their own research and practice. As such, I briefly sketch out the main focus of the coming seven chapters. The reader will notice that chapter length varies somewhat across chapters. One of my aims with this book is to foreground the voices of learners and students. As a result, the empirically-based chapters (especially Chapters 5 and 6), tend to be somewhat longer than the others. As is the case for public deliberation processes that are so important in the capabilities approach, empirical research that places participants centrally cannot be neatly confined to particular conventions, such as chapters of relatively consistent length. The inclusion of multiple learner and student voices in this text is critical to the case being presented here and adds an important level of contextual depth and richness that I trust will overcome any discomfort with the somewhat longer chapters.

While the full argument is developed across the eight chapters of the book, I have sought to present each chapter as a semi-contained whole to allow readers to focus on particular aspects that they find most pertinent. Some readers may wish to read the book from cover to cover. Those who know the access literatures well may decide to skip Chapter 2 in which the literatures on educational transition, the first year at university, meritocracy and access and university readiness are reviewed and interpreted in terms of social justice concerns. Those who are well versed in the capabilities approach may elect to skip Chapter 3 which introduces the capabilities approach for those unfamiliar with the main tenets. The central argument for a capabilities-informed social justice framework for the transition to university, and the empirical data that forms the foundations of the argument, is developed in Chapters 4 to 7. Chapter 4 includes an overview of a series of key studies applying the capabilities approach in the context of education and higher education more specifically. The thorny issue of whether or not to list capabilities is addressed, and an ideal-theoretical capabilities list for the transition to university is developed, drawing on analysis of the rich access literatures as well as capabilities theory and research. The chapter concludes with a consideration of the role of social contexts, the agency of high school learners and university students, and the effects of this on the development of their capabilities. A theoretical capabilities-based framework for the transition to university is then proposed. In Chapter 5 it is the turn of the research participants to speak. Following a brief introduction to the participants, the chapter maps out the transition to university experiences expressed by first-year students, and then reflects on what learners and students have to say about four key domains of university readiness. A concerning discourse of mediocrity and/or failure as being the norm emerges from the learner and student voices, and this discourse is further unpacked by considering university lecturer perspectives on readiness. The focus of Chapter 6 returns to the ideal-theoretical capabilities list that was proposed in Chapter 4. Each of the nine proposed capabilities is interrogated based on the voices of the learners and students. In this way, the participants in the study have an opportunity to 'engage' in the formulation of the capabilities list. The chapter ends with the presentation of a pragmatic capabilities list for the transition to university, grounded on participants' experiences but also drawing on the lessons from existing research. In other writings I have discussed this process of developing a capabilities list as a top-down and bottom-up approach, making use of one capability as an illustrative example (Wilson-Strydom forthcoming). Chapter 6 builds on this paper and presents the 'deliberations' of learners and students across all nine capabilities. In Chapter 7 our focus turns to the interaction of individual agency and social contexts, with particular attention given to understanding the conversion factors operating at personal, social and environmental levels. We return to the empirical data which highlights a series of particularly important conversion factors that should be considered when thinking about access to university. The book is concluded in Chapter 8 where an argument is presented for why the capabilities-based social justice framework developed here potentially helps us to overcome some of the social justice dilemmas in the access terrain. Particular attention is also paid to how the framework might be operationalised. Chapter 8 begins with the following quotation: 'The way things are does not determine the way they ought to be' (Sandel 2010, 165). As we move on to Chapter 2 we begin our excursion in exploring 'the way things are' in the access domain. As the book progresses an argument for how things 'ought to be' is developed, with the overarching aim being to advance social justice within our universities.

Notes

1 http://www.hesa.ac.uk/index.php?option=com_content&task=view&id=2075&Itemid =141 http://www.higheredinfo.org/dbrowser/index.php?submeasure=223&year=200 9&level=nation&mode=graph&state=0
2 Percentage of first time full-time Bachelor's degree seekers who obtain their qualification in three years.
3 Percentage of first time full-time Bachelor's degree seekers who obtain their qualification in six years.
4 http://www.higheredinfo.org/dbrowser/?level=nation&mode=map&state=0&submeas ure=27
5 http://www.hesa.ac.uk/index.php?option=com_content&task=view&id=2064&Itemid =141
6 Model C schools are quasi-government schools that are administered and largely funded by parents and alumni bodies. The schools receive government subsidy and fall under the

jurisdiction of the provincial education department. However, school governing bodies function autonomously and are free to set school fees, appoint additional teachers (who are then not paid by government), invest in school infrastructure, set school rules and admissions policies, and so on. In most cases these schools are those that, under apartheid, served white children only. The term Model C is no longer used officially and it has thus become commonplace to refer to these schools as ex-Model C schools.

7 Following a review of the NSC (Dada et al. 2009), 2011 saw the introduction of another revision to the curriculum called the Curriculum Assessment Policy Statements (CAPS). Since CAPS is being progressively introduced, starting with the foundation phases, this curriculum has not had an influence on the participants in this research. For further details on CAPS please see http://www.education.gov.za/Curriculum/CurriculumAssessmentPolicyStatements/tabid/419/Default.aspx

References

Archer, L, M Hutchings and A Ross. 2003. *Higher Education and Social Class. Issues of Exclusion and Inclusion.* London: RoutledgeFalmer.

Badat, S. 2007. *Higher Education Transformation in South Africa Post 1994. Towards a Critical Assessment. Solomon Mahlangu Education Lecture 2007.* Johannesburg: Centre for Education Policy Development (CEPD).

Bernstein, B. 2000. *Pedagogy, Symbolic Control and Identity. Theory, Research, Critique. Revised Edition.* Oxford: Rowman & Littlefield Publishers, Inc.

Bloch, G. 2009. *The Toxic Mix: What's Wrong with South Africa's Schools and How to Fix It.* Cape Town: Tafelberg.

Bowen, W G, M M Chingos and M S McPherson. 2009. *Crossing the Finish Line. Completing College at America's Public Universities.* Princeton, New Jersey: Princeton University Press.

Bunting, I. 2002. 'The Higher Education Landscape Under Apartheid.' In *Transformation in Higher Education. Global Pressures and Local Realities in South Africa,* edited by N Cloete, R Fehnel, P Maassen, T Moja, H Perold and T Gibbon. Cape Town: Centre for Higher Education Transformation: 58–86.

CHE. 2004. *South African Higher Education in the First Decade of Democracy.* Pretoria: Council on Higher Education (CHE).

———. 2009. *Higher Education Monitor 8: The State of Higher Education in South Africa. A Report of the CHE Advice and Monitoring Directorate.* Pretoria: Council on Higher Education.

———. 2010. *Access and Throughput in South African Higher Education: Three Case Studies.* Higher Education Monitor 9. Pretoria: Council on Higher Education. http://www.che.ac.za.

———. 2012. *Vital Stats. Public Higher Education 2010.* Pretoria: Council on Higher Education. http://www.che.ac.za/documents/d000249/vital_stats_public_higher_education_2010.pdf.

———. 2013. *A Proposal for Undergraduate Curriculum Reform in South Africa: The Case for a Flexible Curriculum Structure. Report of the Task Team on Undergraduate Curriculum Structure.* Pretoria: Council on Higher Education.

Chisholm, L. 2004. *Changing Class. Education and Social Change in Post-Apartheid South Africa.* Pretoria: Human Sciences Research Council Press.

Christie, P. 2008. *Opening the Doors of Learning. Changing Schools in South Africa.* Johannesburg: Heinemann Publishers.

Cloete, N. 2002. 'Policy Expectations.' In *Transformation in Higher Education. Global Pressures and Local Realities in South Africa,* edited by N Cloete, R Fehnel, P Maassen, T Moja, H Perold and T Gibbon. Cape Town: Centre for Higher Education Transformation: 87–108.

Colditz, P, F de Clerq, M Dipholo, J Jansen, C Lubisi, P Lolwana, P Matthews, S Miller, M Roman, J S Roux and A Sanger. 2009. *Ministerial Committee on a National Education Evaluation and Development Unit*. Pretoria: Department of Basic Education, RSA.

Conley, D T. 2005. *College Knowledge. What It Really Takes for Students to Succeed and What We Can Do to Get Them Ready*. San Francisco: Jossey-Bass.

———. 2008. 'Rethinking College Readiness.' *New Directions for Higher Education* Winter (144): 3–13.

Crocker, D. 1995. 'Functioning and Capability: The Foundations of Sen's and Nussbaum's Development Ethic, Part 2.' In *Women, Culture and Development. A Study of Human Capabilities*, edited by M Nussbaum and J Glover. Oxford: Oxford University Press: 153–198.

Dada, F, T Dipholo, U Hoadley, E Khembo, S Muller and J Volmink. 2009. *Report of the Task Team for the Review of the Implementation of the National Curriculum Statement. Final Report*. Pretoria: Department of Education, RSA.

DHET. 2010. *Report of the Ministerial Committee on the Review of the National Student Financial Aid Scheme*. Pretoria: Department of Higher Education and Training. Republic of South Africa.

———. 2013. *White Paper for Post-School Education and Training. Building an Expanded, Effective and Integrated Post-school System*. White Paper. Pretoria: Department of Higher Education and Training. Republic of South Africa.

Dison, A, M Walker and M McLean. 2008. *The Contribution of Higher Education to Transformation, Development and Poverty Reduction: Overview of the South African Higher Education Context*. Background Paper. Nottingham: University of Nottingham.

Fataar, A. 2003. 'Higher Education Policy Discourse in South Africa: A Struggle for Alignment with Macro Development Policy.' *South African Journal of Higher Education* 17 (2): 31–39.

Fiske, E B and H F Ladd. 2004. *Equity. Education Reform in Post-apartheid South Africa*. Washington DC: Brookings Institution Press.

Furlong, A and F Cartmel. 2009. *Higher Education and Social Justice*. Berkshire, England: Society for Research into Higher Education and Open University Press.

Harley, K and V Wedekind. 2004. 'Political Change, Curriculum Change and Social Formation, 1990-2002.' In *Changing Class. Education and Social Change in Post-Apartheid South Africa*, edited by L Chisholm. Pretoria: Human Sciences Research Council Press: 195–220.

Hart, C S. 2009. 'Quo Vadis? The Capability Space and New Directions in the Philosophy of Education Research.' *Studies in the Philosophy of Education* 28: 391–402.

Hurtado, S. 2010. 'Benefits and Barriers.' In *The Next 25 Years. Affirmative Action in Higher Education in the Unites States and South Africa*, edited by D L Featherman, M Hall, and M Krislov. Ann Arbor: University of Michigan Press: 196–207.

Kuh, G D, G Kinzie, J H Schuh and E J Whitt. 2005. *Student Success in College. Creating Conditions That Matter*. San Francisco: John Wiley & Sons, Inc.

Kuh, G D, G Kinzie, J A Buckley, B Bridges and J Hayek. 2007. *Piecing Together the Student Success Puzzle: Research, Propositions, and Recommendations*. ASHE Higher Education Report, 32.

Marginson, S. 2011. 'Equity, Status and Freedom: a Note on Higher Education.' *Cambridge Journal of Education* 41 (1): 23–36. doi:10.1080/0305764X.2010.549456.

Miller, D. 1999. Principles of Social Justice. Cambridge, Massachusetts: Harvard University Press.

MoE. 1997. *Education White Paper 3 – A Programme for Higher Education Transformation*. 18207. Pretoria: South African Ministry of Education.

MoE (RSA). 2001. *National Plan for Higher Education in South Africa.* Pretoria: Ministry of Education.

Morrow, W. 2009a. *Bounds of Democracy. Epistemological Access in Higher Education.* Cape Town: Human Sciences Research Council. http://www.hsrcpress.ac.za.

———. 2009b. 'Entitlement and Achievement in Education (reprint of 1994 Article Published in Studies in Philosophy of Education).' In *Bounds of Democracy. Epistemological Access in Higher Education,* 13. Cape Town: Human Sciences Research Council: 69–86.

Mushi, S L. 2003. 'Chapter 12: Teaching and Learning Strategies That Promote Access, Equity and Excellence in University Education.' In *Access and Equity in the University. A Collection of Papers from the 30th Anniversary Conference of the Transitional Year Programme, University of Toronto,* edited by K S Braithwaite. Toronto: Canadian Scholars' Press: 207–230.

NPC. 2011. *National Development Plan. Vision 2030.* Pretoria: National Planning Commission, Office of the President, South Africa.

Nussbaum, M C. 2000. *Women and Human Development. The Capabilities Approach.* Cambridge, UK: Cambridge University Press.

———. 2011. *Creating Capabilities. The Human Development Approach.* Cambridge, Massachusetts: Harvard University Press.

OECD. 2010. *Education Key Tables from OECD. Tertiary Education Graduation Rates.* Paris: Organisation for Economic Cooperation and Development. http://www.oecd-ilibrary. org/sites/20755120-2010-table1/index.html?contentType=/ns/KeyTable,/ns/Statistical Publication&itemId=/content/table/2075.

Pascarella, E T, and P T Terenzini. 2005. *How College Affects Students. A Third Decade of Research.* Vol. 2. San Francisco: Jossey-Bass.

Quinn, J. 2013. *Drop-out and Completion in Higher Education in Europe Among Students from Under-represented Groups.* Independent report prepared for the European Commission. European Union. http://www.nesetweb.eu/sites/default/files/HE%20Drop%20out%20AR%20 Final.pdf

Republic of South Africa. 1996. *South African Schools Act.*

Ross, R. 1999. *A Concise History of South Africa.* Cambridge, UK: Cambridge University Press.

Sandel, M J. 2010. *Justice. What's the Right Thing to Do?* New York: Penguin Group.

Scott, I. 2008. 'First-year Experience as Terrain of Failure or Platform for Development? Critical Choices for Higher Education.' In University of Stellenbosch First-Year Experience Conference. http://academic.sun.ac.za/fyeconference2008/ Documentation/Powerpoints/Keynote_Diesche_Scott/Ian_Scott_%20FYE%202008. pdf

———. 2010. 'Who Is "Getting Through" in South Africa?' In *The Next 25 Years. Affirmative Action in Higher Education in the Unites States and South Africa,* edited by D Featherman, M Hall and M Krislov. Ann Arbor: University of Michigan Press: 229–243.

Sen, A. 1993. 'Capability and Well-Being.' In *The Quality of Life,* edited by M Nussbaum and A Sen, 30–53. New Delhi: Oxford University Press, India.

———. 1999. *Development as Freedom.* Oxford: Oxford University Press.

———. 2006. ' "What Do We Want from a Theory of Justice?"' *Journal of Philosophy* 103 (5): 215–238.

Simkins, C and A Paterson. 2005. *Learner Performance in South Africa. Social and Economic Determinants of Success in Language and Mathematics.* Pretoria: Human Sciences Research Council.

South African Institute of Race Relations. 2010. *The School Makes All the Difference*. Fast Facts. Johannesburg: South African Institute of Race Relations.

Taylor, N, J Muller and P Vinjevold. 2003. *Getting Schools Working. Research and Systemic School Reform in South Africa*. Cape Town: Maskew Miller Longman (Pty) Ltd.

Teddlie, C and A Tashakkori. 2009. *Foundations of Mixed Methods Research. Integrating Quantitative and Qualitative Approaches in the Social and Behavioural Sciences*. California: Sage Publications.

Tinto, V and B Pusser. 2006. *Moving from Theory to Action: Building a Model of Institutional Action for Student Success*. Washington DC: National Postsecondary Education Cooperative.

Van der Berg, S, C Burger, R Burger, M de Vos, G du Rand, M Gustafsson, E Moses, D Shepherd, N Spaull, S Taylor, H van Broekhuizen and D van Fintel. 2011. *Low Quality Education as a Poverty Trap*. Stellenbosch: University of Stellenbosch.

Vanderyar, S and J Jansen. 2008. *Diversity High. Class, Color, Culture, and Character in a South African High School*. Maryland: University Press of America.

Waghid, Y. 2009. 'Universities as Public Goods. In Defence of Democratic Deliberation, Compassionate Imagining and Cosmopolitan Justice.' In *Higher Education in South Africa. A Scholarly Look Behind the Scenes*, edited by E Bitzer. Stellenbosch: Sun Media: 71–83.

Wilson-Strydom, M G. 2014. *Developing Data Instruments for Researching University Access*. Working Paper. Bloemfontein: Centre for Research on Higher Education and Development.

———. 'A Capabilities List for Equitable Transitions to University: A Top-down and Bottom-up Approach.' *Journal of Human Development and Capabilities*

Wilson-Strydom, M G and H R Hay. 2010. 'Reducing the Gap Between Being Eligible and Being Ready for Higher Education: a Learner Engagement Perspective.' In *Praxis Towards Sustainable Empowering Learning Environments in South Africa*, edited by D Francis, S Mahlolaholo and M Nkoane. Bloemfontein: Sun Media: 239–252.

2   Access and social justice

> [w]hilst public education does benefit everyone, it necessarily also benefits some
> more than others, with those gaining most likely to be those who start out better
> placed, whether that is by nature or circumstance.
>
> (Jonathan 2001, 49)

Does social justice matter?

Social justice is an ambiguous concept with respect to public higher education.
Public universities aim, on the one hand, to make higher education accessible to
all in society (the public). On the other hand, public universities remain elitist
institutions: access is limited to a minority and graduates are commonly granted a
privileged status (Brennan and Naidoo 2008). Higher education researchers and
theorists have long debated challenges and contradictions within higher education
that fall into the realm of social justice. These debates commonly play out through
interrogations of the purposes of higher education which are articulated in
different ways depending on the specific agenda being promoted, or the ideological
underpinnings of a particular organisation or person(s). Even though education
(and higher education) is commonly portrayed in terms of its positive and liberatory
potential – particularly within the access and lifelong learning discourses – there
has also been a long history of theorisation of the various and complex ways in
which education both reproduces and reinforces class inequalities, and how higher
education embodies an ethos of individual achievement and competition, so
reinforcing the hierarchy of social advantage (Archer et al. 2003, 1–2). As the
quotation presented at the start of the chapter reminds us, those who tend to
benefit most from higher education are usually those who started off in a better
position in the first place (Jonathan 2001, 49).

It is precisely these circumstances influencing chances of higher education
access and success, together with how circumstance and individual agency inter-
sect to create or limit opportunity, that I am seeking to understand. The important
body of work on higher education and social justice focuses our attention on range
of inequalities inherent within higher education institutions and systems more
broadly (Unterhalter and Carpentier 2010). The extent of inequality in higher

education systems globally, and the resilience of this inequality to efforts aimed at change, must be approached as an issue of social justice. Depending on the context in which one is located, broadening access or participation might refer to inequalities in access based on gender, race, class, location or a combination of these. Isaac et al. (2003) showed that inequalities in admission to the University of California (UC) were mostly closely related to race, ethnicity and socioeconomic status, with nearly 70 per cent of variance in the percentage of high school graduates gaining a place at UC being explained by parental levels of education. In the UK the focus of broadening participation tends to be on class issues (see for example, Archer et al. 2003; Furlong and Cartmel 2009; Watts and Bridges 2006), while in the US race and/or ethnicity are commonly the focus; so, for example the access challenges faced by African-American and Latino students are typically addressed (for example, Bowen et al. 2009; Del Rios and Leegwater 2008; Hausmann et al. 2007; Taylor Smith et al. 2009). In his analysis of equity and status in Australian higher education, Marginson (2011) points out the inherent tension in higher education equity policy based on whether equity is understood as fairness or inclusion. Equity as fairness argues for, and measures, the growth in the absolute numbers of under-represented groups in higher education, while equity as inclusion considers the proportional representation of under-represented groups in higher education. Related is the important distinction between increased participation and widened participation and the way in which these terms are used in policy discourse and practice. For example, as has been seen in the South African case, it is possible to increase participation (more enrolments) without meaningfully widening participation (proportionally more enrolment from previously under-represented groups) (CHE 2012).

The argument that notions of higher education as a public good has over the past two decades been replaced by neoliberal market models focused on producing a more vocationally skilled workforce in the interests of economic advancement that benefits a few is well known. Furlong and Cartmel (2009, 8) draw our attention to the fact that social justice aims are often in tension and contain competing objectives and understandings of the purpose of education, particularly in the context of globalisation and the neoliberal market ideology underlying the global economic, political and educational environment. Related is the underlying assumption that higher education is an industry serving 'clients' (students) rather than a social institution serving broader social (or public good) purposes, such as the education of a democratically informed and critical citizenry. Although himself arguing strongly for a return to public good purposes of higher education across Africa, Sawyerr reminds us of the complexities and contradictions of higher education in developing country contexts. He notes that:

> This more socially focused conception [e.g. deepening of democracy] of the public good does pose some problems in respect of higher education. How can one justify, for example, spending the same public funds to educate one university student that would support several secondary school pupils – especially when the college graduate also is likely, thereby, to improve her or

his life chances to a much greater degree than the secondary school graduate? Higher education, as we have seen, is an inherently privileging experience, and the situation is compounded by the very nature of university work, which tends to encourage 'meritocratic individualism' by encouraging and rewarding individual success and achievement. Thus, even though its broader social purposes include the equalization of life chances, higher education tends to pull in the direction of individual competitiveness and reproduction of privilege – a contradiction that needs to be addressed by those who advocate the treatment of higher education as a 'public good'.

(Sawyerr 2004, 44)

The complexities that Sawyerr draws attention to can be partly explained by the contradictions inherent in two dominant ideologies underpinning understandings of the purpose of education – human capital based approaches and human rights based approaches. Many argue that the dominant ideology informing education (and higher education) policy, with its foundations deeply rooted in neoliberal ideology and politics, is the human capital understanding of education (for example, Assie-Lumumba 2005; Brock-Utne 2003; Giroux and Giroux 2004; Robeyns 2006; Tikly and Barrett 2011; Walker and McLean 2010). Essentially, human capital approaches to education are based on the assumption that investment in education is required as a prerequisite for economic growth, hence the global focus on massification of higher education. From the perspective of student expectations of the purpose of higher education Giroux (2002, 435) notes that '[W]ithin the neoliberal era of deregulation and the triumph of the market, many students and their families no longer believe that higher education is about higher learning, but about gaining a better foothold in the job market'. Walker (2006) asked UK-based academic staff what they understood the purpose of universities to be. One of her interviewees reported that '[T]he tension between economically desirable pursuits and the expansion of the mind was never far from the surface in discussions about what universities are for' (Walker 2006, 7). Walker argues further that policy trends in higher education, including for example human capital theory, have tended to prioritise the economic returns from higher education. From this perspective, the value or the purpose of higher education lies in the extent to which investment in individual students increases economic productivity and incomes, so producing greater national wealth. In the knowledge economy, higher education has become a prime lever of capitalist growth and development.

In contrast to human capital based purposes of education are human rights based approaches – although policy often draws on both ideologies. South Africa is a case in point, hence the complexities and contradictions described in Chapter 1. Approaching education as a human right is the conceptual opposite of approaching education in terms of human capital, and these differences have consequences for whether human beings are understood as inputs for economic growth or as the ultimate ends of moral and political concerns (Robeyns 2006, 75). The rights based framework for understanding educational purpose emphasises the intrinsic importance of education, irrespective of whether the specific educational opportunity will pay off in human capital or economic terms. Rights based approaches are commonly used in work that has a social justice agenda. However, despite the value of this framework from a social justice perspective, rights based approaches have also been criticised for tending to operate more at the rhetorical level than at the level of actual practices in everyday life. Thus, while declarations might be made stating that equal access to education is a fundamental human right; in practice this is not always achieved. Further, rights based approaches make statements about rights to be achieved (overall outcome statements) but seldom provide precise guidance regarding where the duty to ensure that these rights are actually achieved lies (Robeyns 2006; Spreen and Vally 2006). As I will argue in Chapter 3, the capabilities approach provides a framework for building on and expanding the rights-based understanding of education in a manner that explicitly takes actual lives and everyday injustices into account. For example, while equal access to education may be granted as a right in the South African constitution, the reality on the ground is that major inequalities remain and many young people are unable to realise this right (Cloete 2009). The capabilities approach, arguably, also provides more space for identifying actions towards change than the somewhat more rhetorical language of rights does.

Engaging with what is meant by social justice, and how this translates into policy and practice in the context of university education, is of critical importance. In other writing I have offered a conceptual argument for why the capabilities approach helps us to overcome some of the limitations of the work of John Rawls, Iris Marion Young and Nancy Fraser in the context of higher education (Wilson-Strydom 2014). Although the work of Rawls, Young and Fraser offers important insights for understanding access issues from a social justice perspective, each is limited in specific ways. Rawls's work contributes to access for social justice by advancing a critique of unfair advantage and meritocracy, as well as by drawing attention to the need to focus on benefits for the least well-off when making social justice claims (Rawls 1999). Young's approach details the role of social structures, institutions and group membership in creating and maintaining injustices (Young 2001, 1990). Fraser's multidimensional account of social justice, and in particular her concept of participatory parity, help us to interrogate structural aspects of the access terrain (Fraser 2009). Nonetheless, Rawls's focus on primary goods is limiting in the context of access because conversion of the resource of a place at university into successful performance is not a given. Further, both Young and Fraser's theories that emphasise social and institutional structures do not take sufficient account of students' agency and individual differences. The capabilities approach provides a generative framework for theorising social justice in the context of university access that potentially opens up new ways of understanding these limitations, and then opportunities for overcoming them, by placing students' lives and well-being centrally (Wilson-Strydom 2014).

As noted in Chapter 1, my aim with this book is to present a case for the value of a capabilities-informed approach to social justice through an in-depth analysis of the complexities of university access from the perspectives of learners and students. A useful starting point for such reflection is a consideration of the dilemmas of access presented in the introductory chapter. In order to ground the argument put forward in the coming chapters, I now turn to a discussion of the existing research on access. While it is beyond the scope of this text to present a comprehensive review of all existing access related research, the coming sections cover the key areas of particular relevance to this study, namely: educational transitions, notions of meritocracy and university admissions, the first-year at university, conceptions of the 'under-prepared' student and approaches to understanding and measuring university readiness.

Educational transition

Challenges in the area of educational transition, be it from primary to secondary level or secondary school to higher education have been researched for many years. The analogy of a humpback bridge for understanding educational transition was first used 30 years ago by Steed and Sudworth (1985) in the context of the transition from primary to secondary school in England and Wales. This analogy was used because:

> Traditional in structure, the humpback bridge survives because the volume of traffic wanting to cross is not sufficient to generate demands for change to a more efficient form of bridge. Its narrowness restricts passage to certain categories of road users. Unable to see over it, one forms a view of what is going on at the other side by listening to reports brought back or by making surmises from those activities that create sufficient noise, unless one is prepared to venture across oneself.
>
> (Steed and Sudworth 1985, 23)

This metaphor remains richly descriptive of the transition from school to university today, and is helpful for further theorising this transition (see also, Johnston 2010). The concept of the humpback bridge as an inefficient, traditional structure that has outlived its time is a useful depiction of the current state of access to higher education in South Africa and many other countries. In South African higher education there has been little change in the way that universities and schools collaborate to prepare students for this transition despite the major transformation in the education system, particularly regarding the dramatic increase in student numbers and the changing demographics of the student body since 1994. For most students, an outdated and inefficient humpback bridge remains their principal means of negotiating the transition from school to university. Many students braving the gap between school and university are first-generation students who do not have family members that attended university; they are unable to see over the humpback bridge and so must surmise an understanding of the unknown university world. Marshall and Hargreaves extend this analogy and remind us that 'it is not possible for individuals on *either side* to see across the humpback bridge, such that any judgments or impressions made about conditions on "the other side" have to be based on conjecture or imagination' (Marshall and

Hargreaves 2007, 65, emphasis added). In other words, neither schools nor universities have a clear view of what the other does.

Nonetheless, there are some useful lessons from international experiences of interventions that seek to work on both sides of the humpback bridge. One example is the range of dual enrolment programmes offered in the US, which can take many different forms (Wang Golann and Hughes 2008). These programmes allow high school learners to complete courses that carry credit for both their high school qualification and also at college or university (Hoffman et al. 2008). As such, dual enrolment programmes expose high school students to college or university level coursework and introduce them to the university environment whilst they are in school. Another example is the College Board's[1] Advanced Placement (AP) programme that offers a host of university level courses to high school learners covering a range of different subject areas. Each AP course is modelled on a comparative university level course but is offered at high schools. The culmination of the programme is a suite of university-level assessments. Strong performance in these tests is rewarded by many colleges and universities, some of whom also grant credit for selected first-year courses. Research consistently shows that students who do well in the AP examinations achieve greater success at university (College Board 2009; Lee and Ransom 2010; Saenz et al. 2007; Warburton et al. 2001). First-generation students themselves also report that participating in AP courses better prepared them for college or university, particularly with respect to writing skills and managing the college or university level workload (Reid and Moore 2008). These benefits notwithstanding, we must also consider that access to AP courses differs across schools, with access to the range of available AP courses greater at better resourced schools commonly serving the middle and upper classes. As such, despite the benefits for some students, the provision of AP courses can also further emphasise existing educational inequalities.

Beyond these concrete examples, what does the literature about transitions teach us? The work of Bridges on transitions is well known in the business world, and there are some useful lessons that we can also draw from his thinking for understanding transitions in education. Importantly, Bridges (2004; see also Bridges and Mitchell 2000) distinguishes between change and transition. While change is typically driven by external events or circumstances, Bridges argues that making a transition is an internal process; it is a personal reorientation that some-one making a change must go through. In the contexts of organisational change, he argues further that external change tends to happen more quickly than internal transitions. We could make a similar argument about the transition to university. While the change of being in high school one year and university the next year happens quickly, the personal transition from being a school learner to being a university student might take much longer. For example, Briggs et al. (2012) focus on the formation of a student identity as a central part of the transition process. Bridges (2004) has developed a model of transitions that has three phases. The first of these is the phase of *endings*, where one needs to let go of the way things have been. Applied to school to university transition, this phase would be taking place in the final couple of years of schooling where learners begin making decisions about future study or entry to the job market. The ending phase is followed by a *neutral* phase in which confusion and/or exploration in the direction of the change occurs, for example, the time between finishing final high school examinations and starting at university. The final phase Bridges identifies is the phase of *new beginnings* where one needs to start behaving in new ways. New beginnings would refer to the time in which first-year students are settling in to university life and developing a sense of what university is about. This phase is likely to end towards the end of the first year.

Several authors working specifically in the area of educational transition have also sought to identify stages or phases of transition. For example, Knox and Wyper (2008, 17) identify eight stages in the transition to first year at university. These are: pre-entry, induction, first few weeks, first assessment, end semester one, end semester two, examination 'resits', and transition to the second year. Similarly, working in the South African context, Nel et al. (2009, 985) identify three phases comprising the transition to university: the pre-entry phase (schooling), the enrolment/access phase (application, course selection, registration), and the after-enrolment phase (first few months to the first-year of university). Academic, social, financial and cultural factors operating at each of these levels were identified in an effort to formulate a theoretical framework for a holistic pre-university intervention. Nel et al.'s research usefully highlights the inter-dependence of a complex array of factors at the school level, including the major impact of the unequal South African schooling system, that influence the transition experience. While universities are urged to 'adopt a holistic approach to the school-university process' (Nel et al. 2009, 988), it remains somewhat unclear how this holistic approach might be put into practice by South African universities and schools. Nonetheless, these studies also support the starting assumption noted in Chapter 1; that when we think about and research the transition to university, we need to take into account the last few years of high school as well as the first year of university.

Working with the capabilities approach framework, Hart (2014, 2013) has done some important work on educational transitions beyond schools, including transition into further education and/or the job market. Through her work with young people in the UK, Hart has identified 'techniques of transition' (2014, 207) which refer to the strategies that young people use when transitioning beyond school. The complexity of the notion of transition is emphasised with the transition from high school described as an 'idiosyncratic, dynamic and evolving set of processes' (Hart 2014, 205). The depth of interpretation that is possible when theorising educational transition from a capabilities perspective is also clear, in particular the use of the concept of conversion factors which is integral to the capabilities approach.

The first year at university

Compared to pre-university factors and the interface between schooling and university, it has been more common for research on the transition to university and/or access to focus on the first year of university, sometimes called the first-year experience. It is useful to briefly consider this literature, as it is of direct relevance to the transition, but not on its own sufficient. In a helpful review report Johnston (2010, 30) sums up the literature on the first year and on first-year experience as including the following topics: (1) nature and importance of the first year experience, (2) curriculum imperatives, (3) responses and measures to enhance the first year, (4) institutional priorities and enhancement, and (5) student surveys, assessment, evaluation and measurement of the student experience in the first year. Similar issues have been raised by other authors presenting literature reviews of first-year experience in different contexts.[2] In addition, several studies focus on how students and institutions manage diversity during the adjustment period when entering college or university (Harvey et al. 2006; Hurtado and Carter 1997; Nunez 2009; Strydom and Mentz 2009).

The importance of students developing a sense of belonging as opposed to alienation, social networks, new friendships, and the building of social or cultural capital also receive much attention, and have been noted to have a positive influence on self-esteem, academic performance and social acceptance, although causality has not been established (Mann 2008; Pittman and Richmond 2008; Yorke and Longden 2008). Related is a growing body of research focused on understanding (or advocating, in the case of more policy oriented studies) an increased personalisation of the learning experience within higher education and also during the transition and first-year contexts (Briggs et al. 2012; Dietsche 2009; Knox and Wyper 2008; OECD 2006; Zukas and Malcolm 2007). The importance of better understanding students' expectations of coming to university, the gaps between student and staff expectations, and of recognising the diverse and sometimes contradictory expectations of individual students and across different student groupings have also been noted (Maitland et al. 2005; Pitkethly and Prosser 2001). Given the diversity of students and higher education institutions, Johnston (2010, 3) usefully reminds us that we should rather think of multiple first-year experiences, with nuanced transitions influenced by diverse backgrounds and contexts, rather than a one-size-fits-all format.

A final point that needs to be mentioned in the context of interventions universities put in place to support the variously named 'under-prepared', 'at-risk', 'first generation' students is that, even if not intentionally so, these interventions are usually based on a deficit understanding of students and their capabilities (Smit 2012). Much research on access and transition tends to draw on a deficit view of the student, seeking to identify interventions to reduce problematic drop out and success rates, and so focuses specific attention on groups of students identified as 'at risk' (Whittaker 2008, 26). While understanding risks will always remain important, Whittaker argues that the concept of a successful transition should be measured in terms of the engagement and empowerment of all students and should be rooted in valuing and building on the various strengths, skills and knowledge that individuals bring to higher education, regardless of the specific student profile. Along similar lines, authors drawing on approaches within adult education have criticised 'traditional' university education as being decontextualised and failing to position students in their unique contexts, instead viewing the increasingly diverse student body as a 'set of problems' (Zukas and Malcolm 2007, 21).

While the principle of moving away from a deficit model is a critical component of the capabilities framework being presented here, I believe that we need to be cautious of moving to the opposite extreme at which point we refuse to honestly recognise and challenge contextual or structural deficits which are quite different from individual deficits. For example, it would be short-sighted in the South African context to make the shift away from deficits too emphatically due to the major deficits of both the schooling system and higher education's response which must be named, understood and challenged in the interests of social justice. The critical point is to question whether the explicit recognition of schooling deficit implies personal deficit of the student (Smit 2012). This is where the mistake tends to be made. It has become all too common to adopt a deficit view of the student in response to the deficits operating in the social and educational contexts from which students come. In addition, it is also important for the unit of analysis – educational or institutional systems versus individual students – to be made explicit. My approach is to avoid a deficit model of the individual student by seeking to understand how social and educational environments have limited or enabled the opportunities for students entering university. This is not to assume that students from poor quality educational backgrounds do not have backlogs in their learning that need to be addressed, but it is to assume that under-preparation is not a defining feature of what a student can become. The prevailing ideology of meritocracy that commonly (implicitly and/or explicitly) underpins approaches to access and admission is a particular site through which deficit approaches operate, and so can be challenged.

Meritocracy and access

When considering the myriad of challenges and contradictions of university access, particularly when working through a social justice lens, it is important to think through the 'prevailing and largely unquestioned ideology of merit' that commonly underpins access debates (Oakes et al. 2000, 8). Writing shortly after affirmative action was outlawed in the state of California in favour of merit based approaches for university admissions, Oakes et al. (2000, 8, emphasis in the original) describe the ideology of merit as one which 'conflates the ability to profit from educational opportunities with prior achievement in the traditional academic curriculum, as gauged by conventional measures. Moreover, it positions students with this prior achievement as more *deserving* of these opportunities.' Similarly, Iris Marion Young (1990, 200) refers to 'the myth of merit' and shows how criteria for determining merit 'are normative and cultural rather than neutrally scientific' (1990, 204). Young does not suggest that such criteria cannot be used, but rather emphasises the importance of trying to make the normative and culturally situated nature of merit criteria known rather than presenting merit as a neutral means of making complex admissions decisions.[3] Debates about access and meritocracy are commonly seen as an issue of justice. For example, Cunningham (2007) positions the idea of merit in opposition to that of equal opportunities for those groups traditionally excluded from higher education. The latter position, equal opportunity, focuses greater attention on the role of universities in society and so supports arguments for privileged admission requirements for particular groups of students (e.g. affirmative action) in order to correct for social injustices. Arguments for affirmative action in admissions commonly note that students from traditionally excluded groups need to function within a structural system that defines merit in ways that work against them and as such, fairness or justice requires some form of different treatment for such groups in the interest of broader social gains (Arendale 2010, 3).[4]

Taking these ideas further from a political philosophy stand point, Sandel (2010) describes how the idea of a fair meritocracy seeks to further remedy injustices by correcting for social and economic disadvantage. A fair meritocracy aims to remove obstacles to achievement by providing equal educational opportunities, so that those from poor families (or other disadvantaged groups) can compete on an equal basis with those from more privileged backgrounds. Interventions such as programmes dealing with childhood nutrition, various health related issues, education and skills development and the Head Start scheme, are implemented in the name of establishing a fair meritocracy and bringing everyone, regardless of race, class, gender or family background, to the same starting point. However, Sandel (2010), drawing strongly on the work of Rawls, argues that, while this fair meritocratic conception – particularly common in a market driven society – might correct for some morally arbitrary advantages, such as family background, it still falls short of justice. This is so because the 'natural lottery' means that people have different strengths and weaknesses, and some people will always be more confident, or adapt better to the requirements of formal schooling than others, just as some people are physically able to run faster than others (see also, Rawls 1999). Thus, making admissions decisions based on merit only will always be tainted with some form of moral arbitrariness, and hence cannot be said to be just (Sandel 2010). A related issue is that merit-based decision making, even when placed within the ambit of 'fair meritocracy', places far greater emphasis on individual performance and achievement than on the structural or social conditions that either support or limit achievement for different groups of people. In this way, meritocracy plays an important role as part of broader neoliberal agendas within higher education. Brennan and Naidoo (2008, 290) note that:

[A]longside the arrival of mass higher education we have the growing dominance of a neo-liberal culture emphasising individual competitiveness and responsibility spreading through society, though more advanced in some societies than others. A meritocratic ideology is central to this culture, bringing with it the message that your problems are all your fault. And similarly, your privileges are all your own achievement.

A similar argument is made by Morley and Lugg (2009) who did a study in which they mapped meritocracy at four universities – two in Tanzania and two in Ghana.

Among other findings, they noted that both socioeconomic and gender-based privileges were commonly coded as academic merit.

What do these arguments imply for research on the transition from school to university? What are we to make of these debates in the South African context that is plagued by particularly poor quality schooling for the majority of young black South Africans? Further complicating such questions is the fact that the current higher education system is unlikely to be able to accommodate greater numbers of students without major investment in academic staff as well as teaching and learning facilities. Hence, difficult admissions decisions must be made in a context where supply of available places at university cannot meet the demand. My reading of the access landscape in the South African higher education context is that we can identify two main considerations that bear mention in the context of meritocracy and access. The first is the debate about affirmative action in higher education admissions, including whether this approach is morally defensible and socially just, and also the mechanisms for implementation, such as how to identify students who should benefit from affirmative action. The practice of the University of Cape Town (UCT) in this regard is the most commonly referenced case in academic and public debates in South Africa since UCT explicitly makes use of race-based criteria for admissions.[5] Race-based criteria are also used for making selection decisions in Medical Schools across the country. An edition of the *South African Journal of Higher Education* (vol. 24, no. 2, 2010) was devoted to this debate and highlighted just how challenging and contested is the terrain. Debates about meritocracy and affirmative action are complex, nuanced and also imbued with ideologies and different disciplinary explanations. At the core, however, is the challenge of higher education transformation in a still deeply divided country. While most participants in the debate recognise the importance of higher education providing entrance pathways for prospective students from 'disadvantaged backgrounds', an agreed on definition and way of measuring disadvantage remains elusive.

The second consideration is about the extent to which prospective students demonstrate their likelihood of being able to cope successfully with university study; in other words, their level of preparedness or readiness. This issue can be approached from a limited merit-based perspective with minimum achievement levels at school and on standardised admissions tests taken as a proxy measure of academic preparation. Only the top performers on these tests gain entry. However, the legacy of unequal education in the country and the clear focus on equity and redress from the 1990s has demanded that the notion of readiness be expanded to include potential to succeed. A range of alternative tests that provided access routes to talented students who did not meet the standard admissions criteria were developed in the early 1990s. In addition to providing alternative access, these tests are also important because 'it is essential at admission to assess the learner's level of preparedness for university education, so as to identify areas that require development, if one is serious about equity and redress' (Koch and Foxcroft 2003, 193). This implies that using academic merit as the sole means of gaining entry to higher education (the approach most common at South African universities) is likely to be limited when seeking to build a more socially just higher education environment. Given the importance of understanding and critiquing notions of university readiness, the following section focuses specifically on this issue.

University readiness

Arguably, one of the ways in which some of the difficulties of merit-based admissions discussed earlier have been managed is by focusing greater attention on readiness or levels of preparation for university than strictly on merit or achievement. While readiness and merit need not be different, depending on how each concept is used, it is plausible that a more just approach to university access and admissions might be achieved when the broader concept of 'readiness' (as compared to merit only) is used as the basis for making admissions decisions and for broadening access. However, while the intuitive idea that a broader concept of readiness is likely to be more inclusive than the idea of merit only, the question about how readiness is defined and measured is rather more difficult to answer. Readiness, like merit, is most commonly measured by considering school leaving results which are seen to provide one of the best, albeit imperfect, predictors of success in higher education (Bowen et al. 2009). In addition to school performance, the use of various admissions tests has also played an important role in assessing readiness (and merit), particularly in the US where the Scholastic Aptitude Test (SAT) and American College Test (ACT) are widely used. In the late 1990s it was reported that more than 90 per cent of all public and private higher education providers in the US required their applicants to submit test scores with their application (Beatty et al. 1999). More recently, however, increasing numbers of institutions have adopted what has been termed 'test-optional' admissions policies (Hoover 2011; NACAC 2008). These changes reflect the complex concerns and often polarised debates about the fairness of admissions tests, concerns that have yet to be resolved. Universities in South Africa have also made use of various tests to complement school results, the most recent development being the piloting and then large scale introduction of the National Benchmark Tests (NBTs) which measure prospective students' proficiency in academic literacy, quantitative literacy and mathematics (Yeld 2009). Admissions tests and school leaving results are a useful practical tool for making admissions decisions and do provide some indication of the academic foundation from which universities must build. But, as will be seen in the coming sections, measures of proficiency, aptitude, or content knowledge, as important as they are in access and admissions, remain only a partial component of the multi-dimensional preparation or 'readiness' required for making a successful transition to university.

Readiness as a multidimensional construct

One of the most sustained and thorough accounts of readiness for university that I have encountered is the work of Conley[6] who has developed a multidimensional concept of university or college readiness (Conley 2003, 2005, 2006, 2008a,

2008b, 2010). Conley's model of college readiness draws on research over several years in the North American context, and takes account of a wide range of qualitative and quantitative studies, in different socioeconomic and schooling contexts, together with a wide range of stakeholders' perspectives. I have demonstrated in earlier work that Conley's multidimensional model of university readiness is useful for understanding the transition to university in the South African context (Wilson-Strydom 2010) and I build on that argument here.

Conley's work draws attention to the need to understand the gap between being *eligible* (commonly assessed using school results and admissions testing) for university study, and being *ready* to be successful at university. Similarly, a six-year national study on high school exit standards and higher education entrance standards, conducted by Stanford University's Bridge programme, recommended that it is critical to 'create an awareness that getting into college is not the hardest part [. . .] true college opportunity includes having a real chance to succeed' (Venezia et al. 2003, 4). Conley's multidimensional model of college readiness takes account of four facets of readiness: key cognitive strategies, key content, academic behaviours, and contextual skills and awareness (also called college or university knowledge). Cognitive strategies refer to abilities of problem formulation and problem solving, inquiry and dialogue, reasoning, argumentation and interpretation, and accuracy. Key content knowledge is about having sufficient grounding in the key structures and concepts associated with core academic disciplines. Academic behaviours needed for university readiness include factors such as self-awareness and self-discipline, study skills and time management. University knowledge refers to the formal and informal, stated and unstated information about how universities work, including institutional systems and cultures. Conley (2008, 5) notes that 'because college is truly different from high school, college readiness is fundamentally different from high school completion'. It is thus critical for universities to understand the schooling experiences of their first-year students, the extent to which these experiences have prepared them for university, and also how students are experiencing the transition from the school environment to the university environment.

Conley's work demonstrates that, even though important, it is not enough for learners to complete their schooling with content mastery only (commonly reflected in good school leaving results); they must also develop analytic and writing skills that are consistent with what is required at university. Also important is that learners are supported to understand how they learn best; in other words, they need to learn how to learn (Chickering 2006). In a similar vein, Jacobs (2009, 241) reminds us of the 'need for lecturers to make the hidden disciplinary discourses explicit to students at the first-year level'. This means that epistemological access must be consciously fostered during the first year. This development of analytical and writing skills and the intellectual maturation process that accompanies it is seldom done at schools (Conley 2008a; Johnston and Kockanowska 2009). In addition, the development of academic self-management skills needed to cope successfully with the demands of university study together with an understanding of how the higher education system works are critical (see also, Bell et al.

2009; Perna et al. 2008; Rowan-Kenyon et al. 2008). Tornatzky et al. (2002) usefully describe college knowledge as the instrumental information needed to engage with the college or university environment. Research conducted with students in Scotland highlighted the need for more and better communication about 'what it means to be a student at university today' (Johnston and Kockanowska 2009, 51), with particular emphasis on expectations of students regarding independent learning, self-assessment and writing styles, together with an understanding of the implications for how one approaches the study of a specific discipline(s). In addition, students also called for better communication about what being at university entails at the level of day-to-day activities, such as an idea of the number of lectures each day, what happens in a lecture, tutorial and laboratory requirements, class preparation requirements, reading requirements and the expected size of the entering cohort (Johnston and Kockanowska 2009, 52; see also, Knox and Wyper 2008). Thus, to improve the transition experience, high schools need to provide learners with a more nuanced sense of what readiness for university means, while universities need to have a deeper understanding of students' educational practices at school level. It is not sufficient to consider learners' academic performance, as reflected in their final school leaving marks, only. Readiness implies much more contextual knowledge about the educational experiences and practices of learners whilst at school. Conley sums up the arguments about access and social justice presented in this chapter succinctly as follows:

> Secondary and postsecondary education will need to connect much more systematically and in ways that enable all students, but particularly those who are the first in their families to attend college, to be prepared for the challenges they will face in entry-level college courses. Postsecondary access will be a cruel hoax for these students if success in college is beyond their reach. High school and college will need to change substantially and *in tandem* to achieve the goal of preparing more students for college access.
>
> (Conley 2009, 7 emphasis in the original)

These dilemmas of access that operate in our unequal universities and unequal societies create forms of injustice that may go unnoticed in the global neoliberal context that privileges meritocracy and individual performance. In response I present the capabilities approach as a particularly generative framework for thinking differently about the many access challenges that often undermine social justice.

Notes

1 See http://www.collegeboard.com for additional details.
2 Examples of useful reviews of the literature on the first year include: Gordon (2008), Harvey et al. (2006), Johnston and Kockanowska (2009), Knox and Wyper (2008), Krause et al. (2005), Upcraft et al. (2005) and Yorke and Longden (2008).

3 For additional examples of similar arguments about meritocracy, see James (2007) who works in the Australian context, and Scott's (2009) work in the European and North American contexts.

4 There is also an important body of work focusing on affirmative action debates within critical race theory (for some examples, see Allen et al. 2000; Bell 2000; Carroll et al. 2000; Chang 2000; Delgado and Stefanic 2001; Ladstone-Billings 1998; Ladstone-Billings and Tate IV 1995; Yosso 2005).

5 At the time of writing, UCT was in the in the process of introducing a new admissions policy which makes use of multiple metrics to identity students who are disadvantaged. This includes race, home language, school attended, parental and grandparental education levels, and whether the family depends on social grants. An official news release by UCT on this issue can be found at: http://www.uct.ac.za/dailynews/?id=8716

6 David Conley is the Director of the Centre for Educational Policy Research (CEPR) and the Educational Policy Improvement Centre (EPIC) both located at the University of Oregon. EPIC is a non-profit organisation that works closely with CEPR. EPIC's work is focused on a series of educational policy and practice initiatives that aim to increase student success in college and university but focusing on the public schooling system and the extent to which schooling prepares students for college and university – i.e. school/higher education alignment. EPIC has developed a range of resources to assist both schools and learners/students to prepare for college. These include the CollegeCareerReady School Diagnostic (EPIC 2010a) and the College-Readiness Performance Assessment (C-PAS) (EPIC 2010b). For more information on the work of EPIC, see http://www.epiconline.org and http://cepr.uoregon.edu.

References

Allen, W R, R Teranishi, G Dinwiddie and G Gonzalez. 2000. 'Introduction and Overview: Knocking on Freedom's Door: Race, Equity and Affirmative Action in US Higher Education.' *The Journal of Negro Education* 69 (1/2): 3–11.

Archer, L, M Hutchings and A Ross. 2003. *Higher Education and Social Class. Issues of Exclusion and Inclusion.* London: RoutledgeFalmer.

Arendale, D R. 2010. 'Special Issue: Access at the Crossroads. Learning Assistance in Higher Education.' *ASHE Higher Education Report* 35 (6): 1–145.

Assie-Lumumba, N. 2005. 'Critical Perspectives on the Crises, Planned Change, and the Prospects for Transformation in African Higher Education.' *Journal of Higher Education in Africa* 3 (3): 1–29.

Beatty, A, M R C Greenwood and R L Linn. 1999. *Myths and Trade-offs: The Role of Tests in Undergraduate Admissions.* Washington DC: National Academies Press.

Bell, A D, H T Rowan-Kenyon and L W Perna. 2009. 'College Knowledge of 9th and 11th Grade Students: Variation by School and State Context.' *Journal of Higher Education* 80 (6): 663–685.

Bell, D. 2000. 'Epilogue: Affirmative Action: Another Instance of Racial Workings in the United States.' *The Journal of Negro Education* 69 (1/2): 145–149.

Bowen, W G, M M Chingos and M S McPherson. 2009. *Crossing the Finish Line. Completing College at America's Public Universities.* Princeton, New Jersey: Princeton University Press.

Brennan, J and R Naidoo. 2008. 'Higher Education and the Achievement (and/or Prevention) of Equity and Social Justice.' *Higher Education* 56: 287–302.

Bridges, W. 2004. *Transitions. Making Sense of Life's Changes.* 2nd edition, Kindle. DaCapo Life Long.

Bridges, W and S Mitchell. 2000. *Leading Transition: A New Model for Change*. British Columbia: Berlin, Eaton & Associates Ltd. http://world.edu/wp-content/uploads/2012/10/WilliamBridgesTransitionandChangeModel_000.pdf

Briggs, A R J, J Clark and I Hall. 2012. 'Building Bridges: Understanding Student Transition to University.' *Quality in Higher Education* 18 (1): 3–21. doi:10.1080/13538322.2011.614468.

Brock-Utne, B. 2003. 'Formulating Higher Education Policies in Africa: The Pressure from External Forces and the Neoliberal Agenda.' *Journal of Higher Education in Africa* 1 (1): 24–56.

Carroll, G, K Tyson and B Lumas. 2000. 'Those Who Got in the Door: The University of California-Berkeley's Affirmative Action Success Story.' *Journal of Negro Education* 69 (1/2): 128–144.

Chang, M J. 2000. 'The Relationship of High School Characteristics to the Selection of Undergraduate Students for Admission to the University of California-Berkeley.' *The Journal of Negro Education* 69 (1/2): 49–59.

CHE. 2012. *Vital Stats. Public Higher Education 2010*. Pretoria: Council on Higher Education. http://www.che.ac.za/documents/d000249/vital_stats_public_higher_education_2010.pdf

Chickering, A. 2006. 'Every Student Can Learn – If . . .' *About Campus* May–June: 9–15.

Cloete, N. 2009. *Responding to the Educational Needs of Post-School Youth. Determining the Scope of the Problem and Developing a Capacity-building Model*. Cape Town: CHET and FETI.

College Board. 2009. *The 5th Annual AP Report to the Nation*. New York: College Board. http://www.collegeboard.com

Conley, D T. 2003. *Understanding University Success. A Project of the Association of American Universities and The Pew Charitable Trusts*. Eugene, Oregon: Centre for Educational Policy Research, University of Oregon.

———. 2005. *College Knowledge. What It Really Takes for Students to Succeed and What We Can Do to Get Them Ready*. San Francisco: Jossey-Bass.

———. 2006. *What Must We Do to Create a System That Prepares College Students for Success*. Policy Perspectives. California: WestEd.

———. 2008a. 'Rethinking College Readiness.' *New Directions for Higher Education* Winter (144): 3–13.

———. 2008b. 'What Makes a Student College Ready?' *Educational Leadership* 66 (2): 1–3.

———. 2009. *College Readiness and High School-To-College Success*. Eugene, Oregon: Center for Educational Policy Development. www.epiconline.org/files/pdf/Aspen%20Institute.pdf

———. 2010. *College and Career Ready. Helping All Students Succeed Beyond High School*. San Francisco: Jossey-Bass.

Cunningham, F. 2007. 'The University and Social Justice.' *Journal of Academic Ethics* 5: 153–162.

Del Rios, M and L Leegwater. 2008. *Increasing Student Success at Minority Serving Insitutions: Findings from the Beams Project*. Washington DC: Institute for Higher Education Policy.

Delgado, R and J Stefanic. 2001. *Critical Race Theory. An Introduction*. New York: New York University Press.

Dietsche, P. 2009. 'Small Steps to a Big Idea. Personalising the Postsecondary Experience.' In *Focus on First-Year Success. Perspectives Emerging from South Africa and Beyond*, edited by B Leibowitz, S van der Merwe and S van Schalkwyk. Stellenbosch: Sun Media: 37–46.

EPIC. 2010a. *CollegeCareerReady School Diagnostic*. Eugene, Oregon: Educational Policy Improvement Centre.

———. 2010b. *The College-readiness Performance Assessment (C-PAS). An Innovative, Formative Assessment of Student's Cognitive Abilities.* Eugene, Oregon: Educational Policy Improvement Centre.

Fraser, N. 2009. *Scales of Justice: Reimagining Political Space in a Globalising World.* New York: Columbia University Press.

Furlong, A and F Cartmel. 2009. *Higher Education and Social Justice.* Berkshire, England: Society for Research into Higher Education and Open University Press.

Giroux, H A. 2002. 'Neoliberalism, Corporate Culture, and the Promise of Higher Education: The University as a Democratic Public Space.' *Harvard Educational Review* 72 (4): 425–463.

Giroux, H A and S S Giroux. 2004. *Take Back Higher Education. Race, Youth and the Crisis of Democracy in the Post-Civil Rights Era.* New York: Palgrave Macmillan Ltd.

Gordon, G. 2008. *Quality Enhancement: The First Year Experience. The Nature and Purposes of the First Year: Sharing and Reflecting on International Experiences and Perspectives.* Mansfield, Scotland: The Quality Assurance Agency for Higher Education.

Hart, C S. 2013. *Aspirations, Education and Social Justice. Applying Sen and Bourdieu.* London: Bloomsbury.

———. 2014. 'Agency, Participation and Transitions Beyond School.' In *Agency and Participation in Childhood and Youth. International Applications of the Capability Approach in Schools and Beyond,* edited by C S Hart, M Biggeri and B Babic. London: Bloomsbury: 246–275.

Harvey, L, S Drew and M Smith. 2006. *The First-year Experience: A Review of Literature for the Higher Education Academy.* York: Higher Education Academy.

Hausmann, L, J Ward Schofield and R Woods. 2007. 'Sense of Belonging as a Predictor of Intentions to Persist Among African American and White First-Year College Students.' *Research in Higher Education* 48 (7): 803–839.

Hoffman, N, J Vargas and J Santos. 2008. 'Blending High School and College.' *New Directions for Higher Education* Winter (144): 15–25.

Hoover, E. 2011. 'DePaul Becomes Biggest Private University to Go "Test Optional".' *The Chronicle of Higher Education,* 17 February.

Hurtado, S and D F Carter. 1997. 'Effects of College Transition and Perceptions of the Campus Racial Climate on Latino College Students' Sense of Belonging.' *Sociology of Education* 70 (4): 324–345.

Jacobs, C. 2009. 'Teaching explicitly that which is tactic. The challenge of disciplinary discourses.' In B Leibowitz, A van der Merwe and S van Schalkwyk (eds). *Focus on First-Year Success. Perspectives Emerging from South Africa and Beyond.* Stellenbosch: Sun Media: 241–252.

James, R J. 2007. *Social Equity in a Mass, Globalised Higher Education Environment: The Unresolved Issue of Widening Access to University.* Faculty of Education Dean's Lecture Series. Melbourne: University of Melbourne: Centre for the Study of Higher Education. http://www.edfac.unimelb.edu.au/news/lectures/pdf/richardjamestranscript.pdf

Johnston, B. 2010. *The First Year at University. Teaching Students in Transition.* New York: Society for Research into Higher Education and Open University Press.

Johnston, B and R Kockanowska. 2009. *Quality Enhancement Themes: The First Year Experience. Student Expectations, Experiences and Reflections on the First Year.* Mansfield, Scotland: The Quality Assurance Agency for Higher Education.

Jonathan, R. 2001. 'Higher Education Transformation and the Public Good.' *Kagisano. CHE Higher Education Discussion Series,* 1: 86.

Knox, H and J Wyper. 2008. *Quality Enhancement Themes: The First Year Experience. Personalisation of the First Year*. Mansfield, Scotland: The Quality Assurance Agency for Higher Education.

Koch, E and C Foxcroft. 2003. 'A Developmental Focus to Admissions Testing: Admissions and Placement Standards Development.' *South African Journal of Higher Education* 17 (3): 192–208.

Krause, K L, R Hartley, R James and C McInnis. 2005. *The First Year Experience in Australian Universities: Findings from a Decade of National Studies*. Melbourne, Australia: Centre for the Study of Higher Education, University of Melbourne.

Ladstone-Billings, G. 1998. 'Just What Is a Critical Race Theory and What's It Doing in a Nice Field Like Education?' *International Journal of Qualitative Studies in Education* 11 (1): 7–24.

Ladstone-Billings, G and W F Tate IV. 1995. 'Towards a Critical Race Theory of Education.' *Teachers College Record* 97 (1): 47–68.

Lee, J and T Ransom. 2010. *The Educational Experience of Young Men of Colour. A Review of Research, Pathways and Progress*. College Board. Advocacy and Policy Center. http:// youngmenofcolor.collegeboard.org/sites/default/files/downloads/EEYMC-Research Report.pdf

Maitland Schilling, K and K L Schilling. 2005. 'Expectations and Peformance.' In *Challenging and Supporting The First-Year Student. A Handbook for Improving the First Year of College*, edited by M L Upcraft, J N Gardner and B O Barefoot. San Francisco: Jossey-Bass: 108–123.

Mann, S. 2008. *Study, Power and the University*. Berkshire, England: Open University Press.

Marginson, S. 2011. 'Equity, Status and Freedom: a Note on Higher Education.' *Cambridge Journal of Education* 41 (1): 23–36.

Marshall, N A and D J Hargreaves. 2007. 'Crossing the Humpback Bridge: Primary-secondary School Transition in Music Education.' *Music Education Research* 9 (1): 65–80.

Martin, I, J Karabel, S W Jacquez. 2003. *Unequal Opportunity: Student Access to the University of California*. Berkley, California: University of California Institute for Labour and Employment. http://escholarship.org/uc/item/36h8z95g

Morley, L, and R Lugg. 2009. 'Mapping Meritocracy: Intersecting Gender, Poverty and Higher Educational Opportunity Structures.' *Higher Education Policy* 22: 37–60.

NACAC. 2008. *Report on the Commission of the Use of Standardised Tests in Undergraduate Admission*. Arlington, Virginia: National Association for College Admission Counselling.

Nel, C, C Troskie-de-Bruin and E Bitzer. 2009. 'Students' Transition from School to University: Possibilities for a Pre-university Intervention.' *South African Journal of Higher Education* 23 (5): 974–991.

Nunez, A. 2009. 'Latino Students' Transition to College: A Social and Intercultural Capital Perspective.' *Harvard Educational Review* 79 (1): 22–48.

Oakes, J, J Rogers, M Lipton and E Morrell. 2000. *The Social Construction of College Access: Confronting the Technical, Cultural, and Political Barriers to Low Income Students of Colour*. California: Institute for Democracy, Education and Access, UCLA.

OECD. 2006. *Personalising Education*. Paris: OECD. www.oecd.org/dataoecd/38/45/ 36509488.pdf

Perna, L W, H T Rowan-Kenyon, A D Bell, S L Thomas and C Li. 2008. 'Typology of Federal, State and Local Public Policies Designed to Promote College Access.' *Journal of Higher Education* 79 (3): 243–267.

Pitkethly, A, and M Prosser. 2001. 'The First Year Experience Project: A Model for University-wide Change.' *Higher Education Research and Development* 20 (2): 185–198.

Pittman, L D and A Richmond. 2008. 'University Belonging, Friendship Quality, and Psychosocial Adjustment During the Transition to College.' *The Journal of Experimental Education* 76 (4): 343–361.

Rawls, J. 1999. *A Theory of Justice*. Revised edition. Cambridge, Massachusetts: Harvard University Press.

Reid, J and J L Moore. 2008. 'College Readiness and Academic Preparation for Postsecondary Education: Oral Histories of First-Generation Urban College Students.' *Urban Education* 43: 240–261.

Robeyns, I. 2006. 'Three Models of Education: Rights, Capabilities and Human Capital.' *Theory and Research in Education* 4 (1): 69–84.

Rowan-Kenyon, H T, A D Bell and L W Perna. 2008. 'Contextual Influences on Parental Involvement in College-going: Variations by Socio-economic Class.' *Journal of Higher Education* 79 (5): 564–586.

Saenz, V B, S Hurtado, D Barrera, D Wolf and F Yeung. 2007. *First in My Family: A Profile of First-Generation College Students at Four-Year Institutions since 1971*. California: Higher Education Research Institute. http://www.heri.ucla.edu/PDFs/pubs/briefs/FirstGenResearchBrief.pdf

Sandel, M J. 2010. *Justice. What's the Right Thing to Do?* New York: Penguin Group.

Sawyerr, A. 2004. 'Challenges Facing African Universities.' *African Studies Review* 47 (1): 1–59.

Scott, P. 2009. 'Access in Higher Education in Europe and North America: Trends and Developments.' In Bucharest, Romania, UNESCO Forum on Higher Education in the Europe Region: Access, Values, Quality and Competitiveness.

Smit, R. 2012. 'Towards a Clearer Understanding of Student Disadvantage in Higher Education: Problematising Deficit Thinking.' *Higher Education Research and Development* 31 (3): 369–380.

Spreen, C A and S Vally. 2006. 'Education Rights, Education Policies and Inequality in South Africa.' *International Journal of Educational Development* 26: 352–362.

Steed, E and P Sudworth. 1985. 'The Humpback Bridge.' In *Curriculum Continuity: Primary to Secondary*, edited by R Derricott. Berkshire, England: NFER-Nelson: 23–37.

Strydom, J F and M Mentz. 2009. 'Weaving the Invisible Tapestry. Managing Diversity Through Orientation Innovation.' In *Focus on First-Year Success. Perspectives Emerging from South Africa and Beyond*, edited by B Leibowitz, S van der Merwe and S van Schalkwyk. Stellenbosch: Sun Media: 57–67.

Taylor Smith, C, A Miller and C A Bermeo. 2009. *Bridging the Gaps to Success. Promising Practices for Promoting Transfer Among Low-income and First-generation Students*. Washington DC: The Pell Institute.

Tikly, L and A M Barrett. 2011. 'Social Justice, Capabilities and the Quality of Education in Low Income Countries.' *International Journal of Educational Development* 31: 3–14.

Tornatzky, L G, Cutler, R and Lee J. 2002. *College Knowledge: What Latino parents need to know and why they don't know*. Claremont, California: The Tomas Rivera Policy Institute.

Unterhalter, E and V Carpentier. 2010. *Global Inequalities and Higher Education. Whose Interests Are We Serving?* Hampshire, England: Palgrave Macmillan Ltd.

Upcraft, M L, J N Gardner and B O Barefoot. 2005. *Challenging and Supporting the First-Year Student. A Handbook for Improving the First Year of College*. San Francisco: Jossey-Bass.

Venezia, A, M W Kirst and A L Antonio. 2003. *Betraying the College Dream: How Disconnected K-12 and Postsecondary Education Systems Undermine Student Aspirations*. California: Stanford University Bridge Project.

Walker, M. 2006. *Higher Education Pedagogies*. Berkshire, England: Society for Research into Higher Education and Open University Press.

Walker, M and M McLean. 2010. *Development Discourses: Higher Education and Poverty Reduction in South Africa. ESRC Impact Report*. RES-167-25-0302. Swindon: ESRC.

Wang Golann, J and K L Hughes. 2008. *Dual Enrolment Policies and Practices. Earning College Credit in California High Schools*. New York: Teachers College, Columbia University.

Warburton, E C, R Bugarin, A Nunez and C D Carroll. 2001. *Bridging the Gap. Academic Preparation and Postsecondary Success of First-Generation Students*. Washington DC: National Centre for Education Statistics.

Watts, M and D Bridges. 2006. 'Enhancing Students' Capabilities?: UK Higher Education and the Widening Participation Agenda.' In *Transforming Unjust Structures. The Capability Approach*, edited by S Deneulin and N Sagovsky, 19: Library of Ethics and Applied Philosophy. Netherlands: Springer: 143–160.

Whittaker, R. 2008. *Quality Enhancement Themes: The First Year Experience. Transition to and During the First Year*. Mansfield, Scotland: The Quality Assurance Agency for Higher Education.

Wilson-Strydom, M G. 2010. 'Traversing the Chasm from School to University in South Africa: A Student Perspective.' *Tertiary Education and Management* 16 (4): 313–325.

———. 2014. 'University Access and Theories of Social Justice: Contributions of the Capabilities Approach.' *Higher Education*. doi:10.1007/s10734-014-9766-5.

Yeld, N. 2009. *National Benchmark Tests Project as a National Service to Higher Education. Summary Report*. Pretoria: Higher Education South Africa.

Yorke, M and B Longden. 2008. *The First-year Experience of Higher Education in the UK. Final Report*. UK: Higher Education Academy.

Yosso, T J. 2005. 'Whose Culture Has Capital? A Critical Race Theory Discussion of Community Cultural Wealth.' *Race Ethnicity and Education* 8 (1): 69–91.

Young, I M. 1990. *Justice and the Politics of Difference*. Princeton, New Jersey: Princeton University Press.

———. 2001. 'Equality of Whom? Social Groups and Judgments of Injustice.' *Journal of Political Philosophy* 9 (1): 1–18.

Zukas, M and J Malcolm. 2007. 'Learning from Adult Education.' *Academy Exchange* 6 (Summer): 20–22.

3   The capabilities approach

[T]he crucial good societies should be promoting for their people is a set of opportunities, or substantial freedoms, which people then may or may not exercise in action: the choice is theirs.

(Nussbaum 2011, 18)

In her recent, and very helpful overview, Deneulin (2014, 108) defines Sen's approach to capabilities as '[A] moral approach to assess and judge (and transform) realities from the perspective of human freedom, in its dual aspects of well-being and agency'. This is the sense in which I am using the capabilities approach in this book. There are some differences of interpretation which I will briefly touch on later in the chapter, but for now, Deneulin's definition provides a useful starting point.[1] My aim in this chapter is to present an accessible outline of the capabilities approach for the reader who may not be familiar with the language of capabilities. I begin with a broad introduction to the capabilities approach, and then move on to focus on some of the core concepts on which the approach is built. I recognise that the capabilities approach terminology, with its roots in economics, philosophy and development studies, employs terms that are not always intuitively clear to a multidisciplinary audience. For this reason, in explaining the key concepts, I have included specific examples related to education and higher education in order to ground the concepts in a practical educational setting. In this chapter my argument remains at a relatively broad level, in line with the aim of introducing the approach and presenting an argument for why the capabilities framework is helpful for research looking at higher education from a social justice point of view. In Chapters 4 and 5 these ideas are developed further to theoretically propose a capabilities framework for access and the transition to university.

The capabilities approach was pioneered during the 1980s and 1990s by Amartya Sen, Nobel Prize winning economist and philosopher. Sen sought to provide an alternative to the dominant utilitarian and neoliberal approaches to development and well-being. One of the practical outcomes of Sen's work, developed in partnership with Mahbub ul Haq, has been the Human Development Index (HDI) and Human Development Reports (HDRs) now widely used in the world of international development for comparing relative human development levels of countries. The concept of human development moves discussions about what development means beyond the dominant neoliberal approaches focusing largely on income measured by Gross National Product (GNP) and places people at the centre of development processes. Human development can be defined as follows:

> Human development aims to enlarge people's freedoms to do and be what they value and have reason to value. In practice, human development also empowers people to engage actively in development of our shared planet. It is people-centred. At all levels of development, human development focuses on essential freedoms: enabling people to lead long and healthy lives, to acquire knowledge, to be able to enjoy a decent standard of living and to shape their own lives. Many people value these freedoms in and of themselves; they are also powerful means to other opportunities.
>
> (Alkire 2010, 43)

If we adapt this definition with a specific focus on students within higher education institutions and systems we might propose something along these lines:[2]

> A human development approach within universities would aim to enlarge students' choices to be and do what they value being and doing as students. In practice, this should also include the empowerment of students to actively engage in the development of their university, communities and our shared planet. Universities should be student-centred and enable students to live healthy lives, to acquire knowledge, and to enjoy a decent standard of living (well-being) as students. Students studying at universities that seek to promote human development should have appropriate opportunities to shape their own lives and study paths.

Human development and the capabilities approach are closely intertwined (Boni and Walker 2013), although the capabilities approach has tended to be the focus of academic literatures and human development the focus of development policy research and practice (Alkire 2010). This is one of the strengths of the capabilities approach, that it has a wide disciplinary audience and application, or in Sen's words, there are a 'plurality of purposes for which the capability approach can have relevance' (Sen 1993, 49). The ideas of the capability approach have also been developed further and in a slightly different direction by the well-known feminist philosopher, Martha Nussbaum (Nussbaum 2000). Although the capabilities approach is not a theory of social justice in the traditional philosophical sense, it does provide a normative framework that can be used to guide understandings of individual well-being and social arrangements in a manner that supports a striving for just outcomes (Alkire and Deneulin 2009a, 2009b). Sen describes the aim of his work in the area of capabilities and justice as seeking 'to clarify how we can proceed to address questions of enhancing justice and removing injustice, rather than to offer resolutions of questions about the nature of perfect justice' (Sen 2009, ix). The capabilities approach is thus a framework, with a normative commitment to social justice, that can be used for conceptualising and evaluating a range of social phenomena (Robeyns 2005, 94). At its core, the approach is about what people are effectively able to do and to be, within a comparative frame of reference (Sen 1980, 1985a, 1999). In order to adequately introduce the capabilities approach, it is necessary to focus some attention on the core concepts on which the framework is built. These include well-being, agency, freedom, functioning and capabilities. I will deal with each in the sections that follow, focusing on unpacking the concepts themselves and their importance and interconnectedness within the capabilities approach and in the context of education specifically.

Well-being

The capabilities approach assumes that, in assessing how well someone is doing, the focus needs to be on 'the "wellness" of a person's state of being . . . The exercise, then, is that of assessing the constituent elements of the person's being seen from the perspective of her own personal welfare' (Sen 1993, 36). In this sense, the capabilities approach (which draws on Aristotelian notions of human flourishing) differs from traditional quality of life measures that focus on instrumental outcomes, such as generating wealth or achievements, but say little about personal welfare or human flourishing. As I noted above, the capabilities approach centres on understanding whether people are able to be and do what they value being and doing. These beings and doings constitute a person's well-being. Importantly, well-being should not be confused with opulence or being well-off. Being well-off is about how much someone has (usually measured in terms of wealth), while well-being is about how a person functions and what they are able to be and do – their quality of life (Deneulin 2014). The capabilities approach assumes a rich and multidimensional view of well-being that takes account of the 'links between material, mental, and social well-being, or to the economic, social, political and cultural dimensions of human life' (Crocker and Robeyns 2009, 65). We will return to these links between well-being and context in later sections, as these interconnections are a critically important contribution that the capabilities approach makes to social justice research. But first we need to consider another central concept in the capabilities approach, that of agency.

Agency

Agency refers to the ability of a person to realise the goals that they value and have reason to value. Sen defines an agent as 'someone who acts and brings about change, and whose achievements can be judged in terms of her own values and objectives, whether or not we assess them in terms of some external criteria as well' (Sen 1999, 19). This means that, although well-being and agency are closely related, they are analytically distinct and might sometimes work against each other in a given individual's life. For example, a person who goes on hunger strike in solidarity with those who do not have food chooses to act in a manner that diminishes their own well-being in pursuit of a higher justice-related goal. Being able to make this choice is an expression of agency. Related are notions such as having a voice, self-determination, autonomy and empowerment. The opposite of exercising one's agency is to be forced, oppressed or passive (Alkire and Deneulin 2009b). Thus, the concept of agency includes having opportunities and choices (well-being freedoms) as well as the autonomy to be able to make one's own decisions (agency freedom). Although agency is exercised by individuals, Sen reminds us that his 'work is particularly concerned with the agency role of the individual as a member of the public and as a participant in economic, social and political actions' (Sen 1999, 19). While regarding people as agents is central to the capabilities approach, agency cannot be understood without consideration of the broader social, political, economic and environmental context a person is situated in, which can enable or constrain their agency.

Functionings and capabilities

Functionings can be defined as achieved outcomes, the things that a person is able to be or to do. At a broad level, functionings encompass, for example, being adequately nourished, being employed, being literate, doing a job that is meaningful and fulfilling. If we consider higher education, functionings would include achievements such as being able to read academic texts, being able to take part in university life, taking responsibility for oneself, or being able to pass an examination. The second important element of the concept of functionings is that it refers to outcomes that a person values and has reason to value; as such, individual choice or agency is explicitly recognised. An achievement or outcome is not a functioning if it is not something that is valued by the person concerned (Alkire and Deneulin 2009b, 32). For example, a young man who has just completed an accounting qualification at the instruction of his father, despite the fact that he is a passionate and talented painter who wished to study fine arts, would not necessarily view his accounting qualification as a functioning or an achievement that he has reason to value. He was not able to exercise his agency in selecting his course of study and future career trajectory and this has an impact on his well-being freedom and achievement.

The notion of capabilities combines the concept of functionings with opportunity freedom. Capabilities are the freedom (choices or options) a person has to enjoy valuable functionings (Alkire and Deneulin 2009b; Deneulin et al. 2006; Nussbaum 2000, 2011; Sen 1980, 1999). Put very simply, 'A functioning is an achievement [outcome], whereas a capability is the ability to achieve [potential]' (Sen 1985b, 48; see also Walker and Unterhalter 2007, 4). As such, a functioning can be seen as the active realisation of capabilities (Nussbaum 2011, 24–25). Nussbaum uses the concept of capabilities in a slightly different and perhaps more nuanced way (Nussbaum 2000, 2011; see also, Crocker 1995). In making clear that capabilities should not be reduced to personal abilities, Nussbaum distinguishes between internal capabilities and combined capabilities. Internal capabilities refer to 'states of the person' (Nussbaum 2011, 21) which are fluid and dynamic. Internal capabilities can be described as abilities or traits which are developed through interaction with the broader context in which a person is located. Nussbaum uses the term combined capabilities to encompass the more expansive notion of capabilities as substantial freedoms, which include the 'totality of options [one] has for choice and action in [one's] specific political, social and economic situation' (Nussbaum 2011, 21). Crocker (1995, 161) likens internal capabilities to a form of personal power to act within the constraints of a given social context. The concept of internal capabilities or personal powers also encompasses the notion of skills (Gasper and van Staveren 2003). Yet, importantly, personal powers or capabilities are more than skills. A focus on developing skills rather than capabilities places too great an emphasis on de-contextualised individual abilities and too little emphasis on the interaction with the social, economic, familial and political environments that define what skills can be developed and by whom, and also provide the bounds within which skills may, or may not, be used. As such, 'capabilities are understood both as opportunities, but also as skills and capacities [personal powers] that can be fostered' given a supportive context/environment (Walker 2006, 128). This distinction is particularly important where preparedness for higher education implies more than academic skills alone and where the opportunities to develop the skills and capacities needed for higher education are not equally available to all (see Chapter 2).

The distinction between capabilities and functionings is critical in the context of social justice because understanding outcomes/achievements only does not necessarily provide sufficient information to understand how well someone is really doing, nor do outcomes give an indication of the extent to which a person has agency freedom in their life. Consider the following fictional (although very realistic in the context of my research) example of two young women who both graduate from university with an undergraduate commerce qualification (scenarios adapted from, Walker and Unterhalter 2007, 4–5, drawing on my own experience working with students in South Africa). The first young woman, Judy, attended a middle class suburban high school and came from a reasonably affluent home. Her father had not been to university, as he took over the family business when he completed school. Her mother was a high school teacher. Although Judy had a trainee manager job available at her father's company on completing school, she decided that she wished to experience university before commencing her working life. She did not need to achieve high marks as her future was secure, so she made the most of all the social opportunities available at university. Her schooling had also equipped her relatively well for the demands of university and she enjoyed the discussions and debates in class, but she spent only the minimum time possible on her studies. The second young woman, Bernita, grew up in a semi-urban township area. Her family was poor; her father was unemployed and her mother worked as a domestic worker. The school she attended was under-resourced and there was little commitment to teaching and learning. Bernita was strong academically and with a lot of hard work and studying until late at night she managed to meet the entrance criteria to university on completion of her Grade 12. She was the only learner from her school to go to university. Once at university, Bernita found it difficult to fit in with her peers from a different social class and educational backgrounds to hers. The poor quality of teaching at her school did not prepare her well for discussions in class nor for her written work. At school she was mostly able to talk in Sesotho,[3] her mother tongue, although she officially learned in English, so she felt anxious about speaking in English at university and was unwilling to venture an opinion in class or when doing group work. Bernita worked very hard while at university, but lacked confidence in her abilities and tended to blame herself for poor performance, and as a result she did not ask her lecturers for additional support.

Despite these very different experiences and learning trajectories, both young women obtained second class passes in their commerce degree. Although the educational outcome (functioning) is the same (a second class pass), the capabilities of Judy and Bernita differ tremendously. Considering only the outcome thus masks areas of injustice and inequality that should be addressed (see also, Pendelbury and Enslin 2004; Wolff and de-Shalit 2007). Understanding differences in capabilities such as those highlighted in this fictional example are of particular importance in seeking to facilitate the transition from school to university. As Walker and Unterhalter (2007, 5) remind us:

> The capability approach requires that we do not simply evaluate functionings [outcomes] but the real freedom or opportunities each student had available to choose from and to achieve what she valued. Our evaluation of equality must then take account of freedom in opportunities as much as observed choices. The capability approach, therefore, offers a method to evaluate real educational advantage, and equally to identify disadvantage, marginalisation, and exclusion.

This identification of educational disadvantage, marginalisation and exclusion opens up a space for action towards the overall aim of social justice within higher education and more specifically related to enhancing the transition to university. However, there is some debate in the capabilities literature regarding whether the focus of analysis should be on functionings, on capabilities, or both (for example, Alkire and Deneulin, 2009a; Crocker, 1995; Crocker and Robeyns, 2009; Sen, 1992; Wolff and de-Shalit, 2007). Sen and Nussbaum argue for a focus on capabilities because both place emphasis on the intrinsic value of freedom to choose what one has reason to value (Nussbaum 2000, 2011; Sen 1985a, 1992, 1999). This issue is particularly relevant in the case of education which can be seen as both a functioning (being educated) and a capability (having educational opportunities), both of which support the realisation of other capabilities and functionings. Nussbaum (2011, 25) reminds us that capability and functioning are two sides of the same coin, and if people were never able to function, then it would not make sense to look at capabilities or opportunities to function. Similarly, in much earlier writing, Sen (1992, 50, emphasis in original) states that 'the first thing to note is that capability is defined in terms of the *same* focal variables as functionings'. In seeking to unravel the complexities inherent in operationalising the capabilities approach, Crocker and Robeyns (2009, 71) propose a conceptual way around this debate by arguing that 'one could focus on achieved functioning levels but – where appropriate – include the exercise of choice as one of the relevant functionings'. The key point to note from this debate is that the notions of capabilities (personal powers and opportunities) and functionings (outcomes or achievements) are closely linked. Further, it is not possible to directly observe or assess capabilities. Instead, functionings – which can be observed – need to be used as a proxy for assessing capabilities (Sen 1992). We return to this issue in Chapter 6 where the distinction between capabilities and functionings is unpacked in the specific context of the capabilities framework for the transition to university being developed here.

Conversion factors

The concept of conversion factors plays an important role in bringing together individual agency and the social contexts in which that agency is exercised in the realisation of capabilities and/or functionings. People differ in many ways, and these differences affect the extent to which they can convert resources into opportunities (capabilities), and opportunities into achievements (functionings). While differences do not inherently imply inequality, differences become inequalities when they impact on capabilities, as we saw with the example of Judy and Bernita above. Sen reminds us that 'there is evidence that the conversion of goods to capabilities varies from person to person substantially, and the equality of the former may still be far from the equality of the latter' (Sen 1980, 219). For example, a learner who is blind is different from a learner who can see. This difference is not inherently a form of inequality, but if Braille text books and other learning support needed for blind learners is not provided, then the educational capabilities of the blind learner will be limited compared to the learner who is not blind (see also, Nussbaum 2000, 2003).Paying attention to conversion factors provides a mechanism for understanding what is needed to realise potential outcomes or functionings (Walker and Unterhalter 2007, 10). Sen has identified five ways in which individual variations impact on the conversion of resources, such as income or food for example, into well-being and freedom. These five sources of individual variation are (paraphrased from Sen 1999, 71):

- *Personal heterogeneities*: People have disparate physical characteristics connected with (dis)ability, illness, age, or gender, and these make their needs diverse.
- *Environmental diversities*: Variations in environmental conditions, such as climatic circumstances (temperature ranges, rainfall, flooding and so on), can influence what a person gets out of a given level of income, or other resources available to them.
- *Variations in social climate*: The conversion of personal incomes and resources into quality of life is influenced also by social conditions, including public educational arrangements for example.

- *Differences in relational perspectives*: Conventions and customs which vary between different communities affect commodity requirements and establish patterns of behaviour which impact on the conversion of resources into capabilities and functionings.
- *Distribution within the family*: Incomes (and educational opportunities) are shared within the family. The well-being or freedom of individuals in a family is dependent on how income and resources are distributed within the family, such as families in which the education of male children is prioritised over that of female children.

Consolidating Sen's ideas, Robeyns draws our attention to three groups of conversion factors: *personal conversion factors*, for example metabolism, physical condition, reading ability, intelligence and health status; *social conversion factors*, for example policies, social norms, family relations, practices of discrimination, gender roles, patriarchy and power relations; and *environmental conversion factors*, for example geographical locations, rural versus urban contexts, and climate (Robeyns 2005, 99). These conversion factors impact on the extent to which a person is able to make use of the resources available to them to create capabilities or opportunities. The space within which justice comparisons should then me made, is the space of opportunity or capability. We need to ask whether 'some people get more opportunities to convert their resources into capabilities than others?' (Walker 2005, 109).

Fertile functioning and corrosive disadvantage

The capabilities approach has been used and developed – both theoretically and empirically – by philosophers Wolff and de-Shalit (2007), in their exploration of the meaning of disadvantage. Wolff and de-Shalit argue that disadvantage should be seen as a multidimensional phenomenon where the most disadvantaged are those who experience disadvantage in multiple areas, that is, clusters of disadvantage. There are three aspects of these authors' work of particular relevance in the context of the argument being constructed in this book. The first of these is the notion of risk and, related, that of insecure functionings. Drawing on empirical work in Israel and Britain, Wolff and de-Shalit (2007, 66) argue that one way of identifying disadvantage is to identify those who are exposed to risks that they would not have taken had they had another choice. The argument is not that there should be no risks, but that some people face undue risks and, although they might have certain capabilities in the present, they are not able to count on them in the future (see also, Nussbaum 2011, 43). Further, in many instances 'disadvantages and risks compound each other and cluster together' (Wolff and de-Shalit, 2007, 10). A simplified example in the context of higher education is the student who depends on bursary funding support but is unsure from year to year whether funding would be granted and if so, whether the amount will be sufficient. Such a student has the capability to study, but faces the risk of not being able to pay fees at any time. Further, depending on the amount provided by the bursary, the student may be able to pay for fees but not cover living expenses. As such, the student eats only one cheap and not particularly nutritious meal per day, is inclined to become ill due to poor nutrition, and so misses class. Due to missing classes, and spending a lot of time trying to earn extra money as a part-time waiter, the student performs poorly academically and struggles to earn the minimum credits required for a renewal of funding the following year. The risks continue and, as is seen in this example, cluster together, creating multiple levels of disadvantage.

In developing their theory of disadvantage, Wolff and de-Shalit also add two important new concepts to the capabilities approach, namely, fertile functioning and corrosive disadvantage. Fertile functionings refer to functionings that tend to promote or assist in securing other functionings or capabilities. Corrosive disadvantages are those disadvantages that tend to yield further disadvantage (Wolff and de-Shalit, 2007). Thus, fertile functionings and corrosive disadvantages can been seen as examples of conversion factors. Based on their empirical research, these authors argue that those who are most disadvantaged tend to be in a situation where multiple disadvantages cluster together. As such, they note that special attention should be given to 'the way patterns of disadvantage form and persist, and to take steps to break up such clusters' (Wolff and de-Shalit, 2007, 10). Identifying fertile functionings and corrosive disadvantages provide a means for pinpointing clusters of disadvantage as well as possible steps to remedy them. In seeking to understand the transition to university from a social justice perspective, identifying fertile functionings and corrosive disadvantages holds particular value because they point to specific areas for intervention. In Chapter 5 I investigate the access experiences and the transition to university – from the perspective of learners and students. As will be seen, this analysis points to fertile functionings and corrosive disadvantages on which I then build in later chapters where a capabilities framework for the transition to university is developed.

Capabilities and social justice

Given the pervasiveness of the human capital approach within education and higher education contexts, as well as the overlaps and critical differences between human capital and capabilities, it is helpful to briefly highlight the similarities and differences. Particular emphasis is placed on why the capabilities approach provides a more useful way of understanding social justice in higher education (Boni and Walker 2013). Human capital approaches first emerged within the field of economics. The contribution this work made to traditional economic theories was immense, particularly in demonstrating the human element of development. With a focus on building human capital through investment in education and skills development, this approach was critical in drawing attention to the value of education, and particularly higher education which had been regarded as of less importance than primary education by powerful international players such as the World Bank (Lanzi 2007; Robeyns 2006, 2009; Sen 1997, 1999). However, despite this important contribution, human capital theories are limited in that they focus on the instrumental economic benefits of education;

'human qualities that can be employed as "capital" in production in the way that physical capital is' (Sen 1997, 1959). Further, it is generally assumed that labour markets work rationally and, once someone is educated, the labour market will allocate them to access appropriate employment (Unterhalter 2009). As such, the human capital framework ignores the myriad forms of injustice that operate within education itself and in society more broadly, which limit certain groups' access to opportunities in both education and employment. The capabilities approach extends the human capital conception of education to include both instrumental and intrinsic values of education and the role that education plays in the expansion of individual freedoms, as well as influencing social change. The focus of the capabilities approach on the *actual lives* of people, on what they are able to be and do, means that this approach is directly concerned with *practical, everyday forms of inequality and injustice*. The capabilities approach views each and every individual as an end in themselves, and not the means to some other (larger) end such as the elusive notion of 'development' or in the context of university access – the chasing of equity targets and growth in student enrolment.

The capabilities approach also extends rights based approaches to education, by drawing attention to the fact that just because rights have officially been granted it does not mean they will be realised in practice (Nussbaum 2000, 2006; Sen 1999, 2009). For Nussbaum, the capabilities approach 'provides important precision and supplementation to the language of rights' (Nussbaum 2003, 37). Working from a feminist standpoint, Robeyns argues that, once equal rights have been granted for men and women, it is difficult to make further claims for social change. An example would be where constitutional rights secure equal access to education for both girls and boys, on which basis governments might be satisfied. However, equal access does not say anything about the extent to which educational outcomes might still indicate gender inequalities (Robeyns 2006, 80–81; see also, Nussbaum 2000, 2003).

As I hope is evident from the preceding sections of this chapter, the level and depth of debate and analysis regarding social justice, capabilities, the nature of freedom, human development and so on is extensive and cuts across the disciplines of philosophy, political philosophy, economics, law, social theory and development studies. My focus here is on applying the capabilities approach – which has been shown by various authors to be of immense value in a higher education context – to the issue of university access and the transition from school to university. There is a growing body of research looking at education and higher education from a capabilities perspective and it is to this research that we turn in the coming chapter. Before doing so though, one final theoretical issue requires our attention – the relationship between capabilities, well-being and happiness.

Capabilities, well-being and happiness

In the past decade or so there has been a growing focus on the constructs of well-being, happiness and/or flourishing in the social sciences, including an edited book entitled *Capabilities and Happiness* (Bruni et al. 2008). Deneulin (2014, 39) refers to this as the 'well-being turn' in social research. In the policy sphere we have seen, since 2012, the publication of the annual World Happiness Reports. This well-being turn can also be seen at universities which are increasingly introducing various wellness or well-being interventions targeting both students and staff. Like the human development and capabilities approaches, research on happiness also seeks to move beyond economic or wealth-based assessments of well-being to a deeper consideration of people's lives. However, as Alkire (2010) notes, most of the literature on happiness and well-being (with a few exceptions) adopts a much narrower conception of well-being than is the case in the capabilities approach. It is most common to conceive of happiness as a mood state or as a measure of satisfaction with one's life. When assessing happiness, research participants are generally asked to indicate how happy or how satisfied they are with different aspects of their lives on a quantitative rating scale. As such, the measures of happiness (many of which have been developed within the sub-discipline of Positive Psychology) tend to be based on subjective responses rather than an assessment of the broader life context of the person in question (Diener et al. 2002; Seligman 2012). In contrast, the capabilities approach recognises the importance of subjective happiness and well-being, but also calls attention to the objective circumstances of a person's life in recognition of the fact that people living in abject poverty can still report that they are happy (Deneulin 2014). If happiness is defined as the ultimate normative end point for assessing well-being, then we could plausibly claim that a happy person living in poverty should not be of particular concern from a social justice point of view. Yet, few people would argue that abject poverty is a state of well-being. An example in point is the research conducted by Biswas-Diener and Diener (2006, 2001) with homeless people in Calcutta, California and Portland (Oregon) in which they found relatively high levels of life satisfaction despite dire living conditions. Applied in the context of university students, we would be highly unlikely to conclude that a student who is too poor to afford a meal each day and lives in a shack without basic services, yet does not let this diminish her general sense of satisfaction and happiness at having a place at university, has achieved a state of well-being.

The capabilities approach, which is a normative framework that takes notions of equality, human dignity and social justice as a starting assumption, would explain this apparent contradiction in a different way. Based on her research with poor women in India, Nussbaum notes how women living in unjust situations adapt their preferences and their views about the life they value (their well-being) based on what they know and on what appears to be possible (Nussbaum 2000). The notion of adaptive preferences as used within the capabilities approach refers to 'learning to desire what one is being socially constructed to want, rather than what one has reason to value' (Deprez et al. 2013, 146). In other words, one's personal history and broader context, or as Nussbaum describes it 'people's entire upbringing in society' (Nussbaum 2012, 83), impact on preference formation and, hence, on the type of lives and societies individuals value. The concept of adaptive preferences is a complex and sometimes contested one. A balance must be found between recognising expressions of agency and choice and questioning what one regards as choices made on the basis of adaptive preferences that should be challenged in the interest of equity and fairness. Further, it is also necessary to recognise that in some cases adaptive preferences may serve important purposes for the person who has developed them.[4] Nonetheless, the concepts of adaptive preferences, and the related but distinct concept of conversion factors, provide particularly useful conceptual tools for understanding the broader context within which well-being may or may not be realised. While the happiness literatures and measures provide an important perspective on individual well-being and quality of life, the capabilities approach goes further by integrating both subjective and objective analyses of well-being in the interest of furthering social justice. The coming chapter builds on this introduction to the capabilities approach with an explicit application to the challenges of higher education access for social justice.

Notes

1 Deneulin (2014) explicitly differentiates between Sen's capability approach and Nussbaum's capabilities approach to emphasise that Nussbaum proposes a list of central human capabilities which is not endorsed by Sen. As discussed in the introductory chapter, I am not using this distinction in my work. Instead, I am using the term capabilities to refer to the work of both Sen and Nussbaum. In later works Sen also sometimes refers to the capabilities approach.

2 Two recent books, both published in 2013, that provide important insights into the contribution that a human development and capabilities approach can make to higher education are the collection entitled *Human Development and Capabilities. Re-imagining the university of the twenty-first century* edited by Alejandra Boni and Melanie Walker and the manuscript *Professional Education, Capabilities and the Public Good. The role of universities in promoting human development* authored by Melanie Walker and Monica McLean.

3 South Africa has 11 officially recognised languages, one of which is Sesotho. While there have been moves to allow for mother tongue education in the first three years of schooling, in most cases, the official languages of education are English and Afrikaans. Notwithstanding that most learners in the country officially learn in English, it is very common for teachers to make use of other languages in the classroom when explaining concepts and for questions and answer sessions to also occur in vernacular languages. While this helps with the immediate communicative relationship between teachers and learners, in the longer term, many learners find it difficult to function in a university environment where all learning and communication in the classroom takes place in English or Afrikaans.

4 For example, research conducted by Watts and Bridges (2006) exploring aspirations for higher education and the influence of adaptive preferences showed that young people who chose not to go to higher education, or who did not have aspirations for higher education, were not all responding to adaptive preferences which limited their aspirations. In some cases young people had sound reasons for choosing not to attend university based on the lives that they valued, and not because they did not aspire to university. Thus UK policy that assumes that low participation of particular groups in higher education is largely a result of low aspirations does not take account of the full picture and of the agency of young people who might make specific and informed choices for a life that does not include university education.

References

Alkire, S. 2010. 'Human Development: Definitions, Critiques, and Related Concepts.' Human Development Research Paper 2010/01. New York: UNDP.

Alkire, S and S Deneulin. 2009a. 'A Normative Framework for Development.' In *An Introduction to the Human Development and Capability Approach. Freedom and Agency*, edited by S Deneulin and L Shahani. London: Earthscan: 3–21.

———. 2009b. 'The Human Development and Capability Approach.' In *An Introduction to the Human Development and Capability Approach. Freedom and Agency*, edited by S Deneulin and L Shahani. London: Earthscan.

Biswas-Diener, Robert and Ed Diener. 2001. 'Making the Best of a Bad Situation: Satisfaction in the Slums of Calcutta.' *Social Indicators Research* 55 (3): 329–352.

———. 2006. 'The Subjective Well-Being of the Homeless, and Lessons for Happiness.' Social Indicators Research 76 (2): 185–205.

Boni, A and M Walker. 2013. *Human Development and Capabilities. Re-imagining the University of the Twenty-first Century*. London: Routledge.

Bruni, L, Flavio Comim and M Pugno. 2008. *Capabilities and Happiness*. Oxford: Oxford University Press.

Crocker, D. 1995. 'Functioning and Capability: The Foundations of Sen's and Nussbaum's Development Ethic, Part 2.' In *Women, Culture and Development. A Study of Human Capabilities*, edited by M Nussbaum and J Glover. Oxford: Oxford University Press: 153–198.

Crocker, D and I Robeyns. 2009. 'Capability and Agency.' In *Amartya Sen. Contemporary Philosophy in Focus*, edited by C J Morris. Oxford: Oxford University Press: 60–90.

Deneulin, S. 2014. *Wellbeing, Justice and Development Ethics*. Routledge Human Development and Capability Debates Series. Abingdon: Routledge.

Deneulin, S, M Nebel and N Sagovsky. 2006. *Transforming Unjust Structures. The Capability Approach*. 19. Library of Ethics and Applied Philosophy. Netherlands: Springer.

Deprez, L S, Diane R. Wood, A Boni and M Walker. 2013. 'Teaching for Well-being. Pedagogical Strategies for Meaning, Value, Relevance and Justice.' In *Human Development and Capabilities. Re-Imagining the University of the Twenty-first Century*. London: Routledge: 145–161.

Diener, Ed, R E Lucas and S Oishi. 2002. 'Subjective Well-Beinig.' In *Handbook of Positive Psychology*, edited by C R Snyder and S J Lopez. Oxford: Oxford University Press: 63–73.

Gasper, D and I van Staveren. 2003. 'Development as Freedom – and as What Else?' Feminist Economics 9 (2–3): 137–161.

Lanzi, D. 2007. 'Capabilities, Human Capital and Education.' *Journal of Socio-Economics* 36: 424–435.

Nussbaum, M C. 2000. *Women and Human Development. The Capabilities Approach*. Cambridge, UK: Cambridge University Press.

———. 2003. 'Capabilities as Fundamental Entitlements: Sen and Social Justice.' Feminist Economics 9 (2–3): 33–59.

———. 2006. 'Education and Democratic Citizenship: Capabilities and Quality Education.' Journal of Human Development 7 (3): 385–395.

———. 2011. *Creating Capabilities. The Human Development Approach*. Cambridge, Massachusetts: Harvard University Press.

———. 2012. 'Creating Capabilities: The Human Development Approach.' University of the Free State.

Pendelbury, S and P Enslin. 2004. 'Social Justice and Inclusion in Education and Politics: The South African Case.' *Journal of Education* 34: 31–50.

Robeyns, I. 2005. 'The Capability Approach: a Theoretical Survey.' *Journal of Human Development* 6 (1): 93–114.

———. 2006. 'Three Models of Education: Rights, Capabilities and Human *Capital.*' *Theory and Research in Education* 4 (1): 69–84.

———. 2009. 'Equality and Justice.' In *An Introduction to the Human Development and Capability Approach. Freedom and Agency*, edited by S Deneulin and L Shahani. London: Earthscan: 101–120.

Seligman, M E P. 2012. *Flourish. A Visionary New Understanding of Happiness and Well-Being.* New York: Free Press.

Sen, A. 1980. *Equality of What? The Tanner Lecture on Human Values.* California: Stanford University.

———. 1985a. 'Well-being, Agency & Freedom: The Dewey Lectures 1984.' *Journal of Philosophy* 82 (4): 169–221.

———. 1985b. *The Standard of Living. The Tanner Lectures on Human Values.* Cambridge, UK: Cambridge University.

———. 1992. *Inequality Reexamined.* New York: Russell Sage Foundation.

———. 1993. 'Capability and Well-Being.' In *The Quality of Life*, edited by M Nussbaum and A Sen. New Delhi: Oxford University Press, India: 30–53.

———. 1997. 'Editorial: Human Capital and Human Capability.' *World Development* 25 (12): 1959–1961.

———. 1999. *Development as Freedom.* Oxford: Oxford University Press.

———. 2009. *The Idea of Justice.* Cambridge, Massachusetts: Harvard University Press.

Unterhalter, E. 2009. 'Education.' In *An Introduction to the Human Development and Capability Approach. Freedom and Agency*, edited by S Deneulin and L Shahani. London: Earthscan: 207–227.

Walker, M. 2005. 'Amartya Sen's Capability Approach and Education.' Educational Action Research 13 (1): 103–110.

———. 2006. *Higher Education Pedagogies.* Berkshire, UK: Society for Research into Higher Education and Open University Press.

Walker, M and E Unterhalter. 2007. 'The Capability Approach: Its Potential for Work in Education.' In Amartya Sen's *Capability Approach and Social Justice in Education*, edited by M Walker and E Unterhalter. New York: Palgrave Macmillan Ltd: 1–18.

Walker, M and McLean, M. 2013. *Professional Education, Capabilities and the Public Good. The Role of Universities in Human Development.* London: Routledge.

Watts, M and D Bridges. 2006. 'Enhancing Students' Capabilities?: UK Higher Education and the Widening Participation Agenda.' In *Transforming Unjust Structures. The Capability Approach*, edited by S Deneulin and N Sagovsky. Library of Ethics and Applied Philosophy. Netherlands: Springer: 143–160.

Wolff, J and A de-Shalit. 2007. *Disadvantage.* Oxford: Oxford University Press.

4 Access and the capabilities approach

> The power to do good almost always goes with the possibility to do the opposite.
>
> (Sen 1999, xiii)

We now begin to delve into the specifics of how the capabilities approach can be employed in the context of university access. The chapter begins with a brief discussion of the exiting research on the capabilities approach within education. Studies that have used the capabilities approach for research on access and widening participation are then considered in more detail. The main purpose of the chapter is to present a theoretical rationale and conceptualisation of access for success using the capabilities approach, which proves particularly helpful for tackling the complexities of diversity, inequality and social justice within the domain of university access.

Capabilities approach and (higher) education research

When working within a capabilities framework, it is possible to approach education issues in two broad ways. First, one can consider the 'capability to participate in education', where the focus is on educational opportunities (Vaughan 2007, 116). Second, the fertile functioning of being educated plays an important role in the development of other capabilities, such as finding employment, being able to engage in and understand political processes and so on (Biggeri 2014; Nussbaum 2000; Sen 1999; Vaughan 2007). The first approach, the capability to participate in higher education, is the main focus of this study. Questions about what might prevent a student from engaging in the learning process at school or university, and whether there are specific factors affecting the ability to attend school or university, are thus central. Influences on the ability to effectively participate in education can be found both within and outside of education institutions and include, for example, the social norms and structures within which educational institutions function, personal characteristics of the learner/student and a host of environmental factors (Vaughan 2007).

The capabilities framework has found increasing traction for researching all levels and types of education, and this growing body of work has demonstrated the conceptual depth that the approach provides (for some examples, see Boni and Walker 2013; Hart 2011, 2009, 2007; Hart et al. 2014; Lanzi 2007; Nussbaum 2010; Unterhalter et al. 2007; Walker and McLean 2013). Walker (2006, 142) identifies four reasons why the capabilities approach is of particular value when striving for social justice in education. The first is that both intrinsic and instrumental values of education are recognised, and second, the capabilities approach includes both recognition and redistribution as central elements of social justice. Third, agency is foregrounded as a measure of individual advantage or disadvantage in and through higher education, thus placing the student centrally, and fourth, space is created to consider which capabilities should be fostered in order to achieve educational/pedagogic rights.

It is useful to briefly consider in a little more detail some of the studies that have been done in the areas of education and higher education from a capabilities perspective. These examples of published research highlight the richness and varied applications possible within the broad ambit of the capabilities approach, but by no means cover the full spectrum of research in this field. Because the capabilities approach is based on understanding what people can actually be and do, and on the lives people live in practice, the boundaries between conceptual critique and practical action for change towards more just outcomes are potentially blurred (Walker 2006). As such, the capabilities approach provides both a conceptual lens for theoretically exploring the transition to university from a social justice point of view, as well as a basis for proposing interventions; drawing on the everyday experiences of students.

In a schooling context, Terzi presents a strong argument for why the capability to be educated should be seen as a fundamental entitlement and thus that the provision of quality education for diverse learners is a matter of social justice (Terzi 2007). She also presents a possible list of basic capabilities required for educational functionings. These include literacy, numeracy, sociality and participation, learning dispositions, physical activities, science and technology and practical reasoning (Terzi 2007, 37). A useful review of educational reforms in Queensland, Australia, drew specifically on Sen's book *Development as Freedom* published in 1999 (Harreveld and Singh 2008). These authors conducted a policy analysis of the Queensland Government's Education and Training Reforms – particularly considering 'senior learning'. These reforms sought to reposition senior secondary school to incorporate more flexible and vocational learning opportunities for young people likely to drop out of high school. They found that the flexible learning opportunities introduced did indeed create opportunities for young people with few educational options, and also supported the development of what might be seen as key functionings such as literacy and numeracy. From an educational policy analysis perspective, Harreveld and Singh conclude that 'the usefulness of Sen's (1999) capability approach for policy analysis lies in its potential to engage with the multi-level socioeconomic processes that get worked out over time through complex multi-faceted reforms' (Harreveld and Singh 2008, 222). The capabilities approach has also been used to advance an argument for why post-secondary education is critical for low-income women with children because of what it enables them to be and to do (Deprez and Butler 2007; see also Sen 1999). From a philosophy of education angle, Saito (2003) explores the links between the capabilities approach and education, and concludes her theoretical paper with a call for educationists to explore the new possibilities that capabilities based analyses open up. Unterhalter (2009) has presented a conceptual analysis of the meaning of equity in education drawing on reflections from the capabilities approach, and there is a growing body of research that considers children and youth, including their education and schooling, from a capabilities perspective (Hart et al. 2014).

From a higher education standpoint, and particularly with respect to university access as is the focus here, four further studies bear mention. Walker has presented the capabilities approach as a framework for evaluating higher education peda-gogy and student learning within the context of the social and pedagogical arrangements that influence possibilities for equality of learning opportunities (Walker 2006, 2008, 2009). One of the areas in which she focuses in this work is that of widening participation in the UK higher education context. Working with 14 students who were part of a Widening Participation project, Walker reports that, even though their individual experiences differed and several encountered various difficulties in their studies, all 14 students felt that participating in higher education had helped them to expand their life choices and opportunities. She concludes that understanding widening participation from a capabilities per-spective that considers what widening participation students are able to be and do provides a means of unpacking the ways in which higher education pedagogy can generate both capabilities and capability deprivations, producing both equity and inequity, belonging and exclusion (Walker 2006). Walker's study thus shows how the capabilities approach places research on accessing higher education within the realm of a discourse of ethics.

Marginson (2011, 23) addresses the complex and contradictory ethics of participation in higher education, and sets out to answer the question – 'has socio-economic equity in higher education advanced, concurrent with the growth of participation?' Drawing on Sen's analysis of theories of justice (Sen 2009), Marginson shows how there is an underlying tension in approaches to equity in higher education. He argues that the dominant equity as fairness approaches focus on 'purifying the mechanisms of fair competition' particularly in the context of access, but do not take account of individual's different capacities to compete in the first place (Marginson 2011, 30). The result is that, while participation of under-represented groups increases in absolute numbers, proportional representation remains as unequal as ever. Instead of equity as fairness, which draws on ideal theories of social justice, Marginson (2011, 28, emphasis added) argues that realist approaches to social justice (approaches to which Sen's work is aligned) provide a better means of engaging with the challenges of equity in higher education because the focus is on 'actual human behaviours and the achievement of justice in *real situations*'. He argues further that, when seeking to overcome injustice, the focus should be on understanding, in depth, the various inequalities in higher education and then to identify strategies 'in pursuit of smaller changes at many points, rather than all points at once (and hence in none)' (Marginson 2011, 34).

In their critical considerations of injustices present in widening participation discourse and policy in the UK, Watts and Bridges (2006) also make use of the capabilities approach. Researching working class young people who chose not to enter higher education, these authors use Sen's work to show that combining the agendas of social inclusion and economic development results in reformation of injustice (i.e. new forms of injustice) rather than the resolution thereof (Watts and Bridges 2006, 143). Using the method of life histories to capture the experiences of their sample of young people not in higher education, they were able to move beyond technical widening participation debates that so often focus on statistics indicating access trends. The study showed that some working class young people who chose not to pursue higher education may have in fact made a different decision had they had access to more and better information, and/or lived within social and educational contexts in which higher education was better understood and seen to be of value. However, this argument did not apply to all participants. Indeed, some of the young people with whom Watts and Bridges worked had achieved the functionings (outcomes) they wished to achieve and were living a life they valued and had reason to value without attending university. This was not because of low aspirations or their contextual backgrounds but as a result of reasoned choices that had been made (Watts 2009, 428; Watts and Bridges 2006). Thus, these authors conclude that '[A]lthough wider access is to be applauded, the failure to address the real opportunities people have to enjoy the educational lives they want to lead (including the opportunities to quit education free from the accusation of having low aspirations and achievements) suggests that this may be an enterprise that is doomed simply to establish other educational injustices' (Watts and Bridges 2006, 157). Thus, they highlight the role that hidden assumptions can play in research on access, particularly when the researcher is focused on making a case for social justice gains through widened participation. This argument is not unlike the claim that I put forward at the start of this book – that increasing access without sufficient attention to creating meaningful opportunities for participation, learning and success is leading to new forms of injustices in higher education.

The fourth set of research that is of particular interest for my work was also done in the context of widening participation in the UK. Hart (Hart 2014a, 2013, 2008, 2007) worked with young people attending high school in Yorkshire. Making use of focus groups, surveys and individual interviews, Hart explored the aspirations of learners together with the opportunities and support that was available to them in pursuing these aspirations. Based on her research, Hart argues that the term 'participation' [or access in the South African context] is a loaded term rooted in an incorrect assumption that increasing numbers 'is synonymous with better forms of participation' (Hart 2008, 4). Three broad dimensions of participation emerged from Hart's research with sixth-form learners reported on in a 2008 conference presentation. These dimensions are as follows: (1) participation in the *decision* to engage in education of different types;

(2) the *experience* of participation or non-participation; and (3) the *outcomes* of participation (Hart 2008, 4–5). Hart shows how these three dimensions interplay in various ways for different participants and create multiple advantages or disadvantages for the young people she worked with. Lastly, Hart's (2014a, 249) work has also highlighted the complexity of educational transitions together with the importance of better understanding social structures within which transitions take place, processes of transition, as well as an individual's own experience of the transition. Related is the role of conversion factors in the development of young people's 'capability to aspire'. Working from a model of aspiration formation and transformation that she proposed based on her extensive empirical research, Hart (2014a, 251) argues that '[U]nderstanding more about how conversion factors act to enhance or constrain the possibility of an individual transitioning from one stage of the model to the next is key.' Although this statement was made in relation to the formation of aspirations, the same can be said of transitioning from school to university, as is argued here.

Interestingly, none of the four studies with a particular focus on university access and/or participation have sought to propose a list of capabilities for access or educational transition. Walker (2006) has presented an ideal-theoretical list of capabilities that should be developed *through* higher education. Hart has argued that the capability to aspire should be seen as a 'meta-capability' in the context of educational transitions (Hart 2014b), but she does not identify other capabilities that might underpin the success or not of a specific transition. In contrast, and in building on the existing research, my aim has been to identify transition to university capabilities which could then form a framework for conceptualising university access from a social justice point of view such that interventions for change might be developed. However, it is important to note that there is much debate and disagreement among capabilities scholars about whether or not a capabilities list should be formulated. This is an important debate, and given that I do propose a list, it is necessary for us to briefly detour and to consider the arguments for and against capabilities lists.

Debates about capabilities lists

Several authors have developed capabilities lists as part of their research, although not in relation to university access or transitions. However, as noted already, there is much debate in the capabilities literature – across disciplines – on whether or not one should propose a list of capabilities that we should strive towards ensuring as minimum criteria for justice (Alkire and Deneulin 2009). Sen argues against such a position, preferring to leave the formulation of a possible list of capabilities up to the specific group of people in question, taking their unique context into account (Sen 1999, 2006, 2009). For Sen, the participatory and deliberative process of identifying particular capabilities within a specific context is critical, and hence he does not support a generic or universal list of capabilities. His capabilities approach is intentionally incomplete to explicitly create space for deliberation (Sen 1990, 1993, 1999). As such, Sen's capabilities approach is 'a framework of thought, a normative tool, but it is not a fully specified theory that gives us complete answers to all our normative questions' (Robeyns 2003, 64). Sen argues that there is no problem with listing important capabilities within specific contexts for a particular purpose. He objects to the idea of a predetermined and canonical list of capabilities, that have been identified by theorists without ensuring sufficient space for processes of public reasoning (Sen 2004, 77). Understood from Sen's perspective, specific capabilities lists can provide benchmarks for assessing progress in working towards more just outcomes within a given context. The generation of a list may also help with building mechanisms for identifying and assessing injustice in context and creating spaces for public participation and deliberation. However, any list should always remain open to revision in the light of new evidence and further deliberation, and should not be positioned as universally applicable.

In contrast, in her influential work *Women and Human Development*, Nussbaum puts forth a strong argument for why a list of central human capabilities (see Box 4.1) based on universal values is essential and applicable to all countries and across all contexts. For Nussbaum, Sen's approach is 'too vague' and does not provide sufficient substantive basis to construct a normative conception of social justice (Nussbaum 2003, 33). In her 2003 defence of the list of central human capabilities Nussbaum argues that using the capabilities space in a comparative sense only is not sufficient to direct policy and practice towards a vision of social justice. The list of capabilities Nussbaum proposes is intentionally flexible to take account of human diversity; her list is 'open-ended and humble' and she argues that the details of each capability can be more concretely specified in accordance with the specific context in which it is being used (Nussbaum 2000, 77).

Nussbaum's list of central human capabilities is summarised in Box 4.1. These central capabilities affect all aspects of a person's life, including education and, in line with the notion of personal powers discussed in Chapters 1 and 2, include combinations of skills, abilities and opportunities. Nussbaum's list was developed drawing philosophically on Aristotelian thinking, and empirically on her engagements with poor women in India. Each of the ten capabilities should be seen as separate components of one's overall capability set, which means that the achievement or satisfaction of one by a larger amount does not mean another is not needed. All are of equal importance, although two, practical reason and affiliation, are noted to be of special significance 'since they both organise and suffuse all the others, making their pursuit truly human' (Nussbaum 2000, 81 and 82).Wolff and de-Shalit (2007) have done empirical work and public consultation using interview methods to validate Nussbaum's list of ten capabilities. In addition to this validation these authors proposed to expand Nussbaum's list to include the capabilities of: (1) doing good to others; (2) living in a law-abiding fashion; (3) understanding the law; and (4) the ability to understand and speak the local language (Wolff and de-Shalit 2007).

Despite the fact that Nussbaum's work has been widely used, there have also been specific critiques of her approach which centres on creating a universal list of central human capabilities. Sen's argument against the formulation of one canonical list was noted above (Sen 2004). Various other authors have also critiqued Nussbaum's

Box 4.1   Summary of Nussbaum's central human capabilities (adapted from Nussbaum 2000, 78–80)

1. **Life:** Being able to live to the end of a human life of normal length; not dying prematurely.
2. **Bodily Health:** Being able to have good health, including reproductive health; to be adequately nourished; to have adequate shelter.
3. **Bodily Integrity:** Being able to move freely from place to place; having one's bodily boundaries treated as sovereign; having opportunities for sexual satisfaction and for choice in matters of reproduction.
4. **Senses, Imagination and Thought:** Being able to use the senses, to imagine, think and reason – and to do these things in a 'truly human' way, a way informed and cultivated by adequate education, including, but by no means limited to, literacy and basic mathematical and scientific training. Being able to use one's mind in ways protected by guarantees of freedom of speech.
5. **Emotions:** Being able to have attachments to things and people outside ourselves; to love those who love and care for us, to grieve at their absence; in general, to love, to grieve, to experience longing, gratitude and justified anger.
6. **Practical Reason:** Being able to form a conception of the good and to engage in critical reflection about the planning of one's life.
7. **Affiliation:**
   a. Being able to live with and towards others, to recognise and show concern for other human beings, to engage in various forms of social interaction; to be able to imagine the situation of another and to have compassion for that situation; to have the capability for both justice and friendship.
   b. Having the social bases of self-respect and non-humiliation; being able to be treated as a dignified being whose worth is equal to that of others.
8. **Other Species:** Being able to live with concern for and in relation to animals, plants and the world of nature.
9. **Play:** Being able to laugh, to play, to enjoy recreational activities.
10. **Control Over One's Environment:**
    a. **Political:** Being able to participate effectively in political choices that govern one's life; having the right of political participation, protections of free speech and association.
    b. **Material:** Being able to hold property on an equal basis with others both formally and in terms of real opportunity; having the right to seek employment on an equal basis with others; having the freedom from unwarranted search and seizure.

universalism. For example Charusheela (2008) argues that, despite Nussbaum explicitly drawing on experiences in various countries and across cultures, her work remains ethnocentric (see also, McReynolds 2002). In *Women and Human Development*, Nussbaum presents a deftly argued defence of universal values, taking on particularly the critiques from cultural, diversity and paternalism perspectives.[1] For Nussbaum, specifying a list of capabilities is essential in order to avoid the problems of *omission* and *power* (Alkire and Deneulin 2009, 43; Nussbaum 2000). Omission refers to the challenge that groups may inadvertently overlook a capability that is important, and thus having a list from which to start thinking is useful. This is particularly relevant in the context of the transition to university where, for example, entering students may not yet have a sense of the capabilities that are important for successful university study or may not have considered certain capabilities due to adaptive preferences and the limitations of their schooling and/or social and economic contexts. The problem of power refers to the possibility that the powerful in a specific context will select capabilities in order to advance their own views or agendas, possibly at the expense of marginalised groupings. The debates about meritocracy presented in Chapter 2 are a case in point.

Other authors and researchers using the capabilities approach have argued for the value of lists defined for specific purposes. Robeyns notes that it becomes difficult to *apply* the capabilities approach to a specific concrete issue (as opposed to ideal theorising) if we do not provide some substantive basis from which to 'choose the relevant capabilities and indicate how important each will be in an overall judgement' (Robeyns 2003, 64). Robeyn's argument is not in opposition to Sen's clear commitment to participation and dialogue. The key, though, is to review the processes used to formulate the list of capabilities in the first place, the purpose of the list, and the manner in which specific lists are used. Arguing for a capabilities list for higher education specifically, Walker (2006, 45) provides three overarching reasons. The first is that a targeted list is needed to focus the capability approach on the specificities of higher education, since the broader capabilities approach accommodates the expansive area of human development. Second, this level of specificity provides the basis for arguing for approaches to higher education pedagogy that explicitly seek to foster capabilities and equality. Last, the formulation of a targeted list is needed to test the usefulness and possible applications of the capabilities approach in a higher education context. Similar logic can be applied to the even more specific focus on access and the transition to university. A list of capabilities that underpin a successful transition to university would ensure a focused concentration on the specificity of this particular educational transition, and the role of access in building a socially just higher education environment. Understanding these capabilities and how they can be fostered could then inform the development of interventions that explicitly aim to build or enhance specific capabilities. Proposing and applying such a list would allow us to test the usefulness of the capabilities approach for work on access with success. 'We need to ask not only which capabilities matter, but how well we are doing practically in higher education in fostering these capabilities' (Walker 2006, 142). Conceptualising a capabilities list focused on the transition to university provides a means of identifying what capabilities are important for a successful transition and then presents the basis for an evaluative account of the extent to which these capabilities are being fostered. Such an understanding, ultimately, provides a basis for action. In my work I thus side with Robeyn's and Walker on the issue of lists because a theoretically and empirically grounded capabilities list for the transition to university provides a useful practical tool for advancing social justice in the context of university access (see also, Wilson-Strydom forthcoming). In doing so, the list of higher education capabilities developed by Walker (2006) provides a helpful starting point.

Drawing on her work with widening participation students in the UK as well as other groups of students, and also considering the lists proposed by four other groups of authors, Walker has proposed an ideal-theoretical list of higher education capabilities – capabilities that should be developed through higher education. These are summarised in Box 4.2. She notes that, in the context of her list,

---

Box 4.2 Ideal-theoretical list of higher education capabilities (Walker 2006, 128–129)

1. **Practical Reason:** Being able to make well-reasoned, informed, critical, independent, intellectually acute, socially responsible and reflective choices. Being able to construct a personal life project in an uncertain world. Having good judgement.

2. **Educational Resilience:** Able to navigate study, work and life. Able to negotiate risk, to persevere academically, to be responsive to educational opportunities and adaptive constraints. Self-reliant. Having aspirations and hopes for a good future.

3. **Knowledge and Imagination:** Being able to gain knowledge of a chosen subject – disciplinary and/or professional – and its form of academic inquiry and standards. Being able to use critical thinking and imagination to comprehend the perspectives of multiple others and to form impartial judgements. Being able to debate complex issues. Being able to acquire knowledge for pleasure and personal development, for career and economic opportunities, for political, cultural and social action and participation in the world. Awareness of ethical debates and moral issues. Open-mindedness. Knowledge to understand science and technology in public society.

4. **Learning Disposition:** Being able to have curiosity and a desire for learning. Having confidence in one's ability to learn. Being an active inquirer.

5. **Social Relations and Social Networks:** Being able to participate in a group for learning, working with others to solve problems or tasks. Being able to work with others to form effective or good groups for collaborative and participatory learning. Being able to form good networks of friendship and belonging for learning support and leisure. Mutual trust.

6. **Respect, Dignity and Recognition:** Being able to have respect for oneself and for and from others, being treated with dignity, not being diminished or devalued because of one's gender, social class, religion or race; valuing other languages, other religions and spiritual practices and human diversity. Being able to show empathy, compassion, fairness and generosity, listening to and considering other person's points of view in dialogue and debate. Being able to act inclusively and being able to respond to human need. Having competence in inter-cultural communication. Having a voice to participate effectively in learning; a voice to speak out, to debate and persuade; to be able to listen.
7. **Emotional Integrity, Emotions:** Not being subject to anxiety or fear which diminishes learning. Being able to develop emotions for imagination, understanding empathy, awareness and discernment.
8. **Bodily Integrity:** Safety and freedom from all forms of physical and verbal harassment in the higher education environment.

capabilities should be understood as both opportunities (i.e. opportunity freedom) and capacities that can be fostered (Walker 2006, 128). This understanding of capabilities is in line with Sen's definition of agency, where agency includes the freedom to decide (choice and opportunity) and the 'power to act and be effective' (Crocker and Robeyns 2009, 75). This power to act and be effective can be equated with Walker's notion of capacity that can be fostered and Nussbaum's concept of internal capabilities or personal powers. This distinction is particularly important for education researchers, since one of the purposes of education is to build skills and capacity, and so this component of the notion of capabilities must be factored into capability lists when used in an education context.

In applying Walker's list of capabilities to guide higher education research with a social justice agenda, we need to ask questions about who is able to develop these capabilities and who is not, together with questions about what might enable or constrain individual's agency and/or well-being freedoms. The concept of conversion factors that was introduced in Chapter 3 provides a particularly generative conceptual and analytical tool for doing this and we return to conversion factors later in the chapter. For now it is sufficient to have a broad overview of what is included in Walker's list, and to have made explicit why the formulation of a capabilities list was important in the current study.

Conceptualising a capabilities list for access to university

Having made the case for why a capabilities list specific to the transition to university would be useful, the next step is to review how such a list may be formulated in a manner that does not undermine the agency of individual learners and students that is so central within the capabilities approach, and that ensures some form of public participation in the formulation of the list. Fortunately the path towards the development of capabilities lists has been opened up by several researchers (for some examples, see Alkire and Deneulin 2009; Alkire 2002; Flores-Crespo 2004; Nussbaum 2000; Robeyns 2003; Walker 2006; Walker et al. 2009; Wolff and de-Shalit 2007), and out of this work have emerged specific processes that should underpin the development of a capabilities list. At a broad level, Alkire and Deneulin (2009, 45) note that there are two key questions that must be considered when approaching the task of formulating a capabilities list. First, we need to know which capabilities the people who will enjoy them regard as valuable and of high priority. Second, we need to ask which capabilities are most relevant in a given context. While these questions are helpful as a starting point, I find Robeyn's (2003) more explicitly formulated criteria for developing a capabilities list for assessing gender inequality particularly instructive. The five criteria are as follows (paraphrased from Robeyns, 2003b, 70–71):

1. *The criterion of explicit formulation*: This is the most basic criterion and implies that the list should be explicit, discussed and defended.
2. *The criterion of methodological justification*: The method used for generating a list must be clearly explained, scrutinised and defended as the most appropriate method for the specific issue at hand.
3. *The criterion of sensitivity to context*: The level of abstraction at which the list is pitched should be appropriate to meet the specific objectives for which it was formulated. A pragmatic approach is recommended taking into account that it is important to speak the language of the debate with which one wishes to engage.
4. *The criterion of different levels of generality*: If the list being developed aims at an empirical application or wishes to lead to specific policy and intervention proposals, then at least two stages should be followed in its design. The first stage involves drawing up an 'ideal' list that is unconstrained by the limits of data or measurement, or of socioeconomic or political feasibility. The second stage is focused on drawing up a more pragmatic list that takes such constraints into account.
5. *The criterion of exhaustiveness and non-reduction*: The capabilities included in the list should include all important elements, each of which should not be reducible to the other. While there may be, and often is, some overlap, this should not be substantial. This does not exclude the possibility of a subset having such an important status that it requires consideration on its own, independent of the overall set.

While all five criteria are important and I have sought to adhere to them all, criterion four is of particular relevance, since the list being proposed here, and the broader framework that it will underpin, are explicitly seeking to inform feasible proposals for how universities and schools can partner to foster capabilities formation. The two stage approach has underpinned my method of proposing the list. Drawing on an analysis of the large literatures on access and transitions (summarised in Chapter 2) I propose an ideal-theoretical list as a first step. The empirical work in the coming chapters provides the basis for fleshing out a 'more pragmatic list' (Robeyns 2003, 71), the details of which are presented in Chapter 6.

The ideal-theoretical list of capabilities for the transition to university builds on Walker's list of higher education capabilities shown in Box 4.2. In developing this list, Walker applied all five of Robeyn's criteria for formulating capabilities lists, carefully reviewed six existing capabilities lists, and drew on empirical work with university students together with her own experience working in higher education over many years. Although focused on pedagogy within higher education, I propose that this list provides a useful starting point, with some adaptations and additions, for beginning to understand the transition to university from a capabilities point of view. Walker's list is not the only capabilities list that has been proposed in the context of higher education (for example, Bozalek 2004; Flores-Crespo 2004). However, since the work done by these authors was reviewed by Walker and has informed the list that she has proposed, I have taken her list as the starting point for formulating a conceptual list for the transition to university.

Table 4.1 shows Walker's list with her definitions of each capability. Drawing on the theory and research presented in preceding chapters, specific definitions for an ideal list of capabilities for the transition to university have been proposed. In addition, one extra capability that is critical in the context of access to university has been added. Table 4.1 shows my definitions as well as examples of the literature, theory and existing research that has informed the formulation each definition. I will return to this list in the coming empirical chapters in which the theoretical aspects presented here will be further examined from the point of view of high school learners and first-year university students.

Social contexts, agency and capabilities

One of the key ideas within the capabilities approach is that, in a just world, social structures or social organisations should expand people's capabilities – their freedom to achieve what they value doing and being. As has been argued earlier, capabilities and functionings are influenced by individual circumstances, relationships with others, and social conditions and contexts which create spaces for options to be achieved or not. The capability approach emphasises the basic heterogeneity of individuals as a key aspect of educational equality and provides a conceptual framework for connecting individual histories with social and collective arrangements (Nussbaum 2000; Sen 1980, 1985, 1990, 2009; Walker and Unterhalter 2007). Sen argues that '[T]here is a deep complementarity between individual agency and social arrangements. It is important to give simultaneous recognition to the centrality of individual freedom and to the forces of social influences on the extent and reach of freedom' (Sen 1999, xi–xii). Social norms and opportunities can expand or diminish one's agency. Often social norms construct disadvantages, even where public resources are equally distributed (see also, Crocker and Robeyns 2009; Walker and Unterhalter 2007; Wolff and

Table 4.1 Ideal-theoretical list of capabilities for the transition to university

Ideal-theoretical list of higher education capabilities	Definition (Walker 2006, 128–129)	Proposed definition for transition to university focus	Illustrative examples of literature, theory and research informing the proposed capability
1. Practical reason	Being able to make well-reasoned, informed, critical, independent, intellectually acute, socially responsible, and reflective choices. Being able to construct a personal life project in an uncertain world. Having good judgement.	Being able to make well-reasoned, informed, critical, independent and reflective choices about post-school study and career options.	• Challenge of 'seeing' over the humpback bridge (Hoffman et al., 2008; Marshall and Hargreaves, 2007). • Social class and other factors influencing choice and aspiration (Archer et al., 2003; Furlong and Cartmel, 2009; Hart, 2013; Unterhalter, 2009; Watts and Bridges, 2006). • The idea of building college knowledge (Conley, 2005). • Research on schooling in South Africa (Bloch, 2009; Christie, 2008; Wilson-Strydom and Hay, 2010)
2. Educational resilience	Being able to navigate study, work and life. Able to negotiate risk, to persevere academically, to be responsive to educational opportunities and adaptive constraints. Self-reliant. Having aspirations and hopes for a good future.	Being able to navigate the transition from school to university within individual life contexts. Able to negotiate risk, to persevere academically, to be responsive to educational opportunities and adaptive constraints. Having aspirations and hopes for a successful university career.	• Understandings of the capability to participate in education (Vaughan, 2007) • Schooling challenges in South Africa (Fiske and Ladd, 2004; Simkins and Paterson, 2005). • Risk and resilience in higher education (Hart, 2009; Watts and Bridges, 2006). • Conley's (2010, 2005) work on contextual skills and awareness and academic behaviours as elements of readiness. • Debates about meritocracy (Arendale, 2010; Cunningham, 2007; Morley and Lugg, 2009; Oakes et al., 2000).

Table 4.1 (Continued)

Ideal-theoretical list of higher education capabilities	Definition (Walker 2006, 128–129)	Proposed definition for transition to university focus	Illustrative examples of literature, theory and research informing the proposed capability
3. Knowledge and imagination	Being able to gain knowledge of a chosen subject – disciplinary and/or professional – and its form of academic inquiry and standards. Being able to use critical thinking and imagination to comprehend the perspectives of multiple others and to form impartial judgements. Being able to debate complex issues. Being able to acquire knowledge for pleasure and personal development, for career and economic opportunities, for political, cultural and social action and participation in the world. Awareness of ethical debates and moral issues. Open-mindedness. Knowledge to understand science and technology in public society.	Having the academic grounding needed to be able to gain knowledge of chosen university subjects, and to develop methods of academic inquiry. Being able to use critical thinking and imagination to identify and comprehend multiple perspectives.	• School performance data (DBE, 2011; Simkins and Paterson, 2005; Simkins et al., 2007) • University performance data (CHE, 2012, 2010; Scott et al., 2007). • Aspects of the multi-dimensional model of readiness, including key content knowledge and academic behaviours (Conley, 2010). • Research on epistemological access (Boughey, 2005; CHE, 2010; James, 2007; Morrow, 2009).
4. Learning disposition	Being able to have curiosity and a desire for learning. Having confidence in one's ability to learn. Being an active inquirer.	Being able to have curiosity and a desire for learning. Having the learning skills required for university study. Being an active inquirer.	• Research on expectations – of both students and academic staff (Chickering and Gamson, 1999, 1987; Kuh et al., 2007; Pascarella and Terenzini, 2005; Pikethly and Prosser, 2001; Tinto and Pusser, 2006). • Level of academic challenge (Chickering and Gamson, 1999; Kuh et al., 2007). • National Benchmark test performance data (Prince, 2010; Wilson-Strydom, 2010a). • Academic development research and practice (Johnston, 2010; Krause, 2005; Leibowitz et al., 2009; Upcraft et al., 2005).

5. Social relations and social networks	Being able to participate in a group for learning, working with others to solve problems or tasks. Being able to work with others to form effective or good groups for collaborative and participatory learning. Being able to form good networks of friendship and belonging for learning support and leisure. Mutual trust.	Being able to participate in a group for learning, working with others to solve problems or tasks. Being able to form networks of friendships and belonging for learning support and leisure. Mutual trust.	• Personalisation of the learning experience and learner centred approaches (Dietsche, 2009; Knox and Wyper, 2008; OECD, 2006). • Belonging, friendship and adjustment (Hausmann et al., 2007; Hurtado and Carter, 1997; Pittman and Richmond, 2008). • Research on student involvement (Astin, 1999). • Student engagement research – at school and university levels (Shouping and Kuh, 2002). • Active and collaborative learning (Kuh et al., 2007).
6. Respect, dignity and recognition	Being able to have respect for oneself and for and from others, being treated with dignity, not being diminished or devalued because of one's gender; social class, religion or race; valuing other languages, other religions and spiritual practices and human diversity. Being able to show empathy, compassion, fairness and generosity; listening to and considering other person's points of view in dialogue and debate. Being able to act inclusively and being able to respond to human need. Having competence in inter-cultural communication. Having a voice to participate effectively in learning; a voice to speak out, to debate and persuade; to be able to listen.	Being able to have respect for oneself and for and from others, being treated with dignity, not being diminished or devalued because of one's gender; social class, religion or race. Valuing other languages, other religions and spiritual practices and human diversity. Being able to show empathy, compassion, fairness and generosity; listening to and considering other person's points of view in dialogue and debate. Having a voice to participate effectively in learning.	• Transformation and diversity within schools and universities (Soudien, 2010; Taylor et al., 2003; Vanderyar and Jansen, 2008). • Critiques of deficit-approaches to access (Arendale, 2010; Schreiner and Hulme, 2009; Whittaker, 2008; Zukas and Malcolm, 2007). • Arguments for seeing students as individuals rather than groups or 'numbers' (Arendale, 2010; Astin, 1999; Chickering and Gamson, 1987; Harper and Quaye, 2009; Krause, 2005).

(Continued)

Table 4.1 (Continued)

Ideal-theoretical list of higher education capabilities	Definition (Walker 2006, 128–129)	Proposed definition for transition to university focus	Illustrative examples of literature, theory and research informing the proposed capability
7. Emotional health	Not being subject to anxiety or fear which diminishes learning. Being able to develop emotions for imagination, understanding, empathy, awareness and discernment.	Not being subject to anxiety or fear which diminishes learning.	• Emotional engagement at school (Yazzie-Mintz, 2010). • Supportive campus environment (Kuh et al., 2005). • Issues of discrimination (race, class, gender) (Furlong and Cartmel, 2009; MoE, 2008; Soudien, 2010; Vanderyar and Jansen, 2008). • Academic staff approaches to communicating expectations, and providing suitable support (Chickering and Gamson, 1999; Conley, 2007; Upcraft et al., 2005; Wilson-Strydom, 2010b). • Role of emotion in educational contexts (Boler, 1997; Zembylas, 2003, 2002; Zorn and Boler, 2007)
8. Bodily integrity	Safety and freedom from all forms of physical and verbal harassment in the higher education environment.	Safety and freedom from all forms of physical and verbal harassment in the school and higher education environment.	• Discrimination in higher education (Hurtado et al., 2007; Jansen, 2010; MoE, 2008). • Research on gender issues in education (Arnot, 2002; Meo, 2011; Nussbaum, 2000; Sen, 1999; Unterhalter, 2009).
Additional capability proposed based on the body of access research			
9. Language competence and confidence		Being able to understand, read, write and speak confidently in the language of instruction.	• Academic literacy performance of South African university students (Cliff et al., 2007; Griesel, 2003; Koch and Foxcroft, 2003; Prince, 2010; Wilson-Strydom, 2010a). • Student reports of difficulty with language (Wilson-Strydom, 2010b). • National assessment results in South African schools showing low levels of literacy (DBE, 2011). • Wolff and de-Shalit (2007) identified language competence as an additional capability for understanding the challenges of disadvantage.

de-Shalit 2007). Inequality is evident when people have different capability sets (Alkire and Deneulin 2009). Thus, while agency is an important element of the capabilities approach, it is explicitly recognised that individual functionings (outcomes) are influenced by one's relative advantages or disadvantages in society. A learner's opportunities will be helped or hindered by the choices and actions of others; for example, the quality of teachers, productive peer relationships, policy that enables their learning, and so on.

The concept of conversion factors introduced in Chapter 3 is an important conceptual tool within the capabilities approach that can be used to unpack relative advantages and disadvantages in the conversion of resources into capabilities and, ultimately, well-being achievement. A focus on conversion factors is particularly useful in the context of an unequal education system, and in seeking to formulate ways in which to enhance the capabilities of those who have limited options, often due to the social context in which they find themselves. The provision of educational resources alone is not sufficient to ensure a just higher education system. Rather, it is the relationship between the available resources and the ability of each student to convert these into valued capabilities and then make choices which will inform their actual functionings that ought to be evaluated (Walker 2006, 32–33). Thus, the capabilities approach emphasises the role of individual agency and choice, but reminds us that the freedom of agency individuals have is qualified and constrained by social, political and economic factors and opportunities. As such, we need to research and understand social arrangements and institutional conditions of possibility for educational transitions. In this way, the capabilities framework provides a means for exploring the processes underlying both different and similar outcomes (functionings) of access in a manner that exposes injustices that may be masked by a consideration of outcomes only, such as statistics measuring participation rates.

This interplay of agency and social context can also lead to what has been termed 'adaptive preferences' where the choices individuals make are conditioned by their contexts. For example, Nussbaum has shown how women 'adjust their desires to the way of life they know' (Nussbaum 2000, 136, 2003). Women sometimes 'undervalue basic human capabilities that they later come to value, because of social habituation and social pressure' (Nussbaum 2000, 140). Making a similar argument when using the capabilities approach in an education context Unterhalter (2009, 219) reminds us that we need to question the range of educational choices available to people. She states that 'we would need to ask whether people's educational aspirations had become adapted to their respective circumstances, and whether the low-income group had a range of valued learning opportunities to choose from'. As such, when working within a capabilities framework, we need to ask complex and searching questions that take us beyond the realm of a more narrow focus on satisfaction, preference, or even subjective happiness as the basis for making meaningful choices.

In this research I have sought to understand the agency of school learners in their final years of schooling and students entering university, together with their social and institutional conditions of possibility (at the levels of the school and the university) that might enable or constrain their capabilities for transitioning into higher education. This includes an intentional focus on conversion factors that impact on the extent to which students entering higher education are able to convert their opportunity/resource (a place at university) into capabilities and valued functionings, such as making a successful transition to university from school, being successful in their first year of study, and ultimately completing a qualification that they have reason to value. Such an understanding provides a solid foundation from which to conceptualise interventions that could improve this transition. In Figure 4.1 I draw on the helpful visualisation that Robeyns (2005, 98) presented in her explanation of the importance of distinguishing between means for achievement (resources) and functionings (achievements) which are mediated by capabilities or the freedom to achieve. As I explained above, conversion factors and adaptive preferences influence the extent to which a given person is able to convert their available resources into capabilities and then functionings. Figure 4.1 shows visually how the capabilities approach, and particularly the notion of conversion factors and adaptive preferences, can be applied to conceptualise the essential elements that should be explored in a study of the transition to university.

Having presented a theoretical account of how the capabilities approach can be applied to conceptualise the transition to university in a manner that foregrounds issues of social justice, in the coming two chapters we turn to the learners' and students' experiences and ideas about the transition to university. Including and listening to the voices of high school learners and first-year university students provides a means, albeit limited, of bringing in participation and deliberation with those who are most affected by dilemmas of access. The voices of learners and students help us to interrogate the theoretical conceptualisation presented in this chapter, so moving towards a more practical and actionable capabilities-based framework in pursuit of social justice in the terrain of access and transition to university.

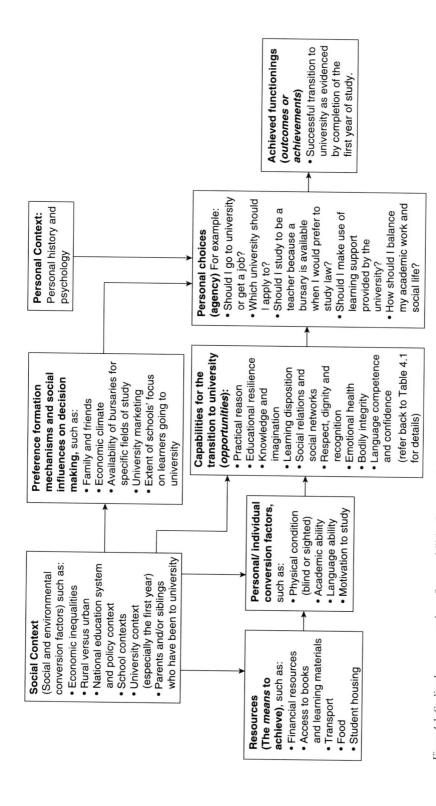

Social Context
(Social and environmental conversion factors) such as:
• Economic inequalities
• Rural versus urban
• National education system and policy context
• School contexts
• University context (especially the first year)
• Parents and/or siblings who have been to university

Personal Context:
Personal history and psychology

Preference formation mechanisms and social influences on decision making, such as:
• Family and friends
• Economic climate
• Availability of bursaries for specific fields of study
• University marketing
• Extent of schools' focus on learners going to university

Resources
**(The *means to*
achieve),** such as:
• Financial resources
• Access to books and learning materials
• Transport
• Food
• Student housing

Personal/ individual conversion factors, such as:
• Physical condition (blind or sighted)
• Academic ability
• Language ability
• Motivation to study

Capabilities for the transition to university (*opportunities*):
• Practical reason
• Educational resilience
• Knowledge and imagination
• Learning disposition
• Social relations and social networks
• Respect, dignity and recognition
• Emotional health
• Bodily integrity
• Language competence and confidence

(refer back to Table 4.1 for details)

Personal choices (agency) For example:
• Should I go to university or get a job?
• Which university should I apply to?
• Should I study to be a teacher because a bursary is available when I would prefer to study law?
• Should I make use of learning support provided by the university?
• How should I balance my academic work and social life?

Achieved functionings
(*outcomes or achievements*)
• Successful transition to university as evidenced by completion of the first year of study.

Figure 4.1 Stylised representation of a capabilities framework for conceptualising the transition to university (adapted from Robeyns 2005, 98)

Note

1 The reader is referred to Chapter 1 of *Women and Human Development* for a comprehensive account of this argument (Nussbaum 2000, 34–110).

References

Alkire, S. 2002. 'Dimensions of Human Development.' *World Development* 30 (2): 181–205.

Alkire, S and S Deneulin. 2009. 'The Human Development and Capability Approach.' In *An Introduction to the Human Development and Capability Approach. Freedom and Agency*, edited by S Deneulin and L Shahani. London: Earthscan.

Archer, L, M Hutchings and A Ross. 2003. *Higher Education and Social Class. Issues of Exclusion and Inclusion*. London: RoutledgeFalmer.

Arendale, D R. 2010. 'Special Issue: Access at the Crossroads. Learning Assistance in Higher Education.' *ASHE Higher Education Report* 35 (6): 1–145.

Arnot, Madeleine. 2002. 'The Complex Gendering of Invisible Pedagogies: Social Reproduction or Empowerment?' *British Journal of Sociology of Education* 23 (4): 583–593.

Astin, A W. 1999. 'Student Involvement: A Developmental Theory for Higher Education (Reprint of Astin 1984).' *Journal of College Student Development* 40 (5): 518–529.

Biggeri, M. 2014. 'Education Policy for Agency and Participation.' In *Agency and Participation in Childhood and Youth. International Applications of the Capability Approach in Schools and Beyond*, edited by C S Hart, M Biggeri and B Babic. London: Bloomsbury: 73–97.

Bloch, G. 2009. *The Toxic Mix: What's Wrong with South Africa's Schools and How to Fix It*. Cape Town: Tafelberg.

Boler, M. 1997. 'Disciplined Emptions: Philosophies of Educated Feelings.' *Educational Theory* 47 (2): 203–227.

Boni, A and M Walker. 2013. *Human Development and Capabilities. Re-imagining the University of the Twenty-first Century*. London: Routledge.

Boughey, C. 2005. ' "Epistemological" Access to the University: An Alternative Perspective.' *South African Journal of Higher Education* 19 (3): 230–242.

Bozalek, V G. 2004. 'Recognition, Resources, Responsibilities: Using Students' Stories of Family to Renew the South African Social Work Curriculum.' Unpublished doctoral thesis, Utrecht Netherlands: Utrecht University.

Charusheela, S. 2008. 'Social Analysis and the Capabilities Approach: a Limit to Martha Nussbaum's Universalist Ethics.' *Cambridge Journal of Economics* 33 (6): 1135–1152.

CHE. 2010. *Access and Throughput in South African Higher Education: Three Case Studies*. Higher Education Monitor 9. Pretoria: Council on Higher Education. http://www.che.ac.za.

———. 2012. *Vital Stats. Public Higher Education 2010*. Pretoria: Council on Higher Education. http://www.che.ac.za/documents/d000249/vital_stats_public_higher_education_2010.pdf

Chickering, A and Z Gamson. 1987. 'Seven Principles for Good Practice in Undergraduate Education.' *AAHE Bulletin* 39 (7): 3–7.

———. 1999. 'Development and Adaptations of the Seven Principles for Good Practice in Undergraduate Education.' *New Directions for Teaching and Learning* 80 (Winter): 75–81.

Christie, P. 2008. *Opening the Doors of Learning. Changing Schools in South Africa*. Johannesburg: Heinemann Publishers.

Cliff, A, K Ramaboa and C Pearce. 2007. 'The Assessment of Entry-level Students' Academic Literacy: Does It Matter?' *Ensovoort* 11 (2): 33–48.

Conley, D T. 2005. *College Knowledge. What It Really Takes for Students to Succeed and What We Can Do to Get Them Ready.* San Francisco: Jossey-Bass.

————. 2007. 'The Challenge of College Readiness.' *Educational Leadership* April: 1–6.

————. 2010. *College and Career Ready. Helping All Students Succeed Beyond High School.* San Francisco: Jossey-Bass.

Crocker, D and I Robeyns. 2009. 'Capability and Agency.' In *Amartya Sen. Contemporary Philosophy in Focus*, edited by C J Morris. Oxford: Oxford University Press: 60–90.

Cunningham, F. 2007. 'The University and Social Justice.' *Journal of Academic Ethics* 5: 153–162.

DBE. 2011. *Report of the Annual National Assessment of 2011.* Pretoria: Department of Basic Education, RSA.

Deprez, L S and S S Butler. 2007. 'The Capability Approach and Women's Economic Security: Access to Higher Education Under Welfare Reform.' In *Amartya Sen's Capability Approach and Social Justice in Education*, edited by M Walker and E Unterhalter. New York: Palgrave Macmillan Ltd: 215–236.

Dietsche, P. 2009. 'Small Steps to a Big Idea. Personalising the Postsecondary Experience.' In *Focus on First-Year Success. Perspectives Emerging from South Africa and Beyond*, edited by B Leibowitz, S van der Merwe and S van Schalkwyk. Stellenbosch: Sun Media: 37–46.

Fiske, E B and H F Ladd. 2004. *Equity. Education Reform in Post-apartheid South Africa.* Washington DC: Brookings Institution Press.

Flores-Crespo, P. 2004. 'Situating Education in the Human Capabilities Approach.' In Pavia, Italy, Fourth Conference on the Capability Approach: Enhancing Human Security.

Furlong, A and F Cartmel. 2009. *Higher Education and Social Justice.* Berkshire, England: Society for Research into Higher Education and Open University Press.

Griesel, H. 2003. 'Controversies of Access to HE Study – The Changing FE-HE Interface.' In Cape Town, 21st Annual AEAA Conference.

Harper, S R and S J Quaye. 2009. 'Beyond Sameness, with Engagement and Outcomes for All. An Introduction.' In *Student Engagement in Higher Education. Theoretical and Practical Approaches for Diverse Populations*, edited by S R Harper and S J Quaye. New York: Routledge: 1–15.

Harreveld, R E and M J Singh. 2008. 'Amartya Sen's Capability Approach and the Brokering of Learning Provision for Young Adults.' *Vocations and Learning* 1: 211–226.

Hart, C S. 2007. 'The Capability Approach as an Evaluative Framework for Education Policy: The Example of Widening Participation in Higher Education in England.' *Prospero* 13 (3): 34–50.

————. 2008. 'What Can Young People Tell Us About Promoting Equality and Inclusion Through Widening Participation in Higher Education in England?' In New Delhi, 5th Annual Conference of the Human Development and Capability Association.

————. 2009. 'Quo Vadis? The Capability Space and New Directions in the Philosophy of Education Research.' *Studies in the Philosophy of Education* 28: 391–402.

————. 2011. *Thinking, Doing, Feeling: Capabilities in Relation to Decision-Making and Transitions Beyond School in the UK.* Working Paper. Cambridge, UK: Cambridge University.

————. 2013. *Aspirations, Education and Social Justice. Applying Sen and Bourdieu.* London: Bloomsbury.

————. 2014a. 'Agency, Participation and Transitions Beyond School.' In *Agency and Participation in Childhood and Youth. International Applications of the Capability Approach in Schools and Beyond*, edited by C S Hart, M Biggeri and B Babic. London: Bloomsbury: 246–275.

————. 2014b. 'The Capability Approach and Educational Research.' In *Agency and Participation in Childhood and Youth. International Applications of the Capability Approach in Schools and Beyond*. London: Bloomsbury: 40–72.

Hart, C S, M Biggeri and B Babic. 2014. *Agency and Participation in Childhood and Youth. International Applications of the Capability Approach in Schools and Beyond*. London: Bloomsbury.

Hausmann, L, J Ward Schofield and R Woods. 2007. 'Sense of Belonging as a Predictor of Intentions to Persist Among African American and White First-Year College Students.' *Research in Higher Education* 48 (7): 803–839.

Hoffman, N, J Vargas and J Santos. 2008. 'Blending High School and College.' *New Directions for Higher Education* Winter (144): 15–25.

Hurtado, S and D F Carter. 1997. 'Effects of College Transition and Perceptions of the Campus Racial Climate on Latino College Students' Sense of Belonging.' *Sociology of Education* 70 (4): 324–345.

Hurtado, S, J C Han, V D Saenz, L L Espinosa and O S Cerna. 2007. 'Predicting Transition and Adjustment to College: Biomedical and Behavioural Science Aspirants' and Minority Students' First Year of College.' *Research in Higher Education* 48 (7): 841–887.

James, R J. 2007. *Social Equity in a Mass, Globalised Higher Education Environment: The Unresolved Issue of Widening Access to University*. Faculty of Education Dean's Lecture Series. Melbourne: University of Melbourne: Centre for the Study of Higher Education. http://www.edfac.unimelb.edu.au/news/lectures/pdf/richardjamestranscript.pdf

Jansen, J. 2010. 'Moving on Up? The Politics, Problems and Prospects for Universities as Gateways for Social Mobility in South Africa.' In *The Next 25 Years. Affirmative Action in Higher Education in the Unites States and South Africa*, edited by D L Featherman, M Hall and M Krislov. Ann Arbor: University of Michigan Press: 129–136.

Johnston, B. 2010. *The First Year at University. Teaching Students in Transition*. New York: Society for Research into Higher Education and Open University Press.

Knox, H and J Wyper. 2008. *Quality Enhancement Themes: The First Year Experience. Personalisation of the First Year*. Mansfield, Scotland: The Quality Assurance Agency for Higher Education.

Koch, E and C Foxcroft. 2003. 'A Developmental Focus to Admissions Testing: Admissions and Placement Standards Development.' *South African Journal of Higher Education* 17 (3): 192–208.

Krause, K L. 2005. 'Understanding and Promoting Student Engagement in University Learning Communities.' In James Cook University, Townsville/Cairns, Queensland.

Kuh, G D, G Kinzie, J A Buckley, B Bridges and J Hayek. 2007. *Piecing Together the Student Success Puzzle: Research, Propositions, and Recommendations*. ASHE Higher Education Report 32.

Kuh, G D, G Kinzie, J H Schuh and E J Whitt. 2005. *Assessing Conditions to Enhance Educational Effectiveness. The Inventory for Student Engagement and Success*. San Francisco: John Wiley & Sons, Inc.

Lanzi, D. 2007. 'Capabilities, Human Capital and Education.' *Journal of Socio-Economics* 36: 424–435.

Leibowitz, B, S van Schalkwyk, A van der Merwe, N Herman and G Young. 2009. 'What Makes a "Good" First-Year Lecturer?' In *Focus on First-Year Success. Perspectives Emerging from South Africa and Beyond*, edited by B Leibowitz, A van der Merwe and S van Schalkwyk. Stellenbosch: Sun Media: 255–270.

Marginson, S. 2011. 'Equity, Status and Freedom: a Note on Higher Education.' *Cambridge Journal of Education* 41 (1): 23–36.

Marshall, N A and D J Hargreaves. 2007. 'Crossing the Humpback Bridge: Primary-secondary School Transition in Music Education.' *Music Education Research* 9 (1): 65–80.

McReynolds, P. 2002. 'Nussbaum's Capabilities Approach: A Pragmatist Critique.' *Journal of Speculative Philosophy* 16 (2): 142–150.

Meo, Analía Inés. 2011. 'The Moral Dimension of Class and Gender Identity-making: Poverty and Aggression in a Secondary School in the City of Buenos Aires.' *British Journal of Sociology of Education* 32 (6): 843–860. doi:10.1080/01425692.2011.614737.

MoE. 2008. *Report of the Ministerial Committee on Transformation and Social Cohesion and the Elimination of Discrimination in Public Higher Education Institutions.* Pretoria: Department of Education, RSA.

Morley, L and R Lugg. 2009. 'Mapping Meritocracy: Intersecting Gender, Poverty and Higher Educational Opportunity Structures.' *Higher Education Policy* 22: 37–60.

Morrow, W. 2009. *Bounds of Democracy. Epistemological Access in Higher Education.* Cape Town: Human Sciences Research Council. http://www.hsrcpress.ac.za

Nussbaum, M. 2003. 'Capabilities as Fundamental Entitlements: Sen and Social Justice.' *Feminist Economics* 9 (2–3): 33–59.

———. 2010. *Not for Profit. Why Democracy Needs the Humanities.* Princeton, New Jersey: Princeton University Press.

Nussbaum, M C. 2000. *Women and Human Development. The Capabilities Approach.* Cambridge: Cambridge University Press.

Oakes, J, J Rogers, M Lipton and E Morrell. 2000. *The Social Construction of College Access: Confronting the Technical, Cultural, and Political Barriers to Low Income Students of Colour.* California: Institute for Democracy, Education and Access, UCLA.

OECD. 2006. *Personalising Education.* Paris: OECD. http://www.oecd.org/dataoecd/38/45/36509488.pdf

Pascarella, E T and P T Terenzini. 2005. *How College Affects Students. A Third Decade of Research.* 2. San Francisco: Jossey-Bass.

Pitkethly, A and M Prosser. 2001. 'The First Year Experience Project: A Model for University-wide Change.' *Higher Education Research and Development* 20 (2): 185–198.

Pittman, L D and A Richmond. 2008. 'University Belonging, Friendship Quality, and Psychosocial Adjustment During the Transition to College.' *Journal of Experimental Education* 76 (4): 343–361.

Prince, R. 2010. 'The National Benchmark Tests Project: 2010 Intake Report.' Presented at the Higher Education South Africa Consultative Forum, Johannesburg, May.

Robeyns, I. 2003. ' Sen's Capability Approach and Gender Inequality: Selecting Relevant Capabilities.' *Feminist Economics* 9 (2–3): 61–92.

———. 2005. 'The Capability Approach: a Theoretical Survey.' *Journal of Human Development* 6 (1): 93–114.

Saito, M. 2003. 'Amartya Sen's Capability Approach to Education: A Critical Exploration.' *Journal of Philosophy of Education,* 37 (1): 18–33.

Schreiner, L and E Hulme. 2009. 'Assessment of Students' Strengths. The First Step to Student Success.' In *Focus on First-Year Success. Perspectives Emerging from South Africa and Beyond,* edited by B Leibowitz, A van der Merwe and S van Schalkwyk. Stellenbosch: Sun Media: 69–78.

Scott, I, N Yeld and J Hendry. 2007. *Higher Education Monitor No. 6: A Case for Improving Teaching and Learning in South African Higher Education.* Pretoria: Council on Higher Education.

Sen, A. 1980. *Equality of What? The Tanner Lecture on Human Values.* California: Stanford University.

————. 1985. 'Well-being, Agency & Freedom: The Dewey Lectures 1984.' *The Journal of Philosophy* 82 (4): 169–221.

————. 1990. 'Justice: Means Versus Freedoms.' *Philosophy and Public Affairs* 19 (2): 111–121.

————. 1993. 'Capability and Well-Being.' In *The Quality of Life*, edited by M Nussbaum and A Sen. New Delhi: Oxford University Press, India: 30–53.

————. 1999. *Development as Freedom*. Oxford: Oxford University Press.

————. 2004. 'Capabilities, Lists, and Public Reason: Continuing the Conversation.' *Feminist Economics* 10 (3): 77–80.

————. 2006. ' "What Do We Want from a Theory of Justice?" ' *Journal of Philosophy* 103 (5): 215–238.

————. 2009. *The Idea of Justice*. Cambridge, Massachusetts: Harvard University Press.

Shouping, H and G D Kuh. 2002. 'Being (Dis)Engaged in Educational Purposeful Activities: The Influences of Student and Institutional Characteristics.' *Research in Higher Education* 43 (5): 555–575.

Simkins, C and A Paterson. 2005. *Learner Performance in South Africa. Social and Economic Determinants of Success in Language and Mathematics*. Pretoria: Human Sciences Research Council.

Simkins, C, S Rule and A Bernstein. 2007. *Doubling for Growth. Addressing the Maths and Science Challenge in South Africa's Schools*. CDE Research no 15. Johannesburg: Centre for Development and Enterprise.

Soudien, C. 2010. 'Race and Class in the South African Higher-Education Sector.' In *The Next 25 Years. Affirmative Action in Higher Education in the Unites States and South Africa*, edited by D L Featherman, M Hall and M Krislov. Ann Arbor: University of Michigan Press: 187–195.

Taylor, N, J Muller and P Vinjevold. 2003. *Getting Schools Working. Research and Systemic School Reform in South Africa*. Cape Town: Maskew Miller Longman (Pty) Ltd.

Terzi, L. 2007. 'The Capability to Be Educated.' In *Amartya Sen's Capability Approach and Social Justice in Education*, edited by M Walker and E Unterhalter. New York: Palgrave Macmillan Ltd: 25–44.

Tinto, V and B Pusser. 2006. *Moving from Theory to Action: Building a Model of Institutional Action for Student Success*. Washington DC: National Postsecondary Education Cooperative.

Unterhalter, E. 2009. 'What Is Equity in Education? Reflections from the Capability Approach.' *Studies in the Philosophy of Education* 28: 415–424.

Unterhalter, E, R Vaughan and M Walker. 2007. 'The Capability Approach and Education.' *Prospero*.

Upcraft, M L, J N Gardner and B O Barefoot. 2005. *Challenging and Supporting the First-Year Student. A Handbook for Improving the First Year of College*. San Francisco: Jossey-Bass.

Vanderyar, S, and J Jansen. 2008. *Diversity High. Class, Color, Culture, and Character in a South African High School*. Maryland: University Press of America.

Vaughan, R. 2007. 'Measuring Capabilities: An Example from Girls, Schooling.' In *Amartya Sen's Capability Approach and Social Justice in Education*, edited by M Walker and E Unterhalter. New York: Palgrave Macmillan Ltd: 109–130.

Walker, M. 2006. *Higher Education Pedagogies*. Berkshire, England: Society for Research into Higher Education and Open University Press.

————. 2008. 'A Human Capabilities Framework for Evaluating Student Learning.' *Teaching in Higher Education* 13 (4): 477–487.

————. 2009. ' "Making a World That Is Worth Living In": Humanities Teaching and the Formation of Practical Reasoning.' *Arts and Humanities in Higher Education* 8: 231–246.

Walker, M and M McLean. 2013. *Professional Education, Capabilities and the Public Good. The Role of Universities in Promoting Human Development.* London: Routledge.

Walker, M, M MClean, A Dison and R Peppin-Vaughan. 2009. 'South African Universities and Human Development: Towards a Theorisation and Operationalisation of Professional Capabilities for Poverty Reduction.' *International Journal of Educational Development* 29: 565–572.

Walker, M and E Unterhalter. 2007. 'The Capability Approach: Its Potential for Work in Education.' In *Amartya Sen's Capability Approach and Social Justice in Education*, edited by M Walker and E Unterhalter. New York: Palgrave Macmillan Ltd: 1–18.

Watts, M. 2009. 'Sen and the Art of Motorcycle Maintenance: Adaptive Preferences and Higher Education.' *Studies in the Philosophy of Education* 28: 425–436.

Watts, M and D Bridges. 2006. 'Enhancing Students' Capabilities?: UK Higher Education and the Widening Participation Agenda.' In *Transforming Unjust Structures. The Capability Approach*, edited by S Deneulin and N Sagovsky, Library of Ethics and Applied Philosophy. Netherlands: Springer:143–160.

Whittaker, R. 2008. *Quality Enhancement Themes: The First Year Experience. Transition to and During the First Year.* Mansfield, Scotland: The Quality Assurance Agency for Higher Education.

Wilson-Strydom, M G. forthcoming. 'A Capabilities List for Equitable Transitions to University: A Top-down and Bottom-up Approach.' *Journal of Human Development and Capabilities.*

———. 2010a. *National Benchmark Tests 2010. Institutional Summary Report.* Bloemfontein: University of the Free State.

———. 2010b. 'Traversing the Chasm from School to University in South Africa: A Student Perspective.' *Tertiary Education and Management* 16 (4): 313–325.

Wilson-Strydom, M G and H R Hay. 2010. 'Reducing the Gap Between Being Eligible and Being Ready for Higher Education: a Learner Engagement Perspective.' In *Praxis Towards Sustainable Empowering Learning Environments in South Africa*, edited by D Francis, S Mahlolaholo and M Nkoane. Bloemfontein: Sun Media: 239–252.

Wolff, J and A de-Shalit. 2007. *Disadvantage.* Oxford: Oxford University Press.

Yazzie-Mintz, E. 2010. *Charting the Path from Engagement to Achievement: A Report on the 2009 High School Survey of Student Engagement.* Indiana: Indiana University, Bloomington.

Zembylas, M. 2002. ' "Structures of Feeling" in Curriculum and Teaching: Theorising the Emotional Rules.' *Educational Theory* 52 (2): 187–208.

———. 2003. 'Caring for Teacher Emotion: Reflections on Teacher Self-Development.' *Studies in the Philosophy of Education* 22: 103–125.

Zorn, Diane and Megan Boler. 2007. 'Rethinking Emotions and Educational Leadership.' *International Journal for Leadership in Education* 10 (2): 137–151.

Zukas, M and J Malcolm. 2007. 'Learning from Adult Education.' *Academy Exchange* 6 (Summer): 20–22.

5 School-university interface
Learner and student voices

It's like getting thrown into the deep end of life . . . without a life jacket!
(student focus group, 2009)

How do students experience the transition to university? The quotation above and drawing below provide some clues about the confusion associated with this experience, but the voices of learners and students still to come highlight the complexity and diversity of transition experiences. This chapter is intentionally constructed around the voices of the research participants, with scant reference to the theoretical topics that have been the focus of earlier chapters. This has been done to provide a space for learners and students to 'participate' in the construction of the capabilities-based social justice framework for the transition to university,

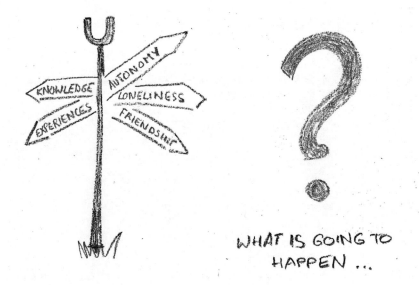

Drawing 5.1 What is going to happen?
(white female first-year student, Economic and Management Sciences, 2010)

without being dominated by theoretical presuppositions. The chapter begins by introducing the participants to the reader. Thereafter, we move on to consider what emerged from the open coding of students' descriptions of coming to university. Conley's multidimensional model of university readiness is then used as an organising framework from which learners and students can 'speak' about readiness challenges and opportunities. The voices of high school learners and first-year university students come together to form a richly descriptive and analytical tapestry depicting the interface between school and university from their perspectives. The learner and student quotations used are presented exactly as provided by the participants. No corrections have been made for spelling or grammar. This is deliberate, because part of the analysis includes a review of language competence and confidence and the quotations included throughout are an important piece in the language puzzle. In Chapters 6 and 7 we will return to the capabilities framework already mapped out in order to interpret and theorise these experiences from a social justice position.

Meet the participants

The value of using a mixed methodology rests, among others, on the depth of analysis and incorporation of multiple perspectives that this methodology allows. One of the challenges, though, is that the inclusion of multiple perspectives and participants creates a complexity of research design that can at times be confusing for those not closely involved in the study. For this reason, and in the interests of the participation of learners and students, in this section I briefly introduce the research participants. This introduction centres on presenting an account of the broader context in which these young people live and go to school and university, since participant demographics were shown in Table 1.1. The starting point for mapping participants' broader social contexts was to better understand their schooling contexts. To do this, a set of four school types was developed based on the geographic locations of schools, annual school fees as an indication of socioeconomic context, and language of instruction at the school (English or Afrikaans). Table 5.1 summarises the school types and presents a short description of each. The vast disparity in annual school fees highlights the range of socioeconomic contexts from which the high school learners came. As is seen in Table 5.1, the suburban HSC schools have been further divided into English and Afrikaans medium of instruction. This was done because, during the analysis of the survey data collected at high schools, I was struck by the differences in responses of learners from English medium of instruction schools compared to Afrikaans medium of instruction schools.

As is to be expected, these schooling contexts generally mirror broader socioeconomic differences. While the school type classifications provide a proxy for socioeconomic context, there were additional questions about this included in the school survey. The data showed how basic nutrition, measured in terms of regularity of eating breakfast, differed across the school types. For example, while 57 per cent of learners attending suburban higher socioeconomic context schools

Table 5.1 School types

School Type	Description	Number of schools per school type
Township	Schools located in township areas, annual school fees less than R1,500 (School fee range among the 7 schools in this group was from R220 per year to R1,300 per year)	7
Suburban lower socio-economic context (Suburban LSC)	Suburban schools, mostly ex-model C, annual school fees range from R1,500 to R5,000, often cater for learners who travel from townships to attend better schools (School fee range among the 4 schools in this group was from R3,000 per year up to R5,000 per year)	4
Suburban higher socio-economic context (Suburban HSC) – English medium of instruction	Suburban schools with annual school fees more than R5,000, usually ex-model C, mostly cater for learners from upper-middle class contexts, English medium of instruction (School fee range among the 3.5 schools in this group was from R11,200 per year up to R20,735 per year)	3.5 (1 parallel medium of instruction)
Suburban higher socio-economic context (Suburban HSC) – Afrikaans medium of instruction	Suburban schools with annual school fees more than R5,000, usually ex-model C, mostly cater for learners from upper-middle class contexts, Afrikaans, medium of instruction (School fee range among the 5.5 schools in this group was from R6,930 per year up to R11,700)	5.5 (1 parallel medium of instruction)

often eat breakfast, only 29 per cent of township learners do. Learners attending township schools spend significantly more time than learners from all other school types caring for family members, doing chores at home, and walking to and from school. In contrast, learners attending the suburban HSC schools spent significantly more time practicing sport and/or playing musical instruments and socialising with friends outside of school. In addition large, differences with respect to parental levels of education were also evident. At HSC schools, while 11 per cent of learners reported that their parents had doctoral degrees, this dropped to only 2 per cent at township schools. At the other end of the spectrum, only 11 per cent of learners attending suburban HSC and LSC schools came from homes where parents had not completed 12 years of schooling, compared with 36 per cent at township schools. Overall, very few of the learners enrolled in township schools came from families where parents or guardians had any post-school education. As such, the vast majority of these young people are the first in their families to go to university.

These socioeconomic differences are further complicated by the complex politics and realities of language in education in South Africa. Most of the high school learners were learning in English (78 per cent), yet only 12 per cent reported that English was their home language. The majority of the high school participants were thus learning in a language other than their mother tongue while at school. In addition to socioeconomic differences across the high school participants, there was also evidence of important gender disparities. There were slightly more female learners that participated in the research (54.3 per cent) compared with male learners (45.7 per cent). Female learners spent more time than male learners doing chores at home, caring for family members and talking on the phone. In comparison, male learners spent more time than female learners working for pay, playing sport, exercising and socialising with friends. These gender differences, like socioeconomic differences, are important conversion factors, and we will return to these issues in greater detail in Chapter 7. Almost all of the high school learners indicated that they planned to attend university in the future, although based on their current school marks it was likely that about 16 per cent of the learners would not qualify for university study.

Moving on to introductions of the university students – as with the high school learners, the basic demographic information about the university students is shown in Table 1.1. Here, the focus is on describing the broader context in which the participating students are located. The vast disparities evident across schooling were described earlier, and it is from those different schooling contexts that the first-year students in the study also came. A total of 56 per cent of the students had attended suburban high schools, from both higher and lower socioeconomic backgrounds, while 36 per cent of students had attended township or rural schools. The remaining 8 per cent attended independent schools, vocationally oriented Further Education and Training Colleges, or were home-schooled. Just over two thirds of the student participants (68 per cent) were living on-campus in university accommodation. Students were enrolled in a multitude of different courses and all academic faculties at the case study university were represented. Thus, in sum, the learners and students participating in this research represented a range of schooling and socioeconomic backgrounds as well as areas of study at university. It is to students' experiences of the transition to university that we now turn.

Transition to university experiences

The central purpose of the qualitative research processes conducted with first-year university students was to explore their experiences of coming to university. The qualitative data gathered using focus group discussions and student drawings of the transition was first analysed using open coding. This open coding pointed to 11 emergent themes describing transition to university experiences. These are summarised in Table 5.2.

It was most common for students to describe feelings of confusion and of being lost and scared. This is not unexpected since students are entering a new and unknown environment and this challenge has been well documented in the

Table 5.2 Summary of emergent themes in student transition to university descriptions and drawings

Transition to university experiences – emergent themes (in alphabetical order)	Number of instances identified in the qualitative data
Confused, lost or scared	110
Diversity experiences (positive and negative)	73
Financial challenges	19
Fun, happy, enjoyable, exciting	53
Independence (learning to become independent)	61
Looking towards the future	24
Orientation experiences (positive and negative)	35
Quality of teaching at university	39
Residence versus commuter students	92
Lack of spaces in large classes	16
Being tired	25

literature. However, what is more significant here is the extent to which this confusion and fear seemed to influence the students' confidence to learn:

> *Sometimes I was confused and felt lost. It took me a while to understand this world (university) and to be part of it. I once thought of giving up when I was exposed to big halls (lecture halls) with lots of people, thought I would not cope. It was just too much for me but never give up. Got advise which lifted me up.*
>
> *(black female first-year student, Natural Sciences, 2010)*

> *For this first month at tertiary I am confused of what is expected from me, I struggle to understand the way in which content are delivered. It is hard for me to compete to my level best, I did not know that there are other modules except the one I wanted to specialise with and that make me underperforming and I really get more confused because I think of the bursary will be cancelled.*
>
> *(black male first-year student, Education, 2010)*

> *I faced the most scary thing I have never faced before, and that was being here. I didn't know what to do, I was shy to ask for help to other people. Its never easy facing the world alone.*
>
> *(black female first-year student, Humanities, 2010)*

Closer scrutiny of the data shows that these feelings of being scared and confused were experienced in relation to space (the physical landscape of the university) and the university system (how things work). This distinction is important when thinking through interventions. For many students leaving home for the first time, part of their confusion and fear had to do with suddenly needing to learn to become independent, as is implied in the student quotation included at the outset of the chapter – 'It's like getting thrown into the deep end of life . . . without a life jacket!' This experience was manifest in a variety of ways, from the difficulty of learning to cook one's own food to the freedom of university where it is one's own responsibility to attend classes and do the required work. Independence is also an important component of university readiness and we will return to this issue a bit later in the chapter.

Students living on campus in university accommodation (residence) commonly made reference to the support networks provided by residence structures during the first few months of university. This support helped students to overcome their feelings of fear and confusion. Several students who did not live in residence remarked about the comparative lack of support they experienced as well as their difficulties meeting people and making new friends:

> *It's a scary experience because if you live in a hostel [residence] you have seniors and stuff, I didn't, I didn't get in a place in a hostel so I had to do everything myself and that was scary because you don't know where that class is and that class and if you ask someone they're like 'why don't you know?' but that was scary for me . . . like why can't we have someone that, a mentor for each hostel, you can ask that person why, where's that, how does this happen. All those things because it's really scary to come here and like, OK I have class in that place but I don't have any idea where it is . . .*
>
> *(student focus groups, 2009)*

> *Confused – didn't quite know where all my classes were. Excited – everything was new. Supported – being in a hostel helped. Independent – I was in control of my own studies and other activities*
>
> *(white female first-year student, Economic and Management Sciences, 2010)*

While university residences were important in helping students adapt to university, many students also lamented the extent of compulsory activities for first-year students which were exhausting and detracted from their academic work. Achieving a better balance between social and academic activities for first-year students in residence is vital for improving the transition experience as well as students' chances of academic success in the first year.

The data related to experiences with diversity highlighted the various challenges first-year students experienced in this area (see also, Wilson-Strydom forthcoming). It was most common for students to report negative experiences related to diversity (or lack thereof):

> *I'm from Kimberley so there's not that much differentiation between black people and white people . . . So when I came here and there's Rag [First-year student fund raising activity] and there's the opening of the new SRC [Student Representative Council] is welcoming them in and you see the division. It's so distinct, like when a white person goes on stage, the other half of the Rag Farm starts screaming and shouting for him but when a black person gets on stage, the other half also starts. So for me, that was shocking and . . . it really, I wasn't prepared for that when I came here.*
>
> *(student focus groups, 2009)*

A small number of students did make specific references to positive diversity experiences, such as 'getting to know different kinds of people', and 'learning another language'. While it was most common for students to reflect on diversity with respect to race, there were also many instances in which diversity was seen in relation to learning in a multilingual environment, with the majority of students who raised this issue describing the challenge of learning in a language that was unfamiliar as well as interacting with lecturers and students who did not speak their chosen language:

> *I don't know, but for me it was a total social adjustment because I'm English so to come to a majority Afrikaans place umm, was very difficult at first, no one wanted to talk to me because I was English so that's also quite a massive culture-shock and that was for me the biggest adjustment, was the Afrikaans.*
>
> *(student focus groups, 2009)*

> *But apart from that, I think for me, because I come from an Afrikaans school, I was brought up in an Afrikaans home so my home language is Afrikaans. So, I come to university, we get forms, I have clearly and explicitly said I want to study in Afrikaans. Now I get my book and my counselling in English . . . have nothing against the English children, really, but it is not so difficult for them because they come from an English school, they grow up in an English home, they study further in English, so for them it is one giant breeze. Yes, they do still struggle with things they do but not as much as we do because I must now go and sit and translate from English to Afrikaans.*
>
> *(student focus groups 2009)*

> *Socially it was worse because it was my first time meeting with different people with a different language. It was a terrible month in all.*
>
> *(black male first-year student, Natural Sciences, 2010)*

The responses of several students emphasised just how difficult it is for students to confront their biases and learn to appreciate diversity. Consider the statement by the student below that clearly shows her difficulty in coming to terms with functioning in a diverse university environment, and is also a further example of how race and language become intertwined in discussions about diversity:

> *and I mean he, he's giving [Business English], it's a language and he can't even speak English. I mean for me in Afrikaans I really need someone to like help me with English because I want to improve my English but now this person's telling me you don't need to attend class and he's just, and then he's speaking about 'comfortable' . . . (LAUGHTER) . . . okaaaay, I'm sorry . . . ja and the thing also, the guy that gives us [Business English], it's a black guy so no, but it's like OK, no, you, they speak umm, softer, but it's like he doesn't, like she said, he doesn't pronounce it correctly and he's like or he doesn't know how to pronounce it so he speaks softer so you don't hear it. You understand, so it's like you don't hear him half the time.*
>
> *(student focus groups, 2009)*

Looking at the results from selected items in the high school learner survey, it is perhaps not surprising that students battle to deal with diversity when entering university. For example, when asked if they had talked to a learner of a different race or culture, only 39 per cent of the large sample of high school learners reported that they had often done so. Particularly concerning was that 10 per cent had never spoken to a learner of a different race or culture. The results were similar when learners were asked if they had talked to or worked with a learner who was different from them in terms of religion, political opinion, family income, or personal values. When analysed across the different school types the results were even more alarming. For example, 26 per cent of Afrikaans learners in suburban HSC schools had often talked to or worked with a learner of a different race or culture and 10 per cent had never done so. Similarly, in township schools 29 per cent of learners had often talked to a learner of a different race or culture and 13 per cent had never done so. Opportunities to engage with diverse learners was most promising at English speaking suburban HSC and LSC schools where 56 per cent and 44 per cent of the learners respectively had often talked with a learner of a different race or culture. Further, very few learners in these schools reported that they had never done so – on average only about 5 per cent.

It was somewhat surprising that relatively few students made reference to financial difficulties when describing their transition to university and their first few months on campus. Financial difficulties faced by students are commonly raised by student organisations and are also well documented in the literature on the first year experience, so one would have expected more reference to this issue by students. We might speculate that financial difficulties emerge a little later in the year because students who had indeed registered to study at the university – and hence were included in the research – had at least overcome the initial financial hurdle faced at registration and had perhaps not reached the next payment deadline. Even though in this specific study, relatively few students spoke of financial issues, the extreme stress students experience when financial resources are insufficient is clear from the quotations below:

> *I find that most people from the school you come from disadvantaged backgrounds and they have like financial aid for their studies, which just pays for their studies and when they get here they have to pay R1000 extra, R4000 for registration, making it difficult for them to come to school . . . So I think they should be more considerate to disadvantaged students and cut off all the extra things that they need to pay for registration and all those things.*
>
> (student focus groups 2009)

> *Yes, it is not only university fees and accommodation, I mean you still need your books and you must buy your food and other stuff and there is a lot of other things that happens that people don't always take into account and this causes problems.*
>
> (student focus groups 2009)

Frustration, no accommodation, no money, clueless, crying, hard work at Rag, challenges with academics, city from rural.

(black male first-year student, Natural Sciences, 2010)

I did find it hard in a way that it was living far from home and the things around campus are expensive so I was always hungry and that was my biggest challenge.

(black male first-year student, Education, 2010)

Compared to the majority of emergent themes that pointed to the various difficulties students experienced during their transition, there were a rather smaller number of examples where students reported experiences that were fun, happy, enjoyable or exciting:

Very great and wonderful, in a nutshell.

(black male first-year student, Economic and Management Sciences, 2010)

Awesome, confusing, fun, confusing, learn lots of new things, get to know yourself and develop, 'n nice and confusing time that everyone should experience in their lives!

(student focus groups, 2009)

It was and still is awesome!

(white female first-year student, Natural Sciences, 2010)

To summarise, on the whole students seem to find the transition to university experience to be one of confusion, being lost, and for some students, scary. While students in university residence are provided with additional support in making this transition, the extent of compulsory activity required of first-year residence students also seems to work against facilitating the transition. This is especially so for students struggling to come to terms with an increased academic load. For a few students, entering a more diverse environment was a positive experience, while for most it was more difficult. In the specific context of the case study university, which has a parallel language policy allowing students to study in either English or Afrikaans classes, issues of diversity and the difficulties experienced in coming to terms with diversity were sometimes intertwined in discussions about the language of instruction. In the coming section we consider what these experiences mean for university readiness.

Readiness for university

The multidimensional model of university readiness proposed by Conley (2008, 2005) that was introduced in Chapter 2 provides a helpful organising framework for presenting the voices of students and learners. The qualitative data collected from high school learners and first-year students was also thematically coded using Conley's four dimensions of readiness. Figure 2 provides a quick visual summary of the four dimensions of readiness in the model and shows the number of

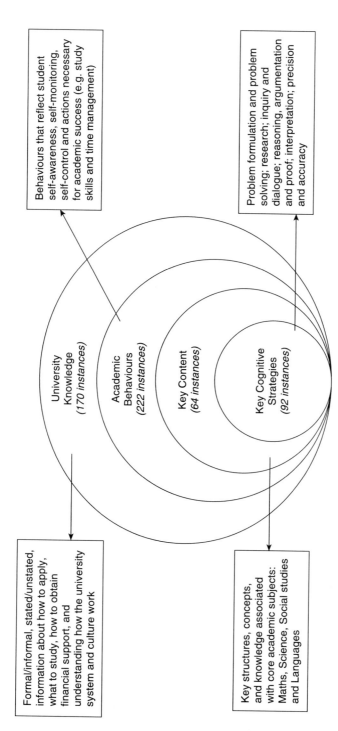

Behaviours that reflect student self-awareness, self-monitoring, self-control and actions necessary for academic success (e.g. study skills and time management)

Problem formulation and problem solving; research; inquiry and dialogue; reasoning, argumentation and proof; interpretation; precision and accuracy

University Knowledge
(170 instances)

Academic Behaviours
(222 instances)

Key Content
(64 instances)

Key Cognitive Strategies
(92 instances)

Formal/informal, stated/unstated, information about how to apply, what to study, how to obtain financial support, and understanding how the university system and culture work

Key structures, concepts, and knowledge associated with core academic subjects: Maths, Science, Social studies and Languages

Figure 5.1 Multidimensional model of university readiness showing qualitative data counts (adapted from Conley 2008, 6)

instances of each dimension found in the qualitative data. Each dimension is discussed in detail thereafter.

Key cognitive strategies

This dimension of readiness refers to the extent to which learners or students have developed their capabilities with respect to problem formulation and problem solving, inquiry and dialogue such as being able to discuss and debate issues, being able to engage in sound reasoning practices, formulate an argument and understand how to back up or 'prove' their argument. Students entering university need to be able to interpret information and arguments and understand different points of view. Conley (2010a, Kindle edition) reminds us that 'students can demonstrate their capabilities only if they are fully challenged and stretched beyond their comfort zones'. Also relevant in this context is the research looking at active learning, academic challenge and student engagement in the learning process (Chickering and Gamson 1999; Kuh et al. 2005a; Yazzie-Mintz 2010). Not only do universities need to actively foster learning environments that support the development of these cognitive strategies. So too should schools be providing spaces in which learners can develop these capabilities.

Unfortunately, substantial gaps in the extent to which high school learners are able to develop more engaged approaches to learning were evident. This was particularly the case in Afrikaans medium of instruction schools, although the trend was found across all the schools. We will return to the differences across school types and also by gender in Chapter 7 when we consider personal, social and environmental conversion factors. For now, our focus is more generally on high school learners and first-year students, irrespective of their schooling contexts or demographic characteristics. The results from the quantitative survey completed by high school learners provides one part of the picture, and this picture is given further depth and clarification using the qualitative comments made by both high school learners and first-year students.

From the quantitative data, it was clear that there is relatively little focus in high schools on discussing questions with more than one answer, exploring learning materials beyond the textbook, solving real world problems, grappling with difficult materials, thinking critically, exploring new ideas and analysing ideas in depth. Only small proportions of learners, less than one third, reported that they 'often' engaged in these sorts of activities. For example, only 27 per cent of learners were often required to solve real world problems, 26 per cent often discussed questions in class that did not have one clear answer, 32 per cent often had to read complex materials, 36 per cent were often encouraged to think critically and only 30 per cent were often asked to analyse ideas in depth. In comparison, 62 per cent of high school learners reported that they often spent a lot of time preparing for examinations. While examination preparation is important, it is concerning that rather more weight seems to be placed on this activity compared to more active and engaging learning activities. High school learners' responses to these statements about learning are instructive because these statements are examples of the type of learning activities that are particularly important in the context of readiness since curiosity, creativity, engagement in discussion, and tackling complex problems are all important cognitive strategies that learners will be required to put into practice when at university.

The implication of this lack of in-depth cognitive engagement at school was powerfully expressed by first-year students who commonly described how different the cognitive demands at university are compared to what they had experienced at school:

> *I don't know, with these new systems they bring into the schools, you don't learn how you now learn at university. You learn so that you, you can still do well because in the exams and tests there are so many case studies and all these sorts of things and that does not allow you to learn the work as you need to learn it now and this was a big adjustment for me. Now you need to know all the work just to get through . . . In the beginning it was really difficult for me at university not to feel like I am writing a lot but actually nothing because that is what you do at school. You wrote like these pages full and waffled and actually said nothing and now at university you need to state facts and your answers must really carry weight to get marks and it was a big adjustment for me to learn to stay with the facts and not waffle to make up your marks and that is what OBE [Outcomes-based education] let me know, because you can . . . /you could get away with that/. . . . yes, you just needed to apply well and not really say 'this is the answer'.*

> *(student focus groups, 2009)*

> *So the gap between what you were taught at school and what was expected from you at school and what is expected from you in your first term of varsity, it's like two completely different worlds and I think that often demotivates students to study something because hey, I used to be good at English and now I'm failing . . . (AGREEMENT) . . . You go home with your marks and your parents are like 'what happened . . . are you pregnant or something?'. . . (LAUGHTER) . . .' why are you failing, why are your marks bad?' And they don't understand that all of a sudden it's on a different level. The teachers, you knew them for long, you could talk to them, if there was something you could go to them afterwards.*

> *(student focus groups, 2009)*

There were three main areas in which the difference between requirements at school and university were described by students, namely: being critical and formulating an argument, being able to integrate theory and practice, and having skills of academic writing and referencing. The first set of student quotations presented below show how students felt under-prepared with respect to critical thinking and being able to formulate academic arguments:

> *At school you just write it, you just basically copy and paste. Here at varsity you must be critical.*

> *(student focus groups 2009)*

To argue your point, to prove it, sometimes I'm not always a hundred percent sure which point I should prove and then I sit there and I spend half an hour just trying to think what am I going to write . . . The reading is not so bad because I enjoy it so I just go through it at the speed of light. Then I sit here and I've got all this info, now . . . What to do with it . . . I mean we did get a crash course on paragraph and essay writing but now you've got to sit and think which points do I want to prove, how am I going to argue those points and that takes a while . . .

(student focus groups 2009)

At school you used, you read a poem, OK, there you go. They didn't expect any, any insight from you, they didn't expect you to go any deeper. At varsity they want you to go and read it and then to go question everything. Remember at school they tried to make you think critically but they don't always succeed all that well because they try to make you think critically within a rigid framework which doesn't work. Think critically means you throw all my ideas away. At varsity they want you to think critically – take this thing and examine every part of it. Do you agree with it, do you not?

(student focus groups 2009)

Here it's more like understanding of the work rather than knowing the words. In high school it's more knowing the words, they just test you if you know OK, the words and how well you know them but they don't understand the understanding of the words so you get, like in Biochemistry we got things that were the same, that we had in high school but now they are testing our understanding, OK, this does this and this and this, not that just is . . .

(student focus groups 2009)

Differences between school and university with respect to the volume of theory that needs to be covered as well as the integration of theory and practical work was also mentioned by students:

Because you come to university and then that is what it is, it is integrating theory with practical because that it what we will need to do outside one day. That is what you are going to do in your work, you are going use theory and practical and that is what the teachers need to teach us more.

(student focus groups 2009)

Challenges specifically related to academic writing were also expressed:

I think the biggest problem is umm, at the beginning of the year we started to do academic writing and we didn't do it at school so we're struggling. I really struggle with academic writing . . . Ja, the referencing, the paraphrasing and that we didn't do at school that much.

(student focus groups, 2009)

I mean we did get a crash course on paragraph and essay writing but now you've got to sit and think which points do I want to prove, how am I going to argue those points and that takes a while . . .

(student focus groups 2009)

Several of the high school learners in their open-ended survey responses also raised concerns about the cognitive demands of their school work which they felt was too low, as well as concerns about the lack of space for thinking critically and questioning:

> *Certain schoolwork isn't challenging enough. S.A has to raise its levels of education if it once to compete with the world in certain areas. There should be certain courses for advanced work. If someone is more intelligent, don't subject him/her to low grade levels!*
> *(white male learner, suburban HSC, 2009)*

> *School is irrelevent, it promotes indoctrination and the stripping of one's identity. you will only get 90% in school if you think in the way they want you to. Any unusual content in projects is disregarded even though the project itself is of a high standard. Christianity is shoved down our throats and teacher's get too personal if for instance, you do not share their religious beliefs.*
> *(white female learner suburban LSC school, 2009)*

> *At my school I have a problem with the teachers on the case of listening to the views or ideas, they only want them to say what they want and don't listen to your views.*
> *(black female learner, township, 2009)*

A final issue related to cognitive challenge that emerged from the data is that of language competence and confidence. Without adequate levels of competence in the language of instruction at university, students are unlikely to be in a position to either develop or make use of the cognitive strategies we have been considering thus far. Several students raised language related issues in the focus groups and also in the written descriptions of their first month at university. Often the challenge noted by students was due to the fact that they were learning in a language other than their home language or mother tongue and so were not as competent in using the language of instruction as they needed to be:

> *A language of education was also challenging course I was not really used to speak English only.*
> *(black male first-year student, Natural Sciences, 2010)*

> *I think they [school] didn't prepare us well – why, because everything they did they, if they do something like social studies they always translate it into Tswana so things become simpler, but now . . . now we don't have Tswana.*
> *(student focus groups, 2009)*

> *It is a very, very difficult subject, really, cos they use, they don't use normal English. They use this high order English and I was like 'oh my word'! And I come from a very, very academic top school and I couldn't do that English because it was too hard. I had to ask my mother to help me to translate it so that I can just pass the subject . . . (LAUGHTER) . . .*
> *(student focus groups, 2009)*

The final quotation in the set above begins to point in the direction of the second language-related theme that emerged from the student voices. In addition to overall competence in the language of instruction, several students made reference to the fact that the type of language being used at university was often difficult to understand, and related that the context in which language was being used was not always clear. These challenges take us in the direction of epistemological access (Morrow 2009) which refers to the importance of students being able to engage with the construction of knowledge within different disciplines and come to understand the language of the discipline itself. In the quotations below students are reflecting on the fact that while they may understand the language of instruction, they do not understand the *specific type* of language being used, which is noted to be at a different level from what they are used to:

> *Umm, didn't you feel that the language use in the textbook that they now have is at a completely different level compared to your comprehensive tests and how the high school textbooks were.*
>
> *(student focus groups, 2009)*

> *I think like, especially when you talk about English, if it could be like bigger, broadened it at high school because I think at the end of the day, whatever module you're doing whether it' s Medicine or you're doing Biology, at the end of the day if you don't know how the question is asked ____(UNCLEAR) and it's asked in English, if they ask you do this and you can't do it or you do that instead, you see it's gonna screw you over because you don't know what the question is . . . how it's being asked basically so English should be our main thing in high school. Even when we get here we should all do English in our first year . . . the broadened version of English where they ask you where did you get stuff instead of just doing an adverb, you know.*
>
> *(student focus groups, 2009)*

> *Because they sometimes used such big words and they use university concepts that we don't understand yet, I mean, now they say this and that and then at the end you have no idea what the first thing was because it is all university concepts, they don't explain the concepts that are important.*
>
> *(student focus groups, 2009)*

These quotations provide examples of students who are having difficulty understanding the type of language used at university, or, in the words of one of the students – the big words or university concepts. In the final quotation below the student reaches a point where s/he begins to understand the context in which language is being used and understands 'how they want me to perform, how they want me to understand' – this is an example of emerging epistemological access:

> *The system here . . . umm . . . the language, like you . . . it was kind of difficult for me, like I had to make sure that if I read this thing, I must know the spelling is correct. If I want to say something, I'll prepare myself before saying it to someone so that someone won't laugh*

*at me when I make a mistake or something, ja. But now . . . ja, it's a bit easier cos I'm used
to the system, I understand lectures, ja, I understand how they want me to perform, how they
want me to understand, that's better.*

(student focus groups, 2009)

These quotations also provide some insight into how insecure students feel when
they are not confidently able to make use of language in the university context.
One of the students above explained how she needed to turn to her mother to help
with translation so that she could just pass the subject, and the student in the final
quotation above worries about someone laughing at him/her should they make a
mistake when speaking. Thus, it seems reasonable to argue that the notion of
language competence and confidence needs to be incorporated within Conley's
dimension of key cognitive strategies since without language competence and
confidence students are unlikely to reach a stage of readiness with respect to the
cognitive demands of university.

Key content

Being ready for university requires that a learner develops the key structures, concepts and knowledge that are associated with core academic subjects such as mathematics, physical science, social studies and languages. Importantly, while school
marks provide some indication of the mastery of content, schools do not always
focus on teaching the key underlying structures, concepts and knowledge (Conley
2010a). This argument is important in the context of epistemological access which
emphasises that students at university need to be aware of the processes of knowledge construction within a university setting – the building blocks of which are key
disciplinary structures, concepts and knowledge (Boughey 2005; Jacobs 2009;
Morrow 2009). Several first-year students made reference to their readiness in this
area during the focus group discussions and in their descriptions of the first month
at university. The following set of quotations shows examples across various subject
areas, including English, Drama, Chemistry and Mathematics:

*I've never failed a language in my entire life at school and I came here and my first English
test – oh hell.*

(student focus groups, 2009)

*I got a distinction for English and I failed most of my tests in English so . . . it's really
scary . . .*

(student focus groups, 2009)

*My school academically, I don't think it prepared me that well cos I remember the first
few lectures of Maths, the guys from rich schools . . . they knew everything what was going
on cos they'd done it the year before they came here so academically my school didn't prepare
me well.*

(student focus groups, 2009)

even today I'm still struggling with Chemistry. I took Chemistry at school and I got sixty percent for Chemistry and I'm still struggling with it.

(student focus groups, 2009)

I also think that umm, like the work here is like a lot harder, like a lot more difficult to understand, so like _____(UNCLEAR). I'm studying Drama so I think that Drama, the subject that they teach at school from Standard 8 till Matric, they should do it more based on the work we're doing now cos now I did Drama at school but it means like almost nothing to me cos it's not anything like we're doing now . . .

(student focus groups 2009)

In addition to the difficulty of finding that a subject that one performed well in at school is now much more difficult, and in some instances 'not anything like we're doing now', some students also pointed to the fact that the content they had learnt at school was sometimes seen as incorrect once at university:

I think as well, ah, school to a certain extent it does give you that background knowledge of a specific subject but then you get, you know, when you go into some lectures and they say, they tell you what you had in high school was . . . was, you know, the wrong thing and this is how you do it. I don't think, I don't think they should be doing that at school level, I think they should be just building a foundation, not like the, a foundation whereby we can build on it. Not a foundation whereby you scrap when you get to varsity and you learn something completely new because what you learn at school, it sticks in your mind and everything.

(student focus groups 2009)

Oh ja, in my major umm, we were doing something, I think it was inventory or something, so we had a specific way of doing it in high school and that's was the way we did it in the umm, common papers and so when we get to our lectures, we had all done it that way, like as part of our homework and then the lecturer told us 'OK, now this is not how you do it, according to the ___(UNCLEAR WORD) financial reporting standards, you do it this way and this way so whatever way you learnt in school, you can just forget about that and you know, learn how to do it this way.

(student focus groups 2009)

In their open-ended survey responses some of the high school learners described difficulties in properly understanding the content being covered at school. In the two quotations below, the learners explain how they do not have sufficient time to cover mathematics and science content in sufficient depth and as a result do not properly understand the key concepts. These learners are likely to find that they are not ready for university in the dimension of key content knowledge should they follow mathematics or science focused courses:

There is not enough time to finish all the work. A bunch of work is rushed and not covered, in Science and Maths.

(white male learner, suburban HSC, 2009)

In Maths we learn something new every day, but we don't get time to practice and time to properly understand. The same with Science, this is why we do so badly.

(white male learner, suburban HSC, 2009)

A final challenge that impacts negatively on readiness for university in the dimension of key content knowledge is the challenge of absent and poor quality school teachers, which is a particularly challenging reality in South African schools (Bloch 2009; Christie 2008). The final three quotations in this section highlight these challenges:

and when I was, I was doing Grade 12, my Physics teacher left June, and since June to December, we had no teacher.

(student focus groups, 2009)

In our school we have problems like the shortage of teacher which is wrong. We don't have the life-Science teacher, the bad thing about this is that, since our teacher left on march we haven't learn anything the problem is that we write the exam without learning something.

(black female learner, township, 2009)

But worse, my English teacher was always drunk . . . He was always drunk, he never taught us, nothing, he was always drunk. Serious . . . serious! Grade 10 to Grade 12, always drunk . . . ja.

(student focus groups, 2009)

Academic behaviours

Academic behaviour was the readiness domain about which students most commonly made mention. This domain refers to skills such as time management, study skills, working in study groups, setting goals, self-awareness of academic strengths and weaknesses, and persistence when academic tasks are challenging. As will be seen below, also important in the South African context is the ability to confidently use a computer for learning. Although the development of many of these academic behaviours is related to maturity, Conley (2010b) reminds us that these skills can also be systematically developed during the high school years so that learners have these skills in place by the time they enter university and so have a greater chance of academic success. Unfortunately this is often not the case. For many students coming to terms with the fact that they are now independent and responsible for their own lives and learning was a major challenge. Making sense of this new personal role is a key aspect of the academic behaviours that students need for successful study at university level. The examples below show some of the responses of students related to being independent, disciplined and having to be responsible for themselves and their own choices:

I academically experience change because here you are given work and there is no one to pressure you, that when I realised that I have to be responsible as I am now :-)

(black female first-year student, Economic and Management Sciences, 2010)

Everything was something I did by choice.

(white male first-year student, Law, 2010)

It was also very tiring and fun even though I had to learn how to make good choices fast.
(black male first-year student, Economic and Management Sciences, 2010)

The thought of having freedom was great feeling but when reality sets in, it was another thing.
(black male first-year student, Economic and Management Sciences, 2010)

That's when you realise that you're, that I'm actually alone here – everything is you, you. You know, you don't have no teachers there, your friends there, you just have to like, depend on yourself.

(student focus groups, 2009)

And also, you know . . . umm, the lecturers they don't care, like . . . umm . . . back in high school if you were failing the teacher would make sure to find out what's wrong with . . . umm, your studying and your techniques but here . . . they really don't care . . . (LAUGHTER) . . .

(student focus groups, 2009)

It was common for students to express a lack of readiness with respect to their study skills. In particular, students made much reference to the volume of work they suddenly faced at university, and the fact that they were now in large classes with less opportunity to ask questions if they did not understand:

My first month at university was very confusing. Although you are continually warned about the increase in the volume of work it was still very intimidating to think you had to complete it and come through. Lecturers are not concerned much about what marks you get and everything becomes your own responsibility.
(white male first-year student, Health Sciences, 2010)

And the amount of work we have to study for a test . . . /I know, I know/ . . . I mean in Matric I had to study ten pages for like a semester test, now I have to study sixty pages for a semester test and you only have two days so I think . . . we had to . . . we had to force ourselves to read faster . . . (AGREEMENT) . . . and to read fast but still remember what we read because there is so much work that we need to learn.

(student focus groups, 2009)

It was hard to pay attention – I was used to much smaller classes where you could ask questions. You feel that you can't ask questions in class, the other students will just laugh at you . . . Yes, there's no spoon-feeding here at university.

(student focus groups, 2009)

The first big shock of class and . . . huge classes. I was sitting at the back and it's this huge class and this dude in front is yap, yap, yap . . . Ja, I remember that whole time concentrating cos I was so used to the thirty minute classes of school and it's fifty minutes so after twenty minutes I was like 'are we leaving now?' . . . (LAUGHTER) . . .

(student focus groups, 2009)

A third aspect of academic behaviours that was described by students was that of learning to manage one's time. For students living in university residences this was partly about trying to balance academic and residence life activities and responsibilities. For many students the fact that they had to now manage their own time and daily schedule, in comparison to the rigidly structured school day, was a challenge:

Tired! The transition was not really easy as I had to learn to motivate myself and plan my time properly. There as also so much to learn and grasp in so little time.

(black female first-year student, Natural Sciences, 2010)

I think, I think varsity is all about time-management . . . (AGREEMENT FROM OTHER STUDENTS) . . . if you manage your time well and you stick by your, your time whatever you call it, timetable you make then you'll be fine. I mean if you tell yourself alright, this is time I'm going to study, then you'll be fine and this is the time for friends, you'll be fine . . .

(student focus groups, 2009)

At high school you have a fixed timetable where you know you've got this at this time. And so you come to university but it's an enormous amount of time and then you have to learn how to group this time in such a way that you can set up enough time for your friends, to study and to keep up with your work. So for me it was a learning experience. I learnt how to manage my time; I learnt how to deal with certain instances because now there is not that barrier. You know in high school you used to this, this, this, this . . . enclosed space, now you're exposed to so many other factors. With freedom comes a lot of responsibility, you know being away from your parents.

(student focus groups, 2009)

Readiness challenges regarding the use of computers were also common in the data. Insufficient meaningful access to computers for learning in schools remains a common problem in South Africa, as well as many other countries of the global South (Brazilian Internet Steering Committee 2013; Farrell and Isaacs 2007; Mdlongwa 2012; Ndlovu and Lawrence 2012; Song 2011). In the context of this study, these difficulties are not surprising when we consider that 31 per cent of township high school learners that completed the quantitative survey reported that their schools do not emphasise the use of computers for school work at all. Consider the following student drawing and quotations:

I was so stupid because I didn't know how to use a computer.

(black female first-year student, Economic and Management Sciences, 2010)

Drawing 5.2 Computer lab fear

(black female first-year student, Humanities, 2010)

> *You don't even have access to the computer . . . /you see/ . . . it's another story . . . minus five marks when you don't type work and you're expected to do it and it's not considered that many people haven't had access to computers . . . (AGREEMENT FROM STUDENTS) . . . as well as, ok fine, we have theory books that we can read before that but it's a total different story to be in front of a computer cos then . . . you're expected to work, you don't know where what is and how what works . . .*
>
> *(student focus groups 2009)*

> *In high school it wasn't compulsory for us to type-in our assignments, but now we have to type-in our assignments but it is something that we're not used to.*
>
> *(student focus groups 2009)*

University knowledge: Views across the humpback bridge

> *there is no manual to tell you this is what you should expect.*
>
> *(student focus groups, 2009)*

The notion of a humpback bridge was introduced in Chapter 2 as helpful analogy for conceptualising the transition to university. In particular, the humpback bridge analogy draws attention to the divide that must be crossed between school and

Drawing 5.3 Across the river

(black male student, Natural Sciences, 2010)

university and the fact that it is not always possible to see across to the other side of the bridge. Several of the students, when asked to draw their experience of the first month at university drew pictures that invoked similar analogies. While no student drew a humpback bridge per se, several students highlighted the disjuncture between school and university and the need for a crossing of this disjuncture. In Drawing 5.3, the student represented the divide between school and university as a river which had to be crossed, in this instance without even the help of a bridge. Drawing 5.4 presents another visual image of the divide between school and university. In this drawing the divide is specifically related to time available for studying, as well as support from parents, with one side of the divide (school) being a happy and sunny picture and the other (university) an unhappy and stormy one. Although Drawing 5.5 does not include a bridge, the idea of not knowing what lies ahead (at the other side) is emphasised by this student in her drawing showing a long and winding road ahead and a question bubble in which she wonders what lies ahead, 'what's up there?'

These three examples of students' visual representations of the transition to university lend further support to the argument made in earlier chapters for the importance of seeking to understand both sides of the humpback bridge that currently joins many of our schools and universities. In unpacking the domain of university knowledge further, it is useful to explore high school learners' expectations of university.

Drawing 5.4 Sunshine and storm clouds

(black female first-year student, Economic and Management Sciences, 2010)

Note: Translation of Afrikaans words used in drawing: leer – learn; sosiaal – social; Huis akt – house/ residence activities; slaap – sleep; Hoërskool – High school; ek – me; Pa – father; Ma – mother

Drawing 5.5 What's up there?

(black female first-year student, Health Sciences, 2010)

What do school learners – who may or may not have seen over the humpback bridge – expect of university? Consider the following quotations showing learner's descriptions of what they expect university to be like. Five quotations taken from the written 'University Knowledge' questionnaire are included. These extracts are long, but provide a strong indication of the humpback bridge at work, and hence are worth quoting at length. Only the first learner would be a first-generation student, the other four learners had one or both parents who attended university and/or a sibling or close family member that is currently at university. All of these learners, based on their school marks at the time of data collection, were likely to meet the minimum admission requirements for entry to university:

I expect that the university is a place where people come and learn many things about the life. In university and I expect university to be where people come and have the information about their study's and I expected it is like living in a different place where by you are going to find new friends, new life and is like your are growing up again but you are developing new things in life and sometimes it is hard to develop new things in life. I expect university to be like everything is there for me things like the metrials that I am going to use on my study's and I expect that all the money are there for me when I work hard on my studys. I expect university is a place where people are been controlled in a equal way no matter what. No matter what you are white or black because in the eyes of God we are all equal.

(*black male learner, township, 2010*)

Well firstly I don't know the subject by name, but I think you only do one subject and you time table is settled refering to your subject. The finances also go with the subjects. In University you only do theory and no practical . . . They is a campus for learners who stays far from school. In most campus you cant do things your own way, they are rules. In classes your not forced to do your work at that time, you can do it at your own time but have to submit in the due date.

(*black male learner, suburban LSC, 2010*)

From what I hear from most people I expect at university to be very busy where every Friday a party is thrown. I expect life at university to be a eat or get eaten kind of life where nobody does not care for you unless you do. That life at university is like survival series where you have to use all material available to you as effectively as possible within the period of time available to you. University to be nothing like High School. instead of a principal standing infront of us in the assembly telling us how disappointed he is that many children take their school work seriously and telling us that we should work hard, to be careful about the people we call friends and to respect our teachers and parents. in university if you want a rope they will give it to you without asking why and they will watch you as you hang yourself with your actions and they will also be there when you regret the choices you have made and when you fail your first year they will just kick you out without mercy. Life at university should be a fast one where is either you do things perfectly or you do not do them at all as lectures are not afraid of putting a zero on your script. they value of time at university is very essential, you have to make sure that you hand all the project and assignments given to you regardless of how many tests or exams you had to study for, on time or you will just simply fail. University is do or die!!!

(*black female learner, township, 2010*)

What I expect in university like academics, I think university don't have theories, having no practical Application everything is conteminared [?] on marks, there only formal test that are written only and which are going to be recorded, the finances, the money is going to be needed when going to university. When you go to university maybe you have a bursary, the goverment will give you money that you can spent while you are in university. Residence life, you have bursary You can Study at university and they will provide you with money, you will be eating free food with no charges and they will give you money to use it on your needs. Focus while you are in class do what you Supposed to do, do your business have a Confident on everything, demand to succes in life. University there are no friends you are alone no one is going to help you. You have to be productive work hard for your own. I expect university to be like at school, do your word therally, Submit it on time. And the lecture should treat children equally.

(black female learner, township, 2010)

Academics: I expect university to be very challenging, classes to have a massive number of students and lectures at night. Most work is self-study and if you miss a lecture, it won't be easy to catch up. No one really cares if you attend lectures or not, it's your own responsibility. It seems like a 'lonely world' and using time productively is vital. There isn't really that 'closeness' with lecturers that you'd get with high school teachers. Social: There are alot of social activities and self discipline is very important. Finances: It seems to me that one has to use money very wisely, as money will be needed often. Managing one's finances might come handy, although it might be quite difficult. Residence life: I expect it to be very awkward, at there'll be different girls from different backrounds. it is also an opportunity to make life-long friends. it's going to be difficult at first, especially for someone who hasn't lived in a hostel before, as mommy won't be around to help you out. independance begins here.

(white female learner, suburban HSC, 2010)

Various themes about university knowledge, or lack thereof, can be identified from these quotations. For example, one learner anticipates that everything he needs will be available and 'money are [sic] there for me', and another that she will be provided with money, 'will be eating free food with no charges and they will give you money to use it on your needs'. Several of the learners appear to be aware that they will be required to take responsibility for their own work and lives and that this would be different from school. A sense of fear and expectation of loneliness is expressed in the quotations, with one learner going as far as to note that 'they will watch you as you hang yourself with your actions' and 'they will kick you out without mercy'. One learner feels that 'there are no friends you are alone no one is going to help you', and another expects to find university a 'lonely world'. On a more upbeat note, there is an expectation of a party being thrown every Friday, the making of life-long friends, and one learner looks forward to meeting new friends and encountering 'new things in life'.

Overall, these quotations highlight the diversity of contextual skills and awareness, or university knowledge, among this group of high school learners. Except for the last quotation where the learner appears to have a relatively good sense of university knowledge, it is not difficult to see why these learners would find the transition to university to be a difficult, and most likely, a confusing and frightening process. This is not surprising when we look at the high school learner survey data where only 20 per cent of learners report that they 'often' talked to a teacher about career goals and 28 per cent had 'often' talked to a teacher about how to apply to university. Perhaps even more disconcerting is that 16 per cent of high school learners had 'never' spoken to a teacher about career goals and 28 per cent had 'never' spoken to a teacher about how to apply to university. This lack of access to information about post school career and university opportunities was also echoed in several of the comments made by learners in their responses to the open-ended survey question that merely asked for 'any additional comments'. One learner made specific mention of the lack of information at her school, stating:

> *I would like to say that in our school we are not given that much information about varsities.*
>
> *(black female learner, suburban LSC, 2009)*

Other learners used the open-ended question space to ask specific questions about university and these questions also highlight the lack of information available for learners at many high schools:

> *I would love to find out how much marks do you need to for the best university of your choice?*
> *(black female learner, suburban LSC, 2009)*

> *I need to know how to apply in the university. What subject should I do if I want to do a course of being a judge in the court.*
>
> *(black learner, no gender given, township, 2009)*

It was also common for first-year university students to raise concerns regarding the lack of information that was provided to them at school with respect to subject choices and the implications of this for further study, as well as information about university more broadly. These experiences were not the same at all schools, as shown in the quotations which follow. At some schools it appears that quite a lot of information and support is provided about subject choices and about further study options. These differences did not seem to be linked to the school type, as per my four school classifications, but rather to particular teachers and/or school principals who went to extra lengths to provide this information. In general, most students reported having little, if any, meaningful support in terms of choosing careers or post-schooling study options:

> *No, we once had a career exhibition programme but then they didn't really explain much, they just gave us pamphlets and then that was it. They didn't really explain what kind of score we want and everything . . .*
>
> *(student focus groups, 2009)*

> *They said 'what do you like doing?' and I told them, well I like cooking . . . (LAUGHTER) . . . and I like reading and then they told me, 'OK you can be a journalist or a chef' . . . (LAUGHTER). So that was my career counseling.*
>
> *(student focus groups, 2009)*

I also think that umm, they don't promote, like they focus specifically on certain . . . /careers/ . . . /faculties/ . . . like Law, Doctor. We always, you know . . . [UNCLEAR DUE TO SIMULTANEOUS SPEECH] . . . and they don't really give you a broader view of 'listen, this is also available, this is also . . .' but they don't and then you only find out halfway in your first year, so like 'oh my gosh', but there's actually this and I always wanted to do that, why don't I swop and then you change and it's another transition and it's a lot of work . . . /and you must catch-up/ . . .

(student focus groups, 2009)

With respect to choice of subjects at school, in some cases learners had little or no say over the subjects they did at school, while for others there was a lot more autonomy granted to learners and their parents in making subject choice decisions. Of particular concern to the first-year students with whom I worked in this study was the confusion over the difference between doing mathematics or mathematical literacy[1] at school and the implications of this for entrance to university. The students in my 2009 sample were the first cohort of South African school learners to have gone through 12 years of the outcomes based National Senior Certificate curriculum that was introduced as a component of the transformation of schooling after apartheid. These students were thus the first group of students to enter the university with the newly introduced subject called mathematical literacy:

There was no relevant information that was given to a learner. That ok, if you want to be a nurse you have to study this subject, if you want to be a, an accountant you have to do this. We just had to think for ourselves.

(student focus groups, 2009)

OK, what happened at our school was that ahh, the teachers made that decision based on, based on a learner's ahh, marks. No parents were involved and the learner was not given a choice, just the teachers made that decision to say 'OK, you will be doing Commerce and you will be doing Science', which served as a disadvantage to others because they wanted to pursue their dreams but they couldn't.

(student focus groups, 2009)

In my school our principal said 'you, you're in the Science class and you, you be in the Tourism class . . . (LAUGHTER) . . . and you, you're in the Accounting class'. You didn't have a choice what to do, even if you know your parents and tell the principal that 'no Sir, I want to do, be an accountant or I want to be what', he'll tell you 'if you don't like it in my school, jy moet gaan' . . . (LAUGHTER)

(student focus group, 2009)

It was Maths or Maths Literacy so I decided to do, I wanted to do Maths but then in the commerce class, there was only three of us who wanted to do Maths so they just decided 'ag man, you guys cannot do Maths because you're gonna mess up the timetable what what what . . . (LAUGHTER) . . . just do Maths Literacy' . . . (LAUGHTER) . . . then you get to varsity and you cannot do some other subjects because we didn't do Maths in high school and it's not like we chose to do umm, we didn't want to do Maths literacy, we wanted to do Maths.

(student focus groups, 2009)

At our school they held a meeting with all the Grade 9 children and their parents before they needed to choose and they said, 'OK, these are the possible subjects, these subjects together will give exemption, these will not. I mean a university exemption, these do not give you a university exemption and they only half, because it was new names the explained to us what they meant in terms of what it was in the old system. It was explain just like that to us and told us what was needed for what types of courses and they went through it with us and with our parent.

(student focus groups, 2009)

Overall then the voices of learners and students, expressed both quantitatively and qualitatively, have highlighted the difficulties that many young people who are getting ready to embark on the journey to university have in seeing over the humpback bridge. Not only are learners often provided little information about what to really expect at university, but their choices and opportunities are also constrained by decisions, often made by others, regarding subject choice as well.

Acceptance of mediocrity or failure

How do students cope with the humpback bridge challenge and their generally poor levels of readiness for university? This study pointed to a concerning coping mechanism that I have called an acceptance of mediocrity or failure. In the qualitative student data there were 58 instances in which first-year students made some reference showing their acceptance of mediocrity or failure. Consider the following:

I think when you come here, they tell you . . . first of all, forget about the A's you got in high school, kiss them goodbye. I think everyone's just so comfortable with failure . . . [LAUGHTER AND AGREEMENT FROM GROUP] . . . it's just ok, you know, I failed so what . . . It's not, it doesn't motivate you to work harder cos in high school, everyone got 70's and then you get 50%. Obviously its gonna, you gonna feel like I have to be a failure.

(student focus groups, 2009)

We were checking our marks last week and this [ ] guy said, 'did you fail? Welcome, welcome to the family!' . . . [LAUGHTER]

(student focus groups, 2009)

When we come here it's completely different to high school and you have to start, like she said, from the really really beginning and . . . there's nobody there to help you start, you're all on your own and nobody wants to help. Everybody's telling you 'if you don't understand it, next year you'll understand it. Next year you will do it over'.

(student focus groups, 2009)

People go with the mentality that I've got forty percent, I'm safe. No matter how much I fail but with a forty percent I know I'm safe.

(student focus groups, 2009)

Ja, ja, but you know what my parents told me, as long as I just pass. So I do work hard to, to pass my subjects but not as hard as I did in school cos in school I studied like to get 80%, now it's really above 50 cos above 50/60 and up costs you my social life and everything is important to me cos I have to socialise and I have to study so I just . . . I just want to pass, just want to pass this year and next year I'll work harder.

(student focus groups, 2009)

These responses provide a different perspective for understanding trends in undergraduate student performance described in Chapter 1. Without appropriate support structures that seek to break down the traditional humpback bridge and replace it with more appropriate and effective mechanisms for negotiating the gap between school and university, it appears that students might cope with their lack of readiness by constructing a university world in which mediocrity or failure is the norm. As was argued in earlier chapters, research shows that institutional expectation of success is a critical factor in student performance (Bowen et al. 2009; Kuh et al. 2005b), yet first-year students report that:

all the lecturers in the first week just told us statistics of who is going to fail, it's very demotivating.

(student focus groups, 2009)

In one of our classes the lecturer said, 'look to your left and now look to your right, only one of you is going to pass.

(student focus groups, 2009)

The first time I entered my Soc [Sociology] class, the lecturer told me 10% of you are gonna pass and then every time I study soc I just have that thing he said in my mind. I'm not gonna pass soc . . . ag, I'm not.

(student focus groups, 2009)

There are lecturers that are going to say, uh man, when you do [the course] the third time around you'll pass it. So that brings you down, it really does bring you down.

(student focus groups, 2009)

At school you could ask a question, here the lecturer won't answer you, he just says 'come back next year'!

(student focus groups, 2009)

But at least if they tell you, study hard, you'll make it, study hard. They must not discourage us . . . [AGREEMENT FROM GROUP] . . .

(student focus groups, 2009)

Are university lecturers, and in this instance particularly those who work closely with first-year students, then complicit in constructing this discourse of mediocrity or failure? Given the large classes often faced in first-year programmes, together with the poor levels of preparation of students exiting a troubled school system, perhaps the discourse of mediocrity and failure also provides a safe haven for academic staff who are unsure of how best to accommodate their students. One might speculate that lecturers use such 'scare tactics' in an effort to ensure that their students are aware that they need to work hard in order to succeed, when in effect the opposite outcome is reached. This issue was not an explicit part of the interviews conducted with academic staff and none of the lecturers made mention of the use of scare tactics. Nonetheless, the perceptions that the majority of lecturers tended to express about the poor academic preparation of students entering university may point in the direction of relatively lower expectations of their students. Although none of the lecturers interviewed themselves reported that these expectations had an influence on how they approached their teaching, it seems reasonable to consider that expectations may be lowered, even if not explicitly:

> *What I pick up, when I look at myself for example, and think about how we were as students. I think this is the bad part, one shouldn't really do this, but they [students] are now very lazy in general. They only want to do the minimum work and just learn what they need to pass. This is the bad part of working with them. So you always have to look carefully, especially when you set tests, not to reduce the quality, but the students always expect that you must do it for them. And they just want to know what they must learn to get through at the end of the day. So they basically only want the basics in the end.*

> *(First-year lecturer, Marketing, 2010)*

> *But then I want to say, when one talks about first-years in general, I think there are people who are a bit, well this is my experience with those I talk to, who have lost contact with what is really happening on the ground. You know, there is a terrible drop in standards with our first-years. I saw it for example last year, when it was our first group that went through the new curriculum, and they were bad in comparison with previous years. And now, I must say, this year I experience the students as even worse.*

> *(First-year lecturer, Education, 2010)*

> *If we want to keep the level of mathematics up at what it was in the past, we don't want it to go down in the standard . . . But then we have to fill the gaps. But we don't have more time. So we are squeezing in new things [additional topics that should have been covered at school] in between that in the past were not there, and of course it's going to also contribute to problems for the student. Because now, these people are not already prepared, but now they have to go though much more foundation topics at the same time, and yet they are the people who are struggling.*

> *(First-year lecturer, Mathematics, 2010)*

I think it's not only a trend or I should say it's not only a problem here but it's a problem I think all over the South African universities in that the skills and the knowledge that they [students] have after finishing high school does not prepare them for learning in higher institutions. So we are inheriting students and perhaps the problems that I have just explained are not the problems of the making of this university. They are problems that we inherited from high schools. I think the problem is with our high schools in that high schools do not prepare students for learning in higher institutions of learning. But if that is the case then the question is what needs to be done? Shouldn't the university put mechanisms in place to ensure that those students then are prepared in such a way that they'll cope.

(First-year lecturer, Political Science, 2010)

To properly unpack and deconstruct the discourse of mediocrity and failure, further research specifically focused on this perplexing issue is needed. Nonetheless, we should not wait until more research is available before introducing targeted interventions to undermine the apparent acceptance of mediocrity, among both students and lecturers, in the interest of a more socially just university system. This sentiment was neatly expressed by one of the lecturers quoted earlier who remarked that 'if that is the case [poor preparation] then what needs to be done? Shouldn't the university put mechanisms in place to ensure that those students then are prepared in such a way that they'll cope?' The capabilities approach provides a new lens for thinking about such interventions, in a manner that recognises backlogs in students' preparation for university without assuming a deficit approach which is likely to result in lowered expectations and, possibly also, the acceptance of mediocrity. One of the ways in which the capabilities approach encourages us to move beyond deficit understandings of learners and students is through a careful analysis of the conditions that enable and constrain readiness for university. In the coming chapter the experiences of learners and students shared here will be theorised from a capabilities perspective as we continue on our journey towards a capabilities-based social justice framework for the transition to university.

Note

1 The difficulty of subject choice at school, particularly decisions regarding Mathematics or Mathematical Literacy have become even more important since 2009 when I did my initial work with students. As of 2012, a student entering university must have passed Mathematics to enter courses in Natural Sciences and Commerce fields. This means that learners who opt to study Mathematical Literacy at school limit their further study options dramatically.

References

Bloch, G. 2009. *The Toxic Mix: What's Wrong with South Africa's Schools and How to Fix It*. Cape Town: Tafelberg.

Boughey, C. 2005. ' "Epistemological" Access to the University: An Alternative Perspective.' *South African Journal of Higher Education* 19 (3): 230–242.

Bowen, W G, M M Chingos and M S McPherson. 2009. *Crossing the Finish Line. Completing College at America's Public Universities*. Princeton, New Jersey: Princeton University Press.

Brazilian Internet Steering Committee. 2013. *ICT Education 2012. Survey on the Use of Information and Communication Technologies in Brazillian Schools*. São Paulo: Center of Studies on Information and Communication Technologies – CETIC.br. http://www.cetic.br/publicacoes/2012/tic-educacao-2012.pdf

Chickering, A and Z Gamson. 1999. 'Development and Adaptations of the Seven Principles for Good Practice in Undergraduate Education.' *New Directions for Teaching and Learning* 80 (Winter): 75–81.

Christie, P. 2008. *Opening the Doors of Learning. Changing Schools in South Africa*. Johannesburg: Heinemann Publishers.

Conley, D T. 2005. *College Knowledge. What It Really Takes for Students to Succeed and What We Can Do to Get Them Ready*. San Francisco: Jossey-Bass.

———. 2008. 'What Makes a Student College Ready?' *Educational Leadership* 66 (2): 1–3.

———. 2010a. *College and Career Ready. Helping All Students Succeed Beyond High School*. San Francisco: Jossey-Bass.

———. 2010b. *Replacing Remediation with Readiness*. NCPR Working Paper. New York: Teachers College, Columbia University.

Farrell, G and S Isaacs. 2007. *Survey of ICT and Education in Africa*. Washington DC: World Bank, Information for Development Programme. http://www.infodev.org/infodev-files/resource/InfodevDocuments_353.pdf

Jacobs, C. 2009. 'Teaching Explicitly That Which Is Tacit. The Challenge of Disciplinary Discourses.' In *Focus on First-Year Success. Perspectives Emerging from South Africa and Beyond*, edited by B Leibowitz, A van der Merwe and S van Schalkwyk, 241–252. Stellenbosch: Sun Media.Kuh, G D, G Kinzie, J H Schuh and E J Whitt. 2005a. *Assessing Conditions to Enhance Educational Effectiveness. The Inventory for Student Engagement and Success*. San Francisco: John Wiley & Sons, Inc.

———. 2005b. *Student Success in College. Creating Conditions That Matter*. San Francisco: John Wiley & Sons, Inc.

Mdlongwa, T. 2012. *Infromation and Communication Technology (ICT) as a Means of Enhancing Education in Schools in South Africa. Challenges, Benefits and Recommendations*. Policy Brief 80. Johannesburg: Africa Institute of South Africa. http://www.ai.org.za/wp-content/uploads/downloads/2012/10/No.-80.-ICTas-a-means-of-enhancing-Education-in-Schools-in-South-Africa.pdf

Morrow, W. 2009. *Bounds of Democracy. Epistemological Access in Higher Education*. Cape Town: Human Sciences Research Council. http://www.hsrcpress.ac.za

Ndlovu, N S and D Lawrence. 2012. 'The Quality of ICT Use in South African Classrooms.' In University of Cape Town. http://www.carnegie3.org.za/docs/papers/197_Ndlovu_The%20quality%20of%20ICT%20use%20in%20South%20African%20classrooms.pdf

Robeyns, I. 2003. 'Sen's Capability Approach and Gender Inequality: Selecting Relevant Capabilities.' *Feminist Economics*, 9 (2–3): 61–92.

Song, Ki-Sang. 2011. '2010 ICT in Education Readiness Report: Lessons to Developing Countries.' In Seoul, Korea. http://siteresources.worldbank.org/EDUCATION/Resources/278200-1121703274255/1439264-1247694138107/6305512-1321460039533/02_Ki_Sang_Song_2010_ICTEducationReadinessReportLessonstoDevelopingCountries.pdf

Wilson-Strydom, M G. Forthcoming. 'Confronting Contradiction: Experiences of Diversity at School and University.' *Perspectives in Education*

Yazzie-Mintz, E. 2010. *Charting the Path from Engagement to Achievement: A Report on the 2009 High School Survey of Student Engagement*. Indiana: Indiana University, Bloomington.

6 A capabilities list for the transition to university

> We are better at critiquing what constrains higher education policy and its misalignment with the social good, but imagine less about what to do in its place, or how to advance the spaces of freedom which persist in universities.
>
> (Walker 2010, 486)

This chapter is about starting to imagine a new way of thinking about access and the transition to university. The tapestry of learner and student voices shared in Chapter 5 has shown quite vividly how complex is the notion of social justice during the transition to university. Drawings 1.1 and 1.2 presented in the introductory chapter provide a particularly stark example of these inequalities and injustices. My intention to formulate a capabilities list for the transition to university is underpinned by a commitment to identify ways of building more accessible bridges between school and university, such that increasing access has a greater chance of leading to success in the first year of study and ultimately a higher education outcome that students have reason to value. The first step in doing so is to interrogate the ideal-theoretical list of capabilities shown in Table 4.1 based on the learner and student voices. This process culminates in the development of a more pragmatic list of capabilities that is shown both theoretically and empirically to underlie a successful transition to university. The chapter thus practically demonstrates a particular methodology for the formulation of a capabilities list (see also, Wilson-Strydom forthcoming).

Drawing on the quantitative and qualitative findings already presented, this chapter reflects on each of the nine proposed capabilities. While the empirical data provides support for the value of all nine, some capabilities emerge as of greater significance than others, and so point in the direction of a refined, pragmatic capabilities list for the transition to university. It is not my intention in interrogating the ideal-theoretical list of capabilities to make comparisons across school type, gender or other variables. These differences will be the focus of Chapter 7 where we explore the role of conversion factors. Part of the process of analysing qualitative data was to code the learner and student responses in terms of the nine capabilities proposed in the ideal theoretical list. This process provided a means of identifying the capabilities that learners and students deem important or valuable.

Table 6.1 Summary of qualitative analysis in terms of the ideal-theoretical capabilities list

Capability	Number of instances identified
1. Practical reason	241
2. Educational resilience	220
3. Knowledge and imagination	106
4. Learning disposition	262
5. Social relations and social networks	146
6. Respect, dignity and recognition	133
7. Emotional integrity	81
8. Bodily integrity	35
9. Language competence and confidence	54

It is important to note that the line of questioning used during data collection did not include specific questions about these nine capabilities. Instead, using questions about how the transition to university was experienced, it was possible to begin to identify the capabilities that learners and students felt had assisted them or created barriers when not yet developed, without specific prompting or directing questions.

Table 6.1 shows the number of instances in which each capability emerged from the qualitative data. This 'quantification' of the qualitative data should be seen as a guide only to understanding the relative importance and relevance of each capability, since in some instances the data implied the achievement of the capability, in others it showed that the capability was needed but not developed and in yet others, either supporting on hindering factors were identified. In many cases a combination of these was evident. It is thus not possible, nor helpful, to try to 'quantitatively' use the qualitative coding to understand the nuances of these capabilities or to rank their importance. Nonetheless, it is useful to show that all nine capabilities did get mentioned by learners and students, and some rather more often than others.

In the coming sections, each of the nine capabilities identified for the ideal-theoretical list is reviewed. For each capability I provide an interpretation of the capability on the basis of participants' voices and present an argument for why, or why not, the capability should be included in a pragmatic capabilities list for the transition to university. In doing so, I have been mindful of the five criteria Robeyns (2003a, 70–71) specified for developing a capabilities list, namely: explicit formulation, methodological justification, sensitivity to context, different levels of generality, and exhaustiveness and non-reduction (refer to Chapter 4 for details). We now consider each capability in turn.

Practical reason

<u>*Definition*</u>: *Being able to make well-reasoned, informed, critical, independent, and reflective choices about post-school study and career options.*

The capability of practical reason, when used in the specific context of the transition to university, is focused on whether high school learners and students entering university are able to make meaningful decisions about post-school study and career options. This capability falls within the readiness domain of university knowledge. The importance of university knowledge, and the lack thereof for many of the school learners and first-year students, was highlighted by both learners and students. The analysis of the qualitative data showed that this domain of university readiness was the second most commonly noted of Conley's readiness dimensions (see Figure 5.2). Similarly, the qualitative coding in terms of the ideal-theoretical capabilities list shows that the capability of practical reason was noted second most frequently. Yet, we saw that, despite the importance learners and first-year students accorded to this capability, only 20 per cent of the learners that completed the survey reported often talking to a teacher about career goals, while 16 per cent have never discussed career goals with a teacher. Given that the learners were in Grades 10, 11 and 12 – the final three years of high school – these findings point to a lack of opportunity to develop the capability of practical reason that underpins a successful transition. Even less support was provided in the area of information about applying to university. In some cases learners may receive this support from their parents or family members, but for first generation students the information provided at school is of critical importance.

Reflections on the challenge of making subject choices at school was another clear theme emerging from the qualitative data – for learners who were provided adequate information and support and for those who were not. Several examples were presented in Chapter 5, and an additional quotation is included here:

> *There was no information in my school. I chose . . . umm, the subject myself. I knew that when I had to be, when I go to Grade 10, I had to choose the subject that I think I can manage, that's all. Then I chose. . .umm, business subjects . . . yeah, till, to Grade 12 but still in Grade 11, I had to change others, they were mixed . . . it was only from, I had to decide for myself, for myself that I'm going to do, umm, Biology, Economics, Business Economics – it was mixed, there was no relevant information that was given to a learner. That ok, if you want to be a nurse you have to study this subject, if you want to be a, an accountant you have to do this. We just had to think for ourselves.*
>
> *(student focus groups 2009)*

Making the choice between mathematics and mathematical literacy was commonly discussed by students since this choice had major implications for their direction of study at university. Many students were unaware of this until they reached university. From a capabilities approach point of view, of particular relevance is the fact that in many instances, even where learners did have information or had a clear sense of study direction, their school determined their subject choices. In this way the agency of high school learners was undermined. Thus while it is quite common for university preparation interventions to provide information to school learners about subject choices, it is clear that this is insufficient when contextual conditions limit what is possible. Even in cases where learners had the personal skill and capacity to make informed choices, their opportunities were limited by teachers and principals who ultimately determined what study directions learners could follow once they entered university. This was highlighted by the example of the learner who wished to study mathematics and was told by her school principal that she would 'mess up the timetable'.

Although it was most common for students to reflect on lack of information and support regarding subject and career choices at school, there were also instances of similar remarks about constraints on choices made at university. The quotation here provides an example:

> *Sometimes the people that work for the university, they're not as clued up as you think. Some of them are not even studying that specific thing and maybe they don't know anything about it. Even at admin when you go register for your modules, the people that give academic advice, my subjects were messed up because the people that were there, they gave me like the wrong information. So I ended up doing second year modules in my first year, it was back and forth. It's the first time I'm doing some of my first-year modules that I was supposed to do and some of the courses are actually written off and I wrote exams on them because I wasn't given proper advice.*

> *(student focus group, 2009)*

Both the existing literature and the voices of learners and students speaking through this study provide evidence of the importance of the capability of practical reason in the context of transitioning to university. In addition, it is also clear that for many young people, the value of the capability for practical reason is highlighted precisely because this capability was not developed, often due to the fact that enabling conditions for this capability were unavailable. The challenge of not having the capability of practical reason for the transition to university is more a result of contextual influences than individual skills and capacities. As such, efforts to foster the development of this capability need to turn attention to the conditions of possibility underpinning, and often undermining, the capability at both school and university levels.

Nussbaum (2000, 2011) includes practical reason in her list of ten central human capabilities. Although Nussbaum's list has a far wider reaching purpose and scope than the specific capabilities list being proposed here, it is useful to return to Nussbaum to better understand the significance of practical reason in the context of accessing university. Nussbaum argues that the capability of practical reason (and affiliation) plays a distinctive role in the context of the other capabilities in her list by being of importance to the development and organisation of them all. She explains as follows, '[W]hat is meant by saying that the capability of practical reason organises all the others is more obvious: the opportunity to plan one's life is an opportunity to choose and order the functionings corresponding to the various other capabilities' (Nussbaum 2011, 39). In other words, if a student entering university was able to develop the other transition to university capabilities and so master all the domains of university readiness, but was not in a position to make meaningful choices about what to study, how to plan their programme of study, or about their future career options, then the achievement of the other capabilities would not lead to an outcome the student had reason to value. The fictional example given in Chapter 3 of the young man who completed an accounting qualification at the instruction of his father even though he wished to pursue his passion and talent for painting is an example of a student who had developed the capabilities needed for the transition to university, but could not put into action the capability of practical reason due to the influence of his father. Similarly, the young woman who was not able to take mathematics due to the timetable concerns of the principal might be capable of making the transition to university, but did not have the capability of practical reason and as a result instead of making an independent choice about what to study, her options were constrained by the actions of the school principal. Thus, in agreement with Nussbaum (2011), it seems reasonable to argue that the capability of practical reason – defined as being able to make well-reasoned, informed, critical, independent, and reflective choices about post-school study and career options – could be seen as a foundational capability (or in the terms of Wolff and de-Shalit, a fertile functioning) for ensuring a successful transition to university.

Educational resilience

> *Definition: Being able to navigate the transition from school to university within individual life contexts. Able to negotiate risk, to persevere academically, to be responsive to educational opportunities and adaptive constraints. Having aspirations and hopes for a successful university career.*

The resilience demonstrated by many of the learners and students who participated in this study is remarkable. Examples abound of learners and students making progress with their education despite overwhelming constraints in their personal contexts, at their schools, and in the broader social, political and economic environment in which they live. Chapter 5 included examples of students who described absent or drunk teachers, unemployed parents, lack of books, poor decision making regarding subject and career choices, lecturers telling them they are likely to fail, and so on. The major challenges evident in the schooling system together with the generally high levels of poverty and unemployment also attest to the resilience of the young people who do indeed successfully transition to university, and ultimately complete their university qualifications, despite the high levels of drop out in the first year and the low proportion of students who actually graduate (Bloch 2009; CHE 2012, 2010; Chisholm 2004; Scott 2010; Scott et al. 2007). The quotation here provides a further example of a particular student's resilience:

> *Well for example, I never _____ (UNCLEAR) cos when I came here two years back, I came here to this university but I've already applied to (NAME OF ANOTHER*

*INSTITUTION) but I didn't have the information . . . I was requiring for the degree that I wanted to study, ja and then I found out that I don't qualify to do that degree so I decided to go over to ahh, the College and then I studied the whole two years at the College, I did my National Certificate there then it was still like high school, it wasn't giving me that challenge . . ./**ja**/ . . . but then after that, after my National Certificate I came to the university where I found more challenges, I feel like I can run away . . . (LAUGHTER) . . . it's good for someone who wants to do something with his life . . . /**yes, yes**/ . . . if you know where you may want to go, if you know the direction that you want to take in your life then I think it's ahh, very much alright.*

(student focus groups 2009)

This example, and several of the other quotations presented in Chapter 5, highlights the role of individual agency in resilient responses of learners and students. Yet, examples of learners and students who show resilience, often in the face of very difficult situations, is not, necessarily, sufficient to ensure successful and just outcomes of university education. Without having several of the other capabilities included in the ideal-theoretical list, it is unlikely that educational resilience (as defined here) will be achieved. Instead, the achievement of educational resilience should rather be positioned as the functioning or outcome demonstrating a successful transition to university. Consider again the proposed definition of educational resilience in this specific context. Being able to navigate the transition from school to university, negotiate risk, persevere, be responsive to opportunities and have aspirations for successful university study is dependent on several of the other capabilities listed in the ideal theoretical list. It is unlikely that a student would successfully navigate the transition or be responsive to opportunities and constraints without some degree of the capability for practical reason, learning disposition, language competence and confidence, and others. As such, it seems preferable to remove the capability for educational resilience from the capabilities list and, instead, position educational resilience as the outcome of a successful transition. In the original formulation of the capabilities framework for the transition to university shown in Figure 1 the outcome or achievement was broadly defined as a 'successful transition to university and success in the first year of study'. The revised formulation, based on the functioning/achievement of educational resilience, is a more clearly defined and precise outcome, whilst still allowing scope for the values of individual students to be incorporated in their own more specified definition of the functioning.

Knowledge and imagination

<u>Definition</u>: *Having the academic grounding needed to be able to gain knowledge of chosen university subjects, and to develop methods of academic inquiry. Being able to use critical thinking and imagination to identify and comprehend multiple perspectives.*

The capability of knowledge and imagination is closely related to the readiness dimensions of key content, and to a lesser extent, key cognitive strategies. Essentially, this capability is about the academic foundations needed when entering university, and encompasses both content knowledge as well as an understanding of methods of inquiry in different subject areas. As such, the capability for knowledge and imagination is also closely related to the concept of epistemological access. First-year students need to have a sound content grounding, as well as be able to understand the knowledge structures and language used in the disciplines that they study. The extensive literature supporting the importance of this capability was shown in Table 5.1. Further support for the inclusion of the capability in a pragmatic capabilities list for the transition to university is provided by the empirical data, where many students made reference to their difficulties with disciplinary knowledge at university even for subjects that they had found relatively unchallenging at school.

The second part of this capability is being able to use critical thinking and imagination to identify and comprehend multiple perspectives. As was shown in Chapter 5, the participants in this research reported that schools place relatively little emphasis on solving real world problems, reading and understanding difficult materials, thinking critically, exploring new ideas and analysing ideas in depth. Further, university students also pointed to the quite limited support with respect to knowledge and imagination that is provided by the university during the first year. As such, it appears unlikely that students entering university would have had sufficient opportunity to develop the capability of knowledge and imagination while at school, and are then also provided with little opportunity to develop the capability during their first year. The inclusion of the capability for knowledge and imagination in the list is thus particularly important in facilitating a successful transition to university.

Learning disposition

Definition: Being able to have curiosity and a desire for learning. Having the learning skills required for university study. Having confidence in one's ability to learn. Being an active inquirer.

The importance of the capability of learning disposition is evident across the empirical data, as well as by the large number of instances in which both learners and students made reference to challenges faced in this area when describing the transition. Most often the comments made by learners and students referred to learning skills required for university, although the other components of this capability were also mentioned. The first component of the learning disposition capability is that of curiosity and desire for learning. The importance of a desire for learning is also highlighted by Barnett (2007a, 2007b) in his theorising about a student's will to learn. He describes the importance of the will to learn as follows:

> 'Will' is the most important concept in education. Without a will, nothing is possible. At any level of education, a pupil, a student cannot make serious progress unless she has a will to do so. Unless she has a will, a will to learn, she cannot carry herself forward, cannot press herself forward, cannot come successfully into new pedagogical situations.
>
> (Barnett 2007b, 15)

Drawing on Barnett, it can be argued that learning dispositions can be seen as an expression of a student's will to learn, or in capabilities terms, an essential part of a student's agency as a learner (Barnett 2007b, 101). A will to learn is the foundational learning disposition on which the others must build. Almost all of the high school learners participating in the study indicated that they wished to attend university, and most learners reported that their school work made them curious to learn new things and that they had opportunities to be creative in their work at school. The vast majority of high school learners noted that they liked to be creative and that they liked discussions that did not have one clear answer, even though schools generally did not provide much space for creativity and debate. The exception in all of these cases was for learners at Afrikaans suburban HSC schools, where the learner responses point towards a possible undermining of the will to learn. We pick up on the school-type issue in the following chapter. On the whole though, it appears that learners exiting the school system have been afforded, at least to some extent, opportunities to develop a curiosity and desire for learning out of which the will to learn in a university context could emerge. A cautionary note is needed here though; the *will* to learn should not be confused with the *confidence* to learn.

In the ideal-theoretical formulation of the capabilities list for the transition to university (Table 4.1), 'having confidence in one's ability to learn' was included in the definition of learning disposition (see also, Walker 2006, 128). However, as the study progressed, it seemed preferable to rather incorporate the notion of confidence to learn in the definition of the capability for emotional health. There are three main reasons for this. First, the definition of the capability for learning disposition already contains several dimensions and was at risk of becoming overly complex and so lacking in clarity. This would undermine the adherence to Robeyn's criterion of explicit formulation. Second, since the notions of the *will* to learn and the *confidence* to learn are related but importantly different, there was a possibility that the one might subsume the other if both were incorporated within the space of one capability. Third, learners and students placed a lot of emphasis on learning skills as a major area of difficulty during the transition to university. A more clearly defined definition of learning disposition encompassing the will to learn and the skills to learn therefore provides a tighter formulation of this capability that is also better aligned with the voices of learners and students. We will return to the issue of confidence to learn when we consider the capability for emotional health.

The majority of the qualitative data coded to this capability included responses of learners and students who felt poorly equipped for university in terms of study skills. First-year students reported that the cognitive demands of university differed from school in three main areas, namely: formulating an argument and/or critique, being able to integrate theory and practice, and having the skills of academic writing and referencing. The volume of work at university compared to school was also regularly described as a challenge by first-year students. In addition, the data pointed to a gap between school and university with regards to writing requirements and learning activities demanding the integration of information from sources other than textbooks. The concept of learning skills also incorporates the student's ability to be an active learner. The high school survey included several items specifically related to active learning such as questions about group work, project work and learning activities that require engagement with people or information outside of the school context. Overall, relatively few learners reported often engaging in these sorts of active learning activities. Both the theoretical and empirical evidence thus point to the importance of building the capability of learning disposition, here defined to encompass both the will and the skills to learn.

Social relations and social networks

Definition: Being able to participate in a group for learning, working with others to solve problems or tasks. Being able to form networks of friendships and belonging for learning support and leisure. Mutual trust.

The capability for social relations and social networks draws attention to the significance of being able to work in groups, having networks of friendships, a sense of belonging and being able to form relationships of mutual trust. This capability aligns with Nussbaum's notion of affiliation which she regards as an architectonic capability, underpinning all others – like practical reason (Nussbaum 2000). The importance of social networks and support has received much attention in the literature on first-year experience, first generation students as well as minority students in various contexts.[1] The role of social relations and social networks was also a theme that emerged quite strongly from the students' descriptions of their transition to university, with the fourth largest number of instances identified for this capability. In some instances students reported that it was their social networks and support systems that helped them to make it through the challenging transition, while for others a lack of social networks was regarded as a key difficulty. Responses in this area also differed between students who were living in university accommodation on campus and those who were not, with the former being more likely to report that the social network of the residence played an important role in their transition. Some students described how their social networks outside of the university supported them when making the transition:

> *Ja, for me I was actually lucky because when I was going to Grade 10, uh, my uncle who's a teacher, so when I was going to Grade 10 my mother set up a meeting with me and my uncle so my uncle asked me what I wanted to do and I was like 'ah, I want to do Maths Literacy and things like that' but when my uncle told me, he was like 'if you do Maths Literacy it's like going to be a problem when you go to varsity' and he told me about things like points, like if you do Maths Literacy, the points, if you take the real Maths, your points are going to be much higher than when you're going to be coming from Maths Literacy. So I think my uncle actually helped me because I knew what I wanted because I told him I want to do Commerce but at school we had a choice between Commerce subjects without the real Maths so he just told me, 'take the real Maths and don't do the Maths Literacy'.*
>
> *(student focus groups, 2009)*

It is difficult for a university to influence the social networks of learners before they enter and it is more likely that the capability for social networks and relations prior to university should be seen as a social conversion factor. However, the value of creating opportunities for first-year students to build new social relations and networks was highlighted by the data and this does fall within the university's realm of influence. This capability appears to be particularly pivotal for students who do not live on campus in university residence. Consider the following examples:

> *It sometimes feels like the students who stay at res have everything and the other students have nothing. At res you always have someone to ask if you don't know something. The university should do more for those who live off-campus ... Yes, those people often just come to class, go to the library and then go home. They also can't take any evening classes because of transport problems so these people are often the loners who know nobody.*
>
> *(student focus groups, 2009)*

> *Socially I suffered a bit in the beginning since I knew no one in Bloemfontein, most of my classmates had gone to other universities and the friend-making process had to start all over again.*
>
> *(white female students, Humanities, 2010)*

Given the prominence accorded to social relations and social networks in supporting students during the transition and the first year, together with the emphasis that many students placed on this capability, we can conclude that this capability would be valued in a pragmatic capabilities list for the transition to university.

Respect, dignity and recognition

Definition: Being able to have respect for oneself and for and from others, being treated with dignity, not being diminished or devalued because of one's gender, social class, religion or race. Valuing other languages, other religions and spiritual practices and human diversity. Being able to show empathy, compassion, fairness and generosity, listening to and considering other person's points of view in dialogue and debate. Having a voice to participate effectively in learning.

This capability has two overarching and closely related dimensions. First, each individual student should be treated with respect and dignity and be accorded recognition for who they are – by themselves, by other students, and by the university itself. Second, students need to be able to treat others, who may or may not be different from themselves, with respect and dignity and be able to recognise and value diversity. These two dimensions are both of critical importance in fostering this capability. If learners and students have the capability to respect others, to treat them with dignity and to recognise injustice then the first dimension is more likely to be realised. Consider the following remark, which falls within the ideology of meritocracy discussed earlier, made by a first-year student during the 2009 focus group discussions:

> *what I feel is that when you come to varsity we are numbers, we are all equal. You went to different schools, different backgrounds, but when you get to varsity, we are all equal. So we can blame the school system all went want, we can blame the past, but we are all equal. Same resources, same lecturers, same everything – we are equal. And that's what I like about varsity.*
>
> *(student focus groups, 2009)*

This quotation provides an example of a student who is not yet capable of recognising difference and, in particular, the varying contexts from which students come and within which students live their lives. This student is likely to find it difficult to understand and respect other students who are different from herself; for example students who are perhaps not able to spend as much time learning as she is due to family commitments, or who do not have money to purchase textbooks, or are not able to join in social events due to lack of finances. The contradictory responses of first-year students with respect to diversity in terms of race and languages presented in the previous chapter highlight the different degrees to which students entering university have developed the capability for respect, dignity and recognition. The results also showed that schools were not providing sufficient opportunity for learners to develop this capability, with only just over one third of the 2,816 learners who completed the high school survey reporting that they often worked with a learner who was different from them in terms of race, culture, political opinion, family income or personal values. Given the growing diversity of the student body in our universities, as well as the concerning extent of injustice and overall poor levels of transformation across the South African higher education sector (MoE 2008), the importance of intentionally creating space for school learners to develop the capability of respect, dignity and recognition is of particular urgency.

The worrying trend towards acceptance of mediocrity and failure at university that was described in Chapter 5 is further evidence for the importance of building this capability in the interests of student success and wellbeing. Learners and students need to recognise their own potential and come to respect themselves as learners/students. Without this self-respect the discourse of mediocrity and failure is likely to find fertile ground for growth as students' confidence in themselves is undermined. This is particularly important in the context of the transition to university and during the first year where it is, to some extent, expected that students will experience some uncertainty and confusion as they enter a new phase of their lives. While first-year students are entering a new domain and stage of life and so need to adjust, the transition is likely to be more successful where students have a sense of confidence in their ability to learn, in other words, recognise their own potential (Arendale 2010; Astin 1993; Bernstein 2000; Conley 2005; Harvey et al. 2006; Johnston 2010; Krause et al. 2005; Upcraft et al. 2005). Upcraft et al. (2005) highlight the importance of treating first-year students with dignity and respect as one of the 11 key principles of good practice in the first year that their research identifies. The quotation below is an example of a high school learner who is not able to recognise his own potential, and does not see himself as worthy of self-respect. What are the implications for this learner in terms of educational opportunities after school?

> *i realy don't feel good about myself as a I am not proud to be me.*
> *(black male learner, township school)*

A further example of the importance of fostering this capability was provided by the learner who stated that 'they will watch you as you hang yourself with your actions' and 'they will kick you out without mercy' (see Chapter 5). The implications for confidence, as well as for the capability of respect, dignity and recognition of the self are highlighted by these worrying comments. Similar conclusions can be drawn from the many examples of students who reported finding the transition to university difficult because they were 'just a number' or had become a 'small fish in a big sea':

> *At school the teachers gave you personal attention, but here the classes are too big for individual attention. At school I was a big fish in a small sea and now I am a small fish in a big sea.*
> *(white female first-year student, Health Sciences, 2010)*

> *Nobody knows you and where I come from everybody's like, every teacher knew you, like they'd know if you're not in class or something so now nobody knows you. You just come in,*

*you're just another person ... /you're just a number/ ... (LAUGHTER AND
AGREEMENT FROM OTHER STUDENTS).*

(student focus groups, 2009)

Ensuring that high school learners and first-year students have opportunities to
develop the capability for respect, dignity and recognition of themselves and of
others is thus a valuable capability to include in the pragmatic list.

Emotional health

Definition: Not being subject to anxiety or fear which diminishes learning.

The role of emotion, of learners/students and teachers/lecturers, in educational
contexts has been convincingly demonstrated by educational researchers (see for
example, Boler 1997; Zembylas 2002, 2003). In the context of the capabilities
approach, the capability for emotional health refers to the extent to which learners
and students are free from anxiety or fear that diminishes learning. The relatively
smaller number of learner/student responses that fell into this category were
almost all related to the confusion and fear students entering a new environment
commonly felt. As was noted in Chapter 5, while it is not unexpected or unusual
for young people entering a new environment to experience some fear and
confusion, the intensity expressed by the students in this study was notable. Also of
concern was the effect that this fear and confusion appeared to have the students'
confidence to learn.

The capability of emotional health, in the specific context of the transition
to university, should thus also take account of learners' and students' confidence or lack thereof, and the impacts this has on learning. Having confidence in
one's ability to learn is crucial (Barnett 2007b; Bernstein 2000; Conley 2008,
2010; Kuh et al. 2007; Smit 2012; Walker 2006). The importance of confidence as a basis for learning has also been strongly emphasised by Bernstein
(2000, xx, Kindle edition) in his work on pedagogic rights. Bernstein defines
three pedagogic rights that are necessary for democratic (or socially just) education
practice. The first of these rights is what Bernstein (2000, xx, Kindle edition)
calls the right to individual enhancement, which is defined as 'the right to the
means of critical understanding and new possibilities' without which 'neither
students nor teachers will have confidence, and without confidence it is difficult to
act' (Bernstein, 2000, xxx, Kindle edition). In a similar vein, Barnett (2007b,
110–111) notes that self-belief or self-confidence underpin a student's learning
dispositions. He argues that, '[G]iven that higher education is a process in which
the student is constantly being stretched, and taken into new and strange places,
self-doubt is always liable to break in. There is a continuing task, therefore, on the
part of the educator in bolstering the student's level of self-confidence' (Barnett
2007b, 111).

Many of the first-year student quotations related to learning skills and transition experiences showed an underlying lack of confidence. A general lack of confidence was also highlighted in the learners' descriptions of their expectations of university where a sense of fear appeared in each quotation, although expressed differently by different learners. A few additional examples are given here to further highlight the importance of incorporating confidence within the definition of the capability of emotional health and reflexivity. The last quotation provides an additional example of a student lacking confidence due to the lack of familiarity and belonging she felt when she entered university:

> *Varsity is not a play-ground. Lecturers were nothing like my highschool teachers. They were fast and there was too much to study. It felt like just a lot for a small brain like mine.*
>
> (black female student, Economic and Management Sciences, 2010)

> *I remember being worried about how will I cope with university pressure, whether will I make it in the end.*
>
> (black male student, Natural Sciences, 2010)

> *My first month was terrible because I was not familiar with such a big school and everything was so complicated and modernised. I did not feel very welcome. I felt like I was lost or in another planet.*
>
> (black female student, Economic and Management Sciences, 2010)

It is thus necessary to expand the definition of the capability for emotional health. The revised definition is then:

> <u>*Definition*</u>: *Not being subject to anxiety or fear which diminishes learning. Having confidence in one's ability to learn.*

In a similar vein to the capability of practical reason, emotional health might also be seen as a foundational capability or fertile functioning needed for the realisation of other capabilities. In particular, the capability of learning disposition – the will and the skills to learn – depends on learners and students having developed confidence in their ability to learn. In this way, the capability of emotional health can become a fertile functioning supporting the achievement of the other transition to university capabilities. Drawing on his work with teachers and schools, Zembylas (2002, 208) reminds us that 'we need to recognise the emotional complexity of schools'. So too, should we consider the emotional complexity of universities, and the emotional complexity of making the transition from school to university.

Bodily integrity

Definition: Safety and freedom from all forms of physical and verbal harassment in the school and higher education environment.

Relatively few learners and students made specific reference to issues of bodily integrity. This was the capability where the fewest instances were found in the qualitative data. The responses that were made by first-year students tended to be related to physical experiences during the orientation week (known as RAG) that includes sports events and other compulsory activities for first-year students such as selling magazines on street corners for charity. Some students described being sunburnt and physically exhausted:

RAG was very much fun, I enjoyed . . . but I got so badly sunburnt even the psalms of my hands were red. The last two days I wore gloves, long-sleeved jackets. Everybody just stared at me cos I'm sweating here but I can't move in the sun.

(student focus groups, 2009)

For me, it's first-years Athletics. They made us stand the whole time and we won so, that was nice but the standing wasn't nice.

(student focus groups, 2009)

Where high school learners made reference to issues of bodily integrity, they were most often referring to bullying, corporal punishment at school and illegal drug use:

Here at school we have a lot of crimes e.g fighting, bulling and jumping outside lot of smoking and selling daga's e.g. Joints.

(black male learner, township, 2009)

Another thing it is that I would also like to change the way we are punished at school because the beating is not nice.

(black female learner, township, 2010)

The teachers of our school are very abusive, They still hit us.

(black male learner, township, 2009)

Some of teachers Drinking Beer in school and other beat us when we are not gilty.

(black male learner, township, 2009)

These are very concerning remarks, and show evidence of criminal activity at schools. This is not an unknown phenomenon in the South African schooling context, and indeed in many others. While limits to bodily integrity should be treated with extreme seriousness across all spheres of social life (including schools and universities), such issues are not specifically related to the transition to university, and hence this capability has not been included in the pragmatic list that is intentionally more narrowly focused on the transition only. Instead, corporal punishment, drug use and abuse should be dealt with by the relevant authorities. While bodily integrity is a capability that should be fostered for all learners and students, this capability is better seen as a general capability of relevance across the entire education system, and, indeed, as Nussbuam argues, at a societal level. As such, the capability for bodily integrity, formulated as a standalone capability, is not sufficiently specific to the transition to university which is the focus of this pragmatic capabilities list. While the capability for bodily integrity does play a valuable role in Walker's (2006) capabilities list for higher education as a whole, this capability has not been included it in this pragmatic list in the interest of ensuring the formulation a very specific and defined focus on the transition to university.

Language competence and confidence

> *Definition: Being able to understand, read, write and speak confidently in the language of instruction.*

The final capability included in the ideal-theoretical list for the transition to university was that of language competence and confidence. This was an additional capability not originally included in Walker's list of capabilities for higher education. The inclusion of language competence and confidence was supported by the work of Wolff and de-Shalit (2007) who included the capability of language competence in the process of developing their capabilities list in which they extended the work of Nussbaum to philosophically and empirically explore the concept of disadvantage. Further, there is much evidence in the transition to university literature as well as the literature on student success, epistemological access, and the first year at university that emphasises the importance of language competence. The theoretical relevance of this additional capability has thus been established (see Chapter 2). In this section we focus on the extent to which the voices of learners and students also support the inclusion of this capability in a pragmatic capabilities list for the transition to university.

Based on the coding of the qualitative data, a relatively small number of learners and students made direct mention of language competence and confidence, compared to other capabilities. Where language was specifically referred to in the context of the transition to university three main thematic areas emerged. The first related to the multilingual environment of university, which for some students was difficult to adapt to, and for a few was a positive experience. The second focused on the difficulty of learning in a language other than one's home language or mother tongue. Third, several students described their difficulty with coming to understand the type of language used at university. The insecurity of students who did not feel comfortable in the language of instruction was evident in many of the quotations shared in Chapter 5.

Perhaps even more telling than the students' own comments about language related challenges is the generally poor quality of language evident in written qualitative responses of both school learners and university students. As noted earlier, the learner and student quotations used as examples throughout this text have been presented in their original form, without spelling and grammar corrections. Several examples of poor language competence can be seen in many of the preceding quotations. A few additional examples are given here. The first two are taken from the school learner data, and the second three from first-year university students:

> *Our school doesnt have any oppertunitiyes so many of use fail to understand anything.*
> *(black learner, no gender given, township, 2009)*

> *Getting educated is what I want, my Future come First and my education is my First Priority. Sometimes things be difficult at school and Iam working hard to achieve my goals. and i try so hard to be perfect and work on the subjects I strangle on like mathematics and I enjoy school and teacher's company and they have a lot of care For us and I work hard because I want a bursary to go to varsity.*
> *(black female learner, township, 2009)*

> *I was the most difficult month on my life. I stuggle lot in my academic and able to make new friend. It was difficult to balance academic life. I found send end give up. In term of social I found so few problem in terms of cultural differences.*
> *(black male first-year student, Economic and Management Sciences, 2010)*

> *It was exciting to be at the university level of which in my life I have never thought of being to further my studies up the university – because I knew I would not manage to pay fees for this standard. But fortunately God provides always.*
> *(black female first-year student, Education, 2010)*

> *For this first month at tertiary I am confused of what is expected from me, I struggle to understand the way inn which content are delivered. It is hard for me to compete to my level best, I did not know that there are other modules except the one I wanted to specialise with and that make me underperforming and I really get more confused because I think of the bursary will be cancelled.*
> *(black male first-year student, Education, 2010)*

These examples, together with the data available about students' performance in the academic literacy test of the National Benchmark Tests nationally highlight the importance of building the capacity for language competence and confidence (Prince 2010). The National Benchmark Tests results for the case study university specifically have shown consistently over the three years that the tests have been administered that only approximately 30 per cent of first-year students are proficient in academic literacy. Further, the many challenges students have with quality of their written language were also commonly raised by the first-year lecturers that were interviewed. As such, the importance of including the capability of language competence and confidence in the final capabilities list for the transition to university is clear.

A pragmatic capabilities list for the transition to university

Summarising the arguments made in the preceding sections of this chapter, the following pragmatic capabilities list for the transition to university has been formulated drawing on both comprehensive theoretical analysis as well as 'deliberation' by high school learners and first-year university students.

The overall purpose of developing these capabilities among high school learners and students entering university is to build the educational resilience needed for a successful transition to university. In this context educational resilience is defined

Table 6.2 Pragmatic capabilities list for the transition to university

Capability	Definition
1. Practical reason	Being able to make well-reasoned, informed, critical, independent and reflective choices about post-school study and career options.
2. Knowledge and imagination	Having the academic grounding needed to be able to gain knowledge of chosen university subjects, and to develop methods of academic inquiry. Being able to use critical thinking and imagination to identify and comprehend multiple perspectives.
3. Learning disposition	Being able to have curiosity and a desire for learning. Having the learning skills required for university study. Being an active inquirer.
4. Social relations and social networks	Being able to participate in a group for learning, working with others to solve problems or tasks. Being able to form networks of friendships and belonging for learning support and leisure. Mutual trust.
5. Respect, dignity and recognition	Being able to have respect for oneself and for others as well as receiving respect from others, being treated with dignity, not being diminished or devalued because of one's gender, social class, religion or race. Valuing other languages, other religions and spiritual practices and human diversity. Being able to show empathy, compassion, fairness and generosity, listening to and considering other person's points of view in dialogue and debate. Having a voice to participate effectively in learning.
6. Emotional health	Not being subject to anxiety or fear which diminishes learning. Having confidence in one's ability to learn.
7. Language competence and confidence	Being able to understand, read, write and speak confidently in the language of instruction.

as being able to navigate the transition from school to university within individual life contexts; being able to negotiate risk, to persevere academically; to be responsive to educational opportunities and adaptive constraints; and to have aspirations and hopes for a successful university career. The seven capabilities making up the list encapsulate existing knowledge about factors impacting on the transition to university and provide a framework that accommodates the perspectives of learners and students. The list provides a possible guide for action, and while encompassing the various dimensions of readiness that Conley identified, also goes further due to its roots in an explicit social justice agenda that takes the well-being of individual students as a starting point. As such, this list provides the basis for a normative framework for understanding what is needed for access to university in order to strive towards more just outcomes that take the well-being of individual students into account (Alkire and Deneulin 2009). The preceding discussions about each of the capabilities also highlighted the manner in which this list allows for a focus on both the agency of the student as well as contextual factors that may, or may not, limit this agency.

The seven capabilities provide a basis for moving towards a different language for talking and thinking about the transition to university in a manner that overcomes the deficit model language of under preparation and at risk students (Smit 2012). The capabilities language also takes us beyond, but still incorporates, the traditional focus of access research on measurable performance as a basis for making admissions decisions and predicting the likelihood of success. As such, a capabilities approach to access and the list of capabilities identified as valuable moves access debates forward by focusing on the creation of opportunity for a successful transition and the removal of barriers to this opportunity. The agency of students is recognised and valued, but not in a naïve manner that assumes that agency can be exercised without contextual influences, both positive and negative. The capabilities approach draws attention to the ways in which contextual factors support or hinder students' agency and resultant opportunities (see Chapter 7). In addition, as will be argued in Chapter 8, these seven capabilities have the potential to open up specific possibilities for actions to facilitate the transition from school to university.

We now return to Robeyn's (2003, 70–71) five criteria for developing a capabilities list in order to present a summary and final word of explanation regarding the value of the list, and the methodological soundness thereof (see also, Wilson-Strydom forthcoming). The first criterion is that of *explicit formulation*. This was achieved by detailed explication of an ideal-theoretical list based on a comprehensive analysis of a wide body of literature which was then followed by further interrogation based on the voices of the high school learners and university students who are the target audience of this list. *Methodological justification* was ensured through the research design that allowed for incorporation of multiple perspectives and data gathered over time to ensure consistency. Further, the research instruments were specifically developed for their relevance to the topic of transitioning to university, but were not structured according to the proposed capabilities list such that the views of learners and students could emerge rather than be primed in the direction of the ideal-theoretical list through the line of questioning used. Criterion three, *sensitivity to context* was achieved by explicitly aligning the development of the list with the expansive literature on university access and transitions, as was shown in Table 4.1. Further, by using Walker's (2006) list of capabilities for higher education specifically as the foundation from which to construct the list, the development of the list was firmly rooted within the higher education context. The final seven capabilities were formulated by incorporating the voices of high school learners and first-year university students in a reflexive manner to ensure that the final list and definitions of each capability represent a clear expression of the context and perspectives of learners and students themselves. In meeting the requirements of criterion four, *different levels of generality*, the study was aligned with the two stages proposed by Robeyns, starting with an ideal list and then refining this to present a more pragmatic list that is particularly targeted to the realities of the contexts in which it will be used. Finally, according to the criterion of *exhaustiveness and non-reduction* all important elements should be reflected in the list of capabilities, each capability should not be reducible to others, even though there might be some overlap. The final list of seven capabilities incorporates the important lessons from the analysis of the literature and the points raised by learners and students. All the themes that emerged from both the open coding presented in Chapter 5, and the more specific coding according to each capability shown in this chapter, are reflected in the final list. In the interrogation of each ideal-theoretical capability the value thereof was explained and justified drawing on the empirical data. The capability of educational resilience was shown to encapsulate the other capabilities, and so was removed from the capabilities list and instead positioned as the outcome of a successful transition to university.

Capabilities and/or functionings

A final issue requires attention before concluding this chapter. When introducing the capabilities approach, reference was made to the analytical and measurement tension between capabilities and functionings, as two sides of the same coin (Nussbaum 2011, 25), closely related, yet explicitly different concepts. This tension centres on the fact that functionings (achieved outcomes) can be observed and 'measured' while capabilities (realisable opportunities to function) cannot, because a person may have developed a particular capability but may choose not to exercise the opportunity and hence the capability would not be observable. Despite this challenge, the distinction between capabilities and functionings is fundamental to the capabilities approach in order to ensure space for the exercise of agency – being able to choose whether or not to exercise a particular capability. As was discussed in Chapter 3, the distinction between capabilities and functionings is also important in assessing the relative well-being of different individuals, since equality of outcome does not necessarily translate into equality of opportunity or well-being.

Deciding whether to focus on capabilities and/or functionings is somewhat more complicated when used in an educational setting where the functioning of being educated is fundamental for the realisation of many other capabilities, and where the opportunity to participate in education is also a valuable capability in its own right. Further, since the process of education is about facilitating learning and the development of ideas, even when learners or students are seen as active participants or agents in the learning process, the teacher or lecturer necessarily has a role of guiding that process in a particular direction or towards a particular set of outcomes (however broadly defined). In some ways then, the agency of the learner or student is always limited to some extent by the guidance of the teacher in an educational setting. Further, when assessing equality in the context of education, we do wish to observe equality of outcomes (learning), as well as equality of opportunity in achieving those outcomes.

One of the ways in which this challenge can be resolved in the context of the list of capabilities for the transition to university is to see the list as both a list of opportunities to function (capabilities) and functionings (achievements or outcomes), depending on when the list is being used.[2] In an ideal world, a student entering university should be able to be and do all the elements included on the list, although it is more likely to assume that these capabilities would be developed by the end of the first year for most students. In other words, these should be functionings that a student can demonstrate having achieved by the end of the first year. When considered from the point of view of high school learners, who may or may not choose to attend university, the list should be viewed as a list of capabilities or opportunities to function that should be fostered for all high school learners. It is then a matter of individual choice and the exercise of individual agency that determines whether or not the young person puts the capabilities into practice as functionings important for the transition to university. By the end of the first year at university that marks the end of the transition to university phase, given appropriate enabling conditions, all students should be in a position to demonstrate that they have achieved these seven transition to university functionings. As such, the list of capabilities for the transition to university should be seen as both a list of opportunities to function (capabilities) and of functionings themselves. In the coming chapter we move on to consider the conditions that enable and/or constrain the development of these capabilities and the translation of these capabilities into functionings, by analysing the personal, social and environmental conversion factors that impact on learners and students during the transition.

Notes

1 For selected examples, the reader is referred to the following sources (Hurtado and Carter 1997; Hurtado et al. 2007; Krause 2005; Krause et al. 2005; Mann 2001, 2008; Pascarella and Terenzini 2005; Perna and Titus 2005; Pike and Kuh 2005; Pittman and Richmond 2008; Savitz-Romer et al. 2009; Shouping and Kuh 2002; Tinto 1975, 1999; Tinto and Pusser 2006; Yorke and Longden 2008; Yosso 2005).

2 Biggeri (2007) put forward a similar argument about capabilities in childhood. Depending on the age and stage of development of the child, certain capabilities will be more or less

relevant, and for a young child it may be necessary for someone else – a parent, guardian or perhaps a teacher – to determine which capabilities should be developed (Hart 2014).

References

Alkire, S and S Deneulin. 2009. 'A Normative Framework for Development.' In *An Introduction to the Human Development and Capability Approach. Freedom and Agency*, edited by S Deneulin and L Shahani. London: Earthscan: 3–21.

Arendale, D R. 2010. 'Special Issue: Access at the Crossroads. Learning Assistance in Higher Education.' *ASHE Higher Education Report* 35 (6): 1–145.

Astin, A W. 1993. *What Matters in College? Four Critical Years Revisited*. San Francisco: Jossey-Bass.

Barnett, R. 2007a. 'Willing to Learn: Being a Student in an Age of Uncertainty.' In Trinity College Dublin. http://www.google.co.za/url?sa=t&rct=j&q=barnett%20will%20to%20learn&source=web&cd=3&ved=0CFQQFjAC&url=http%3A%2F%2Fwww.brookes.ac.uk%2Fservices%2Focsld%2Fisl%2Fisl2007%2Fbarnett_keynote.ppt&ei=A2bxT7b0I5KwhAfcjfTrBQ&usg=AFQjCNHdcIGPLKGXC6ToGpyt9ly78y9QFg&cad=rja

———. 2007b. *A Will to Learn. Being a Student in an Age of Uncertainty*. Berkshire, England: Society for Research into Higher Education and Open University Press.

Bernstein, B. 2000. *Pedagogy, Symbolic Control and Identity. Theory, Research, Critique. Revised Edition*. Oxford: Rowman & Littlefield Publishers, Inc.

Biggeri, M. 2007. 'Children's Valued Capabilities.' In *Amartya Sen's Capability Approach and Social Justice in Education*. Basingstoke: Palgrave Macmillan Ltd.

Bloch, G. 2009. *The Toxic Mix: What's Wrong with South Africa's Schools and How to Fix It*. Cape Town: Tafelberg.

Boler, M. 1997. "Disciplined Emptions: Philosophies of Educated Feelings." *Educational Theory* 47 (2): 203–227.

CHE. 2010. *Access and Throughput in South African Higher Education: Three Case Studies*. Higher Education Monitor 9. Pretoria: Council on Higher Education. http://www.che.ac.za.

———. 2012. *Vital Stats. Public Higher Education 2010*. Pretoria: Council on Higher Education. http://www.che.ac.za/documents/d000249/vital_stats_public_higher_education_2010.pdf

Chisholm, L. 2004. *Changing Class. Education and Social Change in Post-Apartheid South Africa*. Pretoria: Human Sciences Research Council Press.

Conley, D T. 2005. *College Knowledge. What It Really Takes for Students to Succeed and What We Can Do to Get Them Ready*. San Francisco: Jossey-Bass.

———. 2008. 'What Makes a Student College Ready?' *Educational Leadership* 66 (2): 1–3.

———. 2010. *Replacing Remediation with Readiness*. NCPR Working Paper. New York: Teachers College, Columbia University.

Hart, C S. 2014. 'The Capability Approach and Educational Research.' In *Agency and Participation in Childhood and Youth. International Applications of the Capability Approach in Schools and Beyond*. London: Bloomsbury: 40–72.

Harvey, L, S Drew and M Smith. 2006. *The First-year Experience: A Review of Literature for the Higher Education Academy*. United Kingdom: Higher Education Academy.

Hurtado, S and D F Carter. 1997. 'Effects of College Transition and Perceptions of the Campus Racial Climate on Latino College Students' Sense of Belonging.' *Sociology of Education* 70 (4): 324–445.

Hurtado, S, J C Han, V D Saenz, L L Espinosa and O S Cerna. 2007. 'Predicting Transition and Adjustment to College: Biomedical and Behavioural Science Aspirants' and Minority Students' First Year of College.' *Research in Higher Education* 48 (7): 841–887.

Johnston, B. 2010. *The First Year at University. Teaching Students in Transition.* New York: Society for Research into Higher Education and Open University Press.

Krause, K L. 2005. 'Understanding and Promoting Student Engagement in University Learning Communities.' In James Cook University, Townsville/Cairns, Queensland.

Krause, K L, R Hartley, R James and C McInnis. 2005. *The First Year Experience in Australian Universities: Findings from a Decade of National Studies.* Melborne, Australia: Centre for the Study of Higher Education, University of Melbourne.

Kuh, G D, G Kinzie, J A Buckley, B Bridges and J Hayek. 2007. *Piecing Together the Student Success Puzzle: Research, Propositions, and Recommendations.* ASHE Higher Education Report 32.

Mann, S. 2001. 'Alternative Perspectives on the Student Experience: Alienation and Engagement.' *Studies in Higher Education* 26 (1): 7–19.

———. 2008. *Study, Power and the University.* Berkshire, England: Open University Press.

MoE. 2008. *Report of the Ministerial Committee on Transformation and Social Cohesion and the Elimination of Discrimination in Public Higher Education Institutions.* Pretoria: Department of Education, RSA.

Nussbaum, M C. 2000. *Women and Human Development. The Capabilities Approach.* Cambridge, UK: Cambridge University Press.

———. 2011. *Creating Capabilities. The Human Development Approach.* Cambridge, Massachusetts: Harvard University Press.

Pascarella, E T and P T Terenzini. 2005. *How College Affects Students. A Third Decade of Research.* 2. San Francisco: Jossey-Bass.

Perna, L W and M Titus. 2005. 'The Relationship Between Parental Involvement as Social Capital and College Enrolment: An Examination of Racial/ethnic Group Differences.' *Journal of Higher Education* 76 (5): 485–518.

Pike, G R and G D Kuh. 2005. 'First- and Second-Generation College Students: A Comparison of Their Engagement and Intellectual Development.' *Journal of Higher Education* 76 (3): 276–300.

Pittman, L D and A Richmond. 2008. 'University Belonging, Friendship Quality, and Psychosocial Adjustment During the Transition to College.' *Journal of Experimental Education* 76 (4): 343–361.

Prince, R. 2010. 'The National Benchmark Tests Project: 2010 Intake Report'. presented at the Higher Education South Africa Consultative Forum, Johannesburg, May.

Savitz-Romer, M, J Jager-Hyman and A Coles. 2009. *Removing Roadblocks to Rigor. Linking Academic and Social Supports to Ensure College Readiness and Success.* Washington DC: Institute for Higher Education Policy.

Scott, I. 2010. 'Who Is "Getting Through" in South Africa?' In *The Next 25 Years. Affirmative Action in Higher Education in the Unites States and South Africa,* edited by D Featherman, M Hall and M Krislov. Ann Arbor: University of Michigan Press: 229–243.

Scott, I, N Yeld and J Hendry. 2007. *Higher Education Monitor No. 6: A Case for Improving Teaching and Learning in South African Higher Education.* Pretoria: Council on Higher Education.

Shouping, H and G D Kuh. 2002. 'Being (Dis)Engaged in Educational Purposeful Activities: The Influences of Student and Institutional Characteristics.' *Research in Higher Education* 43 (5): 555–575.

Smit, R. 2012. 'Towards a Clearer Understanding of Student Disadvantage in Higher Education: Problematising Deficit Thinking.' *Higher Education Research and Development* 31 (3): 369–380.

Tinto, V. 1975. 'Dropout from Higher Education: A Theoretical Synthesis of Recent Research.' *Review of Educational Research* 45 (1): 89–125.

———. 1999. 'Taking Student Retention Seriously: Rethinking the First Year of College.' http://faculty.soe.syr.edu/vtinto/Files/Taking%20Student%20Retention%20Seriously.pdf

Tinto, V and B Pusser. 2006. *Moving from Theory to Action: Building a Model of Institutional Action for Student Success*. USA: National Postsecondary Education Cooperative.

Upcraft, M L, J N Gardner and B O Barefoot. 2005. *Challenging and Supporting the First-Year Student. A Handbook for Improving the First Year of College*. San Francisco: Jossey-Bass.

Walker, M. 2006. *Higher Education Pedagogies*. Berkshire, England: Society for Research into Higher Education and Open University Press.

———. 2010. 'A Human Development and Capabilities "Prospective Analysis" of Global Higher Education Policy.' *Journal of Education Policy* 25 (4): 485–501.

Wilson-Strydom, M G. forthcoming. 'A Capabilities List for Equitable Transitions to University: A Top-down and Bottom-up Approach.' *Journal of Human Development and Capabilities*

Wolff, J and A de-Shalit. 2007. *Disadvantage*. Oxford: Oxford University Press.

Yorke, M and B Longden. 2008. *The First-year Experience of Higher Education in the UK. Final Report*. UK: Higher Education Academy.

Yosso, T J. 2005. 'Whose Culture Has Capital? A Critical Race Theory Discussion of Community Cultural Wealth.' *Race Ethnicity and Education* 8 (1): 69–91.

Zembylas, M. 2002. ' "Structures of Feeling" in Curriculum and Teaching: Theorising the Emotional Rules.' *Educational Theory* 52 (2): 187–208.

———. 2003. 'Caring for Teacher Emotion: Reflections on Teacher Self-Development.' *Studies in the Philosophy of Education* 22: 103–125.

7 Diversity, conversion factors and capabilities

Higher education is neither neutral nor natural. It affects people's lives, it is implicated in relations of power within society, and the way it is organised and undertaken is a function of social and historical choices.

(Mann 2008, 3)

In the introductory chapter, I began by juxtaposing two student drawings. In the first, a young woman saw a whole world of opportunities before her as she entered university. In the second, a young man was up against a brick wall. These two drawings visually echo Mann's (2008, 3) statement quoted above, that '[H]igher education is neither neutral nor natural'. How is it that two young people, both having succeeded in getting a place at the same university, can tell such different stories about their transition experiences?

The capabilities approach, in particular the concept of conversion factors, provides a helpful analytical lens that we can use in trying to understand – with the aim of changing – this state of affairs. The notion of conversion factors draws attention to the points at which individual agency and context come together, and so provides a mechanism for researching the interaction between agency and contexts such that we can identify enablers and constraints on this agency. The key question then, (following Walker 2005) is whether some learners and students have more opportunities than others to convert their resource of a place at university into capabilities? Drawing on Sen (1999, 71) and Robeyns (2005, 99), an analysis is presented here of the personal, social and environmental conversion factors that impact on the formation of transition to university capabilities. These conversion factors can be likened to the bricks in the wall faced by many students entering university. Before we can break down the brick wall, we need to understand more about the types of bricks from which it is built so that we know what tools are needed to break it down most effectively. This is the main focus in this chapter, which concludes by bringing together the capabilities list proposed in Chapter 6 and the conversion factors discussed here to present the full capabilities-based social justice framework for the transition to university.

In his one of his earliest writings making a case for the capabilities approach, the 1979 Tanner Lecture entitled 'Equality of What?' Sen argued that neither income nor resources were sufficient metrics to use in assessing inequality

(Sen 1980). He argued against the use of income because it is only a means towards other ends that actually determine well-being. With respect to resources, Sen noted that, since all people are different, people are not necessarily all in the same position to convert the resources at their disposal into valued functionings. Equality of resources does not guarantee equality in the space of capabilities and well-being. In Sen's words; '[I]f human beings were very like each other, this would not have mattered a great deal, but there is evidence that the conversion of goods into capabilities varies from person to person substantially, and the equality of the former may still be far from the equality of the latter' (Sen 1980, 219). The concept of diversity, and understanding what diversity means with respect to equality of capability, is thus accorded central place in the capabilities approach. This centrality of diversity is a further reason why the capabilities approach is particularly helpful for exploring inequality and social justice in higher education, where we see a growing diversity of the student body globally. As universities, we cannot assume that ensuring equal access to resources at university will lead to just outcomes. In fact the capabilities approach tells us that equality of resources can mask inequalities in the space of capabilities. This means that, while universities need to ensure that all students entering have access to the basic resources they need for studying – such as financial aid, housing, food, learning materials, and so on – universities also need to go further than resource provision in the interests of building more socially justice higher education institutions. Understanding the factors that influence the conversion of resources into capabilities for the diverse body of first-year students at university is one means of doing this. Once conversation factors have been identified and understood, then universities are in a better position to develop policies and put in place relevant interventions in an effort to enhance positive conversion factors (fertile functionings) and minimise negative conversion factors (corrosive disadvantages). In this way, high school learners and first-year students will be better placed to develop transition to university capabilities and to put these capabilities into action in order to achieve the overall functioning of educational resilience which I argued in the previous chapter should be seen as the outcome of a successful transition to university.

Personal conversion factors

Personal conversion factors encompass individual (personal) factors that impact on the development of capabilities and the achievement of valued outcomes (functionings). Examples include an individual's physical condition, personality, health status, and so on (Robeyns 2005; Sen 1999). Personal conversion factors in the form of academic performance, commonly taken as a measure of ability, have tended to be the focus of much of the research on readiness. This is particularly so in the context of global higher education that privileges ideologies of meritocracy. While measures of ability, potential and competence are important for the transition to university, a focus on these factors alone does not present the full picture and does not take account of social justice challenges so prevalent in the domain of access to higher education. As such, the focus here is more on social conversion factors as a point of entry to identify the ways in which injustices are manifested. Nonetheless, there are three, somewhat inter-related, personal conversion factors that emerged strongly from the data. They are the will to learn, the confidence to learn, and home language.

Both the will to learn and the confidence to learn are also elements that are included in the definitions of the seven capabilities for the transition to university. Why is it important to include these both as capabilities to be fostered and as personal conversion factors? If the will and confidence to learn were only included as conversion factors, then we would be implicitly assuming that these are properties of individuals which either support or impede the transition. While will and confidence are individual characteristics, these abilities are fostered (or undermined) in contexts, and some contexts are more conducive to fostering their development than others. This means that we cannot see the absence of a will to learn or confidence to learn as something inherent to a given person, or as an individual fault that needs to be corrected. This understanding is what underlies deficit approaches to readiness. Rather, we need to understand the social conditions that enable or constrain their development and this can be done when we consider these abilities as capabilities. Nonetheless, it is also important to recognise that an individual's will to learn and confidence to learn also act as conversion factors that can help us to understand differences in transition experiences. Not having a will to learn or the confidence to learn can become corrosive disadvantages, while having a will to learn and confidence to learn are likely to be fertile functionings. The analysis presented in the previous chapter showed that, while the will to learn was generally quite strong amongst both students and learners, in most cases the confidence to learn was lacking, often because schools and the broader social environment do not foster its development. Although not specifically mentioned by the research participants, the extremely negative media reporting about the quality of schooling in South Africa, and of the quality of school leaving examination results (commonly known as 'matric') in particular, is likely to further undermine first-year students' confidence in their ability to learn. Examples of recent newspaper headlines include: '2013 Matric Pass Rate: Proof of good education or failing the youth?' (Mail & Guardian 2013); 'SA has worst maths, science education in the world' (News24 2014, 24); 'Employers lament poor matric quality' (eNCA 2014); and 'Why the matric pass rate is not a reliable benchmark of educational quality' (Wilkinson 2014). While the media plays a critically important role in noting issues of educational quality that should be debated in the public domain, we also need to think about what this means to the young people who are completing these qualifications and then moving on to university. Several of the bricks making up the wall faced by many students are likely to be comprised of a lack of confidence to learn at university.

Learners and students who needed to function in a language of learning that was not their home language, or was not a language in which they felt confident, experienced a range of difficulties at university. Relevant examples were shared in the previous two chapters, but it is worth repeating some of them again here. It is also important to recognise how language competence impacts on the confidence to learn. Further complicating the issue of language competence is the fact that the type of language used at university is different from what many students have been used to at home and school. Students described academic language used at university as being of a higher level than they were used to, and some even gave examples of how they could not understand what they were learning even though they were mother tongue speakers. As before, no grammar or spelling corrections have been made when presenting these quotations as the quality of language used also supports the case for positioning language as a personal conversion factor:

> *I think like, especially when you talk about English, if it could be like bigger, broadened it at high school because I think at the end of the day, whatever module you're doing whether it's Medicine or you're doing Biology, at the end of the day if you don't know how the question is asked ___(UNCLEAR) and it's asked in English, if they ask you do this and you can't do it or you do that instead, you see it's gonna screw you over because you don't know what the question is . . . how it's being asked basically so English should be our main thing in high school. Even when we get here we should all do English in our first year . . . the broadened version of English where they ask you where did you get stuff instead of just doing 'this is an adverb . . .'*
>
> *(student focus groups, 2009)*

> *I'm under the impression that South African schools, they really try but once getting into varsity, you find that there's a huge gap. There is a huge. . .I don't lie. Our schools are all great, I was. . .I was in private schools most of my life but getting to varsity you find they'll tell you your English is insufficient and yet you were getting A + and that in high school. And then, even, even the manner in which you have to study – high school, varsity, two different things. You just feel as if you're just out of your depth.*
>
> *(student focus groups, 2009)*

> *A language of education was also challenging course I was not really used to speak English only.*
>
> *(black male first-year student, Natural Sciences, 2010)*

The challenges expressed by students in the quotations above can be juxtaposed with the confidence of the student in the quotation here who had achieved the fertile functioning of language competence and confidence:

> *I think my school really did like groom us for varsity in terms of the English, I had one of the best English teachers and they like caused me to do a whole lot of writing and a whole lot of referencing and that. So that kind of helped cos I didn't really have such a difficult time in terms of, umm, writing essays or building some campaign or something. So it was really easy for me and ja . . .*
>
> *(student focus groups, 2009)*

Given that the majority of young people at high school and those entering university are learning in a language other than their mother tongue, the issue of language competence and confidence requires special attention by both schools and universities. In the capabilities framework for the transition to university that is developed here, like the will and confidence to learn, language competence and confidence has been included as both a capability to be fostered and a personal conversion factor that impacts on the development of other capabilities and ultimately on the achievement of valued educational functionings. As such, this is an area requiring careful and urgent attention by universities in multilingual contexts.

Social conversion factors

Included in the realm of social conversion factors are social institutions (including schools and universities), policies, social norms, family norms, patriarchy, gender roles, power relations, and so on. As such, social conversion factors are aligned to the sociological concept of social structures. Several important social conversion factors emerged during this study. The most striking was the school context within which a learner was located, with the most challenges identified for learners in Afrikaans HSC schools and learners attending township schools. The concept of school context operates at the intersection of socioeconomic background as well as learning cultures within different types of schools. In township schools it was common to find examples of absent and poor quality teachers, general lack of resources and limited subject choices. Across the board, learners at Afrikaans HSC schools reported much lower levels of engagement in effective educational practices, poorer levels of motivation for learning, and fewer opportunities to engage with diversity of ideas and people. For example, when asked how regularly they discussed questions without one clear answer in class, only 16 per cent of learners attending Afrikaans suburban HSC schools reporting doing this often, compared with 33 per cent at English suburban HSC schools, 29 per cent at township schools and 26 per cent at suburban LSC schools. Further, only 20 per cent of learners at Afrikaans suburban HSC schools reported that they often asked questions in class. This is compared with 41 per cent of learners in English suburban HSC schools, 38 per cent of learners in suburban LSC schools and 37 per cent in township schools. Learning to question and engage in academic debate is an important aspect of cognitive readiness for university, so it is likely that these learners will find the transition to an environment in which more critical thinking is needed to be difficult. Learners at township schools report engaging in group work more often than learners at the other school types, with 48 per cent of township school learners reporting that they do this 'often', compared with only 32 per cent at suburban LSC schools, 24 per cent at Afrikaans suburban HSC schools and 35 per cent at English suburban HSC schools.

The high school learner survey also included a series of questions about the extent to which schools placed a strong emphasis on engaged learning activities.

The access and readiness research reviewed in earlier chapters highlighted that ideally schools should place greater emphasis on pedagogic practices that encourage critical thinking, exploration of new ideas, being able to analyse information or ideas in depth, reading and understanding complex materials, and solving real world problems, rather than practices such as preparation for examinations and rote memorisation. Across all of the questions about schools' emphasis on pedagogical practices, learners at Afrikaans medium of instruction schools reported significantly less emphasis on engaged learning. For example, only 20 per cent of learners at Afrikaans suburban HSC schools reported that their school placed 'very much' emphasis on solving real world problems compared with 32 per cent at both township and suburban LSC schools and 27 per cent at English suburban HSC context schools. Even starker were the differences with respect to the emphasis placed on thinking critically. While only 21 per cent of Afrikaans learners reported very much emphasis on critical thinking, this number increased to 37 per cent for English HSC schools, 42 per cent for township schools, and 44 per cent for suburban LSC schools. Similarly, when reporting on the emphasis placed on reading and understanding difficult materials, 22 per cent of Afrikaans suburban HSC learners reported strong emphasis on this by their schools, compared with 33 per cent for English suburban HSC schools, 36 per cent for township schools and 37 per cent for suburban LSC schools. Very similar patterns were seen for the extent of emphasis placed on exploring new ideas and analysing ideas in depth. Thus, high school learners who attend Afrikaans medium of instruction schools appear to have far fewer opportunities to learn to work with and appreciate new and different ideas, something that is given much emphasis at university. As such, Afrikaans learners are less likely to have had sufficient opportunities to develop the capabilities of knowledge and imagination and learning disposition. These quantitative findings were well summed up by a remark made by a first-year student who had attended an Afrikaans suburban HSC school:

> *At school you were very much constrained and you thought in a little box.*
> *(student focus groups, 2009)*

Evidence of fewer opportunities to engage with diverse peers was also evident for learners attending township schools and Afrikaans suburban HSC schools. For example, compared with the 56 per cent of learners at English suburban HSC schools who had often talked to or worked with a learner of a different race or culture, only 29 per cent of learners at township schools had often done so, and even fewer, 26 per cent, at Afrikaans suburban HSC schools. Similarly, while only 6 per cent of learners at English suburban HSC schools at never talked to or worked with a learner of a different race or culture, this percentage jumped to 10 per cent at Afrikaans suburban HSC schools and even higher to 13 per cent at township schools. Thus, high school learners who have attended township or Afrikaans high schools appear to have had much fewer opportunities to positively engage with diversity. When entering university, many of these students find encounters with diverse peers, lecturers and ideas particularly difficult, as was discussed in Chapter 5.

A further way in which school type functions as a conversion factor for young people making the transition to university relates to the quality of teachers typically found at different types of schools. While we should be careful of making sweeping generalisations, on the whole, learners attending township schools have teachers who are not as well qualified as their counterparts in suburban schools (Bloch 2009; Christie 2008). In addition, several examples of teachers using corporal punishment, being drunk at work, or being absent were shared by the learners from township schools. This learning environment creates a barrier to the development of capabilities for the transition to university.

Broader socioeconomic context including life outside of school was also an important social conversion factor for the transition to university. In particular, the influence of socioeconomic context was seen in the comparisons across school types in how learners spend their time outside of the formal school day. The data showed that learners living in township areas (typically amongst the poorest areas in the country) spent significantly more time than learners living in other socioeconomic contexts walking to school, caring for family members and doing chores at home, and significantly less time engaging in educational enrichment activities such as volunteer work, exercise and sport, playing musical instruments and participating in cultural activities. Learners from this poor socioeconomic context generally came from families where parents' level of education was low, and many are or will be first generation university students. The data also showed that learners from lower socioeconomic contexts often lacked supportive social networks that could assist them during the transition. Last, the proxy measure for nutritional status – regularity of eating breakfast – showed that learners in the lower socioeconomic context environments (both township and suburban lower socioeconomic contexts) were less likely to regularly eat breakfast. Although this is a crude measure of nutritional well-being, research has shown the importance of breakfast in the context of educational performance (see for example, Mahoney et al. 2005; Taras 2005).

The final group of social conversion factors that emerged as relevant to the transition to university were those related to gender. Interestingly, gender as a conversion factor appears to operate in somewhat conflicting ways. When considering activities outside of school time, the results showed that girls spent significantly more time than boys doing household chores and taking care of family members. This means that girls tend to have more responsibilities in the home compared to boys, which we would expect to have a negative impact on their educational practices. However, in contrast, the results related to engagement in effective learning activities at school showed that in some areas, most notably academic behaviours, girls tended to be better prepared for university than boys. For example, girls spent more time on educational activities such as writing and doing homework and across several items were more likely than boys to report that their schools placed strong emphasis on active and deep learning activities, including the use of computers for learning.

While it does appear that gender is an important conversion factor operating in varying ways in the home and school contexts, more nuanced analysis of the quantitative data points to important intersectionalities between gender and socioeconomic context, and also sometimes cultural background. While girls spend more time on household chores and caring work than boys within each of the socioeconomic groupings (evidence of gender as a conversion factor), the differences across socioeconomic contexts are far greater. For example, when we look at time spent on chores at home by both gender and socioeconomic context, we find that girls from higher socioeconomic contexts spend less time on chores than boys living in townships do. Girls living in townships spend the most time on chores, with 32 per cent spending more than 6 hours per week on chores, and boys in higher socioeconomic contexts spend the least time doing chores, with only 18 per cent reporting that they spend more than 6 hours on chores. Even starker socioeconomic context differences are evident in time spent caring for family members. While in suburban higher socioeconomic contexts, only 6 per cent and 8 per cent of boys and girls respectively spend more than 6 hours a week on caring tasks, these numbers jump to 10 per cent and 12 per cent for suburban lower socioeconomic contexts and 20 per cent and 21 per cent for boys and girls living in township areas. On average boys reported spending more time working for pay than girls did. We once again find important intersectionalities with socioeconomic context in this instance. While boys and girls in suburban higher socioeconomic contexts spend equally little time working for pay, in township contexts 14 per cent of boys spend 6 hours or more working compared with only 6 per cent for girls. It thus seems that young men living in poor contexts bear a greater burden of earning income for their families than young women do, while young women bear greater responsibility for caring work.

Intersectionality of gender and socioeconomic context was also evident with respect to educational practices, both inside and outside of school. In general, girls spent more time doing homework, reading and studying for school as well as reading for personal enjoyment. With respect to time spent on written homework, learners attending township schools, both girls and boys, spent relatively less time on this activity than learners across the other school types. Only 18 per cent of township-based girls and boys reported that they spent six hours or more doing written homework per week. Learners attending HSC schools spent the most time doing homework. Girls within this school type reported spending more time on homework than boys, but the differences were small. At suburban LSC schools, gender appeared to have a greater effect with boys from these schools spending about the same time doing homework as boys from township schools. In contrast, girls at suburban LSC schools spent about the same time as learners from HSC schools. Thus, outside of the school day, we also see evidence of the complex interaction between responsibilities such as working for pay and caring for family members and time spent doing school work. This is likely to be further complicated by the time spent travelling or walking to school for learners attending township schools and suburban LSC schools.

Slightly larger numbers of girls than boys reported that their teachers encouraged them to engage in classroom discussions across all socioeconomic contexts. The difference was largest (although still small) for learners at suburban LSC schools. There were no gender differences in responses regarding opportunities to be creative in the classroom for learners at township schools and suburban LSC schools. However, girls at both English and Afrikaans HSC schools reported more opportunities for creativity than boys did. Across all types of schools, except for Afrikaans schools, boys tended to ask questions in class more often than girls did. In each case the gender difference was very small, except in township schools where boys reporting asking questions in class much more often than the girls did. Boys attending Afrikaans schools were the least likely of all learners to often ask questions in class. Similarly, fewer boys attending Afrikaans schools compared to all other learners reported that learning was important to them. Overall, fewer learners at Afrikaans schools liked discussions where there was no one clear answer, compared to all other school types. However, there was also a large gender difference in response to this item, at Afrikaans schools only, where 47 per cent of boys, compared with 67 per cent of girls, liked complex discussions. This can be compared to 83 per cent of boys and 82 per cent of girls at township schools who like to engage in complex discussions. The same trend was evident with respect to enjoyment of solving difficult problems. Afrikaans boys at HSC schools were less likely to agree that they liked to work on difficult problems. These findings remind us that, although socioeconomic context has a critical impact on young people's opportunities to learn as well as their broader well-being, this impact does not occur in isolation. The intersectionality of socioeconomic context with gender and culture are important parts of the story.

Environmental conversion factors

Factors related to geographical locations and climate conditions are examples of environmental conversion factors. Environmental conversion factors were of less significance than social conversion factors, since the geographical area in which the research was located is not unduly affected by harsh climatic events, such as flooding for example. Nonetheless, the results did point to the impact of geographical location, in particular, living on campus as opposed to commuting, had on the lives of students. In most cases, students who had a place in university residence reported better support systems and an easier process of forming friendships and social networks. However, living in residence could also sometimes create a barrier to success, in particular due to the greater time pressures and tiredness as a result of the many compulsory first year activities for residence students. Geographic location also had an effect on the high school learners' lives in various ways. For example living and attending school in a township meant spending more time than other learners walking to school. The phenomenon of many learners living in townships but travelling long distances to attend better resourced suburban lower socioeconomic context schools was also noted, with these learners spending a significant amount of time each day in taxis.

Capabilities framework for the transition to university

This complex mix of conversion factors, and the intersectionality of gender, socioeconomic context and school cultures, helps us to understand the diversity of bricks that are making up the brick wall limiting access and success. It also highlights the intricate manner in which the bricks are held together, both within and outside of educational institutions. Such an understanding potentially provides a foundation from which we can begin to formulate strategies and interventions to bring the wall down. The analysis of conversion factors has pointed to the complex intersectionality of socioeconomic contexts, learning cultures in schools, gender, and broader personal and cultural influences, such as home language for example. Although not a major focus in this chapter, Chapter 5 documented the ways in which learning cultures at university also play a role in the transition and performance in the first year. In bringing together the various threads of the argument for a capabilities-based social justice understanding of the transition to university, it is helpful to return to the stylised representation of a capabilities framework shown in Figure 4.1. Drawing on the voices of learners and students, it is now possible to concretise and make practical the stylised framework in order to map out the various aspects that must be considered, and tackled, in order to work towards more socially just approaches to the transition experience. Figure 7.1 brings together the empirical research presented in Chapters 4, 5 and 6, with the broader literature on access to university, and so presents an overarching framework in which a capabilities-based social justice approach for the transition is conceptualised. The overall outcome of a successful transition is the achievement of educational resilience, here defined as students who have (1) navigated the transition to university within their own life context; (2) been able to negotiate risks they faced, have shown perseverance academically, and have been responsive to opportunities; and (3) have clear aspirations and hopes for a successful university career. While it is important to recognise all the complexities inherent in the transition to university, in order to facilitate action for change, we also need to identify the points at which universities and schools can intervene together with those aspects that, although important to consider as researchers, fall outside of the realm of influence of educational institutions. Possible points of intervention for both schools and universities are highlighted in Figure 7.1 using bold and underlined text. How this framework can be applied in practice for schools and universities is the focus of the final chapter.

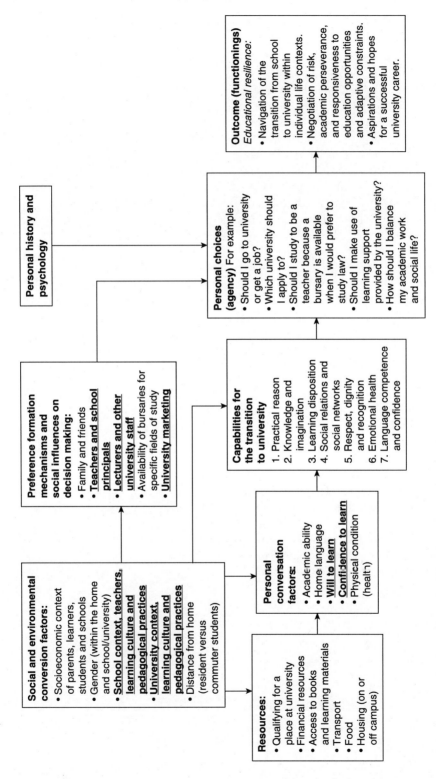

Figure 7.1 Capabilities-based social justice framework for the transition from school to university

Personal history and psychology

Social and environmental conversion factors:
- Socioeconomic context of parents, learners, students and schools
- Gender (within the home and school/university)
- **School context, teachers, learning culture and pedagogical practices**
- **University context, learning culture and pedagogical practices**
- Distance from home (resident versus commuter students)

Preference formation mechanisms and social influences on decision making:
- Family and friends
- **Teachers and school principals**
- **Lecturers and other university staff**
- Availability of bursaries for specific fields of study
- **University marketing**

Resources:
- Qualifying for a place at university
- Financial resources
- Access to books and learning materials
- Transport
- Food
- Housing (on or off campus)

Personal conversation factors:
- Academic ability
- Home language
- **Will to learn**
- **Confidence to learn**
- Physical condition (health)

Capabilities for the transition to university
1. Practical reason
2. Knowledge and imagination
3. Learning disposition
4. Social relations and social networks
5. Respect, dignity and recognition
6. Emotional health
7. Language competence and confidence

Personal choices (agency) For example:
- Should I go to university or get a job?
- Which university should I apply to?
- Should I study to be a teacher because a bursary is available when I would prefer to study law?
- Should I make use of learning support provided by the university?
- How should I balance my academic work and social life?

Outcome (functionings)
Educational resilience:
- Navigation of the transition from school to university within individual life contexts.
- Negotiation of risk, academic perseverance, and responsiveness to education opportunities and adaptive constraints.
- Aspirations and hopes for a successful university career.

References

Bloch, G. 2009. *The Toxic Mix: What's Wrong with South Africa's Schools and How to Fix It*. Cape Town: Tafelberg.

Christie, P. 2008. *Opening the Doors of Learning. Changing Schools in South Africa*. Johannesburg: Heinemann Publishers.

eNCA. 2014. 'Employers Lament Poor Matric Quality.' http://www.enca.com/south-africa/employers-lament-poor-matric-quality

Mahoney, C R, H A Taylor, R B Kanarek and P Samuel. 2005. 'Effect of Breakfast Composition on Cognitive Processes in Elementary School Children.' *Physiology and Behaviour* 85 (7): 635–645.

Mail & Guardian. 2013. '2013 Matric Pass Rate: Proof of Good Education or Failing the Youth?' *The M&G Online*. http://mg.co.za/article/2014-01-07-2014-matric-pass-rate-proof-of-good-education-or-failing-the-youth/

Mann, S. 2008. *Study, Power and the University*. Berkshire, England: Open University Press.

News24. 2014. 'SA Has Worst Maths, Science Education in World.' *News24*. http://www.news24.com/SouthAfrica/News/SA-has-worst-maths-science-education-in-world-20140602

Robeyns, I. 2005. 'The Capability Approach: a Theoretical Survey.' *Journal of Human Development* 6 (1): 93–114.

Sen, A. 1980. *Equality of What? The Tanner Lecture on Human Values*. California: Stanford University.

———. 1999. *Development as Freedom*. Oxford: Oxford University Press.

Taras, H. 2005. 'Nutrition and Student Performance at School.' *Journal of School Health* 75 (6): 199–213.

Walker, M. 2005. 'Amartya Sen's Capability Approach and Education.' *Educational Action Research* 13 (1): 103–110.

Wilkinson, Kate. 2014. 'Why the Matric Pass Rate Is Not a Reliable Benchmark of Education Quality.' *Africa Check*. http://africacheck.org/reports/why-the-matric-pass-rate-is-not-a-reliable-benchmark-of-quality-education/

8 University access for success

The way things are does not determine the way they ought to be.

(Sandel 2010, 165)

Starting with the juxtaposition of two students' strikingly different experiences of coming to university, one of the central threads running through this book has been that of the extent and complexity of injustices at play within schools and universities. This injustice can be metaphorically visualised as the wall against which the student in Drawing 1.2 was pushing and which was blocking his view and chances of success. An overarching ideology of meritocracy currently underpins most approaches to access, particularly given the strong neoliberal agenda operating globally at this time. It was argued earlier that this becomes a site through which injustices, particularly deficit understandings of certain groupings of students, operate. Another important thread was related to the complexity of university readiness which, following Conley, should be seen a multidimensional construct. A failure to adequately take account of this complexity in the way in which university admissions as well as access initiatives are conceived, implemented and measured adds further layers of injustice. However, as Sandel (2010, 165) states in the quotation earlier, 'the way things are does not determine the way they ought to be'. The brick walls of injustice need not remain, and the capabilities-based social justice framework developed here provides a means of better understanding why the brick wall exists in the first place, and then provides ideas for how we might begin to break it down.

Since readers may have engaged with the book in different ways, focusing on the chapters of most relevance to their own needs, I start this concluding chapter with a quick summary of the main argument. My starting point was the observation that, despite the progressive post-apartheid higher education policy context and the significant gains that have been made in broadening access, the South African higher education environment remains plagued by a host of injustices. Similar injustices and inequalities in the global context were also noted, even though the particular historical trajectory might be different. The more specific focus has been on accessing university and the fact that increased and broadened access, in many instances, does not lead to success for large numbers of students, and may indeed be creating new forms of injustices. I argued upfront that much of the research on access to university has tended to focus on either schooling or the first year at university, but seldom both.

Using one South African university and a group of 20 local schools as my case study, I have sought to understand the transition from school to university from the perspective of high school learners and first-year university students. Drawing on Sen, I argued that many of the injustices inherent to the transition to university are remediable and thus we have a responsibility to work towards their elimination. The study was firmly rooted within a social justice agenda and I argued that the capabilities approach provides a particularly rich and generative theoretical starting point and normative framework for exploring the transition to university from a social justice perspective. In Chapter 3 the key tenets of the capabilities approach were introduced, followed by a review of how the approach has been applied in (higher) education settings in Chapter 4. While I do not wish to repeat the details, it is useful to briefly restate the main ideas from the capabilities approach, as they highlight why the approach helps us to think differently about access.

The capabilities approach takes as the starting point the well-being of individuals and asks about the extent to which people are able to be and do what they have reason to value being and doing. This can be contrasted with commonly used access statistics that count enrolment numbers of students from different demographic groupings to create statistics that can be used to track access related changes. Although an important part of the bigger picture, these statistics do not tell us anything about students' well-being. Capabilities refer to opportunity freedoms, or the freedom an individual has to enjoy the functionings (outcomes/achievements) necessary for their well-being. When we consider issues of justice or injustice, we cannot merely ask whether different people have achieved the same outcome, but rather, whether different people have had the same opportunities to achieve the outcome. The particular importance of this for understanding educational inequalities was shown with the example of Judy and Bernita in Chapter 3. Individual agency is central, together with notions of freedom and choice. However, agency is not given primacy to the extent to which social structures, institutions and contexts are insufficiently accounted for. I argued in Chapter 4 that it is the manner in which the capabilities approach foregrounds agency together with the interaction of agents and social contexts that I find particularly useful for my work. The conceptual device used within the capabilities approach for bringing structure and agency together is the notion of conversion factors.

Personal, social and environmental conversion factors impact on the extent to which a given individual is able to make use of available resources to create capabilities and functionings. As such, the capabilities approach emphasises agency and choice, but also draws our attention to the fact that the opportunity freedoms (capabilities) of individuals/agents are qualified and constrained or supported by social arrangements. My focus has thus been on understanding the agency of both high school learners and first-year university students, together with the social and institutional conditions of possibility that might either enable or constrain their capabilities for making a successful transition to university. To do this it was necessary to identify the capabilities that are needed when making the transition from school to university. Identifying these capabilities involved a two stage process carried out according to the five criteria for developing a capabilities list specified by Robeyns (2003). The first stage was theoretical in which an ideal-theoretical capabilities list (see Table 4.1) was proposed, drawing on Walker's (2006) higher education capabilities list and integrating the theory and research on access to university that was reviewed in Chapter 2. This ideal-theoretical list of nine capabilities was then subjected to 'deliberation' on the basis of the empirical data – voices of learners and students – in order to propose what I have called a pragmatic capabilities list for the transition to university (see Table 6.2). The pragmatic list consists of seven capabilities that should be fostered in the interest of promoting a more socially just approach to university access that takes the achievement of educational resilience as a measure of success (rather than enrolment statistics). Bringing together the capabilities list and enabling and constraining conditions that operate in the space of the transition to university, Chapter 7 ended with a visualisation of what a capabilities-based social justice framework for the transition to university might look like. In this final chapter the potential implications of this framework are explored with a focus on points of intervention.

Confronting injustice – towards interventions

In the introductory chapter I included a short section reflecting on my personal positioning as researcher. I noted, as the inspiration for this research, that I was committed to the cause of students entering university often with little chance of success given the schooling contexts from which they come, and the university environment in which they find themselves. This book, and my own journey, would not be complete without some consideration of possible ways that these injustices might be remedied. Nonetheless, the analysis and findings highlight the complexity of the transition to university and should serve as a warning that there are unlikely to be any quick fix solutions. Instead, a comprehensive and long term approach is needed, rooted in a commitment to improve the transition to university in a manner that impacts positively on the well-being of students first and foremost, with measurable access gains being of secondary importance. I believe that rooting such efforts in a capabilities-based framework provides a helpful starting point and ensures that student well-being is placed centrally, that students are recognised as individuals and are seen as inherently valuable in their own right.

While the capabilities-based social justice framework presented in Figure 7.1 pointed to various factors that impact on the transition experience, many remain outside the realm of influence of universities and schools, and hence cannot be a site of productive intervention for these educational institutions. This does not mean that injustices operating outside of school and university realms of influence should be ignored. Indeed, I would argue that it is the responsibility of higher education scholars and researchers to make such injustices known and to take the impact thereof into account. However, for pragmatic reasons, it is necessary to concentrate, at least initially, on the areas in which interventions would be most likely to lead to change. This is in line with Sen's call to focus on the remediable injustices we see around us, even if we are not yet clear on what complete justice would look like or how it would be achieved (Sen 2009). Sen's argument applies well to universities, which as was noted in Chapter 2 occupy an ambiguous space with respect to social justice. While higher education creates opportunities for those who are able to access it and can serve public good purposes, it remains elitist, with places limited and graduates commonly granted privileged status in society. Although we cannot neatly resolve this dilemma, we can still identify particular injustices operating within and through higher education. In terms of the metaphor of the brick wall standing between students and their success at university, while we may not be able to knock down the entire wall at one go, we can certainly start to identify which bricks can most easily be removed.

Drawing on the arguments and data that have been covered in this book, it seems prudent to consider the following points of intervention as possible priority areas (or bricks in the wall) for action within both schools and universities. First, there are social and environmental conversion factors at both schools and universities. This includes the learning cultures and activities in schools and universities. Second, personal conversion factors, in particular fostering the will to learn and helping learners and students to develop the confidence to learn as well as language competence and confidence are also important. Third, various social influences on learners' and students' decision making (preference formation mechanisms) can be addressed. Falling into this category are the actions of school teachers and principals, actions of university lecturers and other staff; and approaches to university marketing.

What could universities do differently?

The starting point is for universities to embrace the more comprehensive understanding of access and readiness presented here, taking into account the seven capabilities identified as important for the transition to university together with the effects of conversion factors. This approach to the transition takes account of the complexities of university readiness as a multidimensional construct together with the need to ensure epistemological rather than only physical access for students entering the university system. Further, readiness is located within the complex personal, social, economic and educational environments in which it is developed. The voices of students provided ample evidence of the fear and confusion experienced by many in relation to the unknown physical space of the university and, perhaps more importantly, the unknown rules of the university system (university knowledge). This is particularly so for first generation students who do not have support networks that assist them to make sense of their new environment. The lack of university knowledge that emerged from the student and learner data, as well as the difficulties experienced by learners and students in developing the capability of practical reason (making informed choices about study and career options) highlights the immense value that an educationally intentional approach to university marketing could have as a significant social influence on learners' decision making. Against the neoliberal trend of seeing students as clients to whom the university sells a service, it is critical for universities to recognise that the marketing of a university is substantively different from marketing in a commercial sense. This is particularly important if the purpose of the university is understood from a public good perspective, emphasising the intrinsic value of education in the building of just societies, rather than as simply the production of human capital to serve economic advancement – although this purpose will always remain relevant. Rather than interacting with schools in an effort to 'sell' the university and increase the number of applications received, marketing efforts should focus on building university knowledge amongst high school learners and providing advice and support that enable learners to make well-reasoned, informed, critical, independent and reflective choices about post-school study and career options (i.e. foster the capability of practical reason). One way that this could be facilitated is through the development of well-defined, long term partnerships with schools from which students at a given university are regularly recruited. In this way, schools and universities can work together to build the capabilities for the transition to university.

Within the university environment, intentional measures need to be identified at the levels of student support, pedagogy and curriculum to ensure that first-year students are provided with the tools to access and understand the unspoken 'rules' of the university, understand and interrogate the key knowledge structures of their disciplines (key content knowledge), and be afforded safe spaces to develop language competence and confidence. The fact that so many first-year students reported difficulties in relation to learning dispositions and academic behaviours, in particular study skills and learning to function independently, highlights the need for a much greater focus on student support initiatives, academic advice and mentoring during the transition phase. While the case study university, like many others in South Africa and beyond, does provide a range of academic support services, in few cases is this support really integrated into the core functioning of the university such that it is not seen as an add on for 'at risk' students. Pedagogic approaches facilitating the development of academic behaviours that can be integrated into the core teaching and learning project of the university so that students have an opportunity to learn and build these skills in meaningful and authentic academic contexts are thus needed. This has the potential to impact on students' will and confidence to learn – two important personal conversion factors that are currently limiting the progress of many students. Related is the need to challenge and subvert the growing acceptance of mediocrity that emerged among both students and lecturers in this research. While it appears that young people have a strong will to learn, in many instances this did not translate into the confidence to learn. The relatively shallow emphasis on complex ideas and meaningful engagement at high school is also likely to be undermining the confidence to learn among students.

Putting these ideas into practice

How might we begin to put these ideas into practice within our universities? An initial, very modest, concrete example is shared here. After listening to a seminar about this research and the capabilities for a successful transition to university, colleagues in the Social Work department approached me to begin exploring ways in which we might share these ideas with first-year students. We decided to begin with an afternoon workshop with first-year students during the first two weeks of the new academic year. The workshop was called: 'Facilitating the transition to university: Capabilities for success'. Following initial introductions and a short presentation on the seven transition to university capabilities, each of the 23 students participating in the workshop was asked to complete a form in which they assessed the extent of their own development of each of the capabilities at this stage of the transition – so identifying their personal strengths as well as areas in which additional work or support might be needed. This individual exercise was followed by group discussions during which students reflected on the seven capabilities with their peers and debated the relevance and importance of each as well as which capabilities they felt they needed to work on most. Each group then did a short report back to the large group. Discussions were lively and students appeared to find the process of deliberating the capabilities enriching. The substance and depth of the discussions and report backs was also impressive. The analysis of the group report backs as well as the individual level data collected through the individual exercise showed that all seven capabilities were regarded as important, but priorities differed somewhat from student to student. These individual differences in terms of capability realisation and prioritisation provide support for the foundational assumption within the capabilities approach – that of individual heterogeneity. Based on the individual student responses, students recorded the lowest levels of realisation of the capability for emotional health, followed by knowledge and imagination. Based on the group report backs and group prioritisation exercise, the capability for learning disposition emerged as a particular priority for further support and development.

In addition to providing an opportunity for deliberation on the value of the capabilities included in the capabilities list for the transition to university and hence further verification thereof, the workshop also seemed to be helpful for the students in making sense of their own transition experiences. The value of discussions of this nature for the students was highlighted in the responses that students gave when evaluating the workshop. One of the questions posed on the evaluation form was: 'The most useful thing I learnt today was . . .' Students provided insightful responses, demonstrating how thinking about transition capabilities helped them to position themselves within the transition process:

> We all think differently and find things particularly strange, but exciting to be here at varsity.

> That we have so much to learn and that everything impacts on everything.

Things are not as obvious as they seem.

You need to think critically and ask why sometimes.

That these sessions truly help you to understand why we do what we do at university.

Further, almost all the students reported that they would recommend the workshop to their peers, and supporting statements were made in the open comments section of the workshop evaluation:

This workshop must be compulsory for all first years enrolling at the university.

Thank you for your time, I surely hope that workshops such as these will be held more often.

It is too soon to assess the extent to which students drew on their reflections on their transition to university capabilities during the rest of their first year. However, further research will be conducted to track these 23 students and to explore with them if and how knowledge of the transition capabilities helped them to negotiate their first year.

What could universities and schools do in partnership?

In addition to the work that universities themselves need to engage in to become better ready to welcome the diversity of students entering in the first year, it is also critical for schools and universities to work together in facilitating the transition. School and university partnership initiatives are not new, although in many cases the focus tends to be on partnerships for pre-service teaching education rather than the transition to university more specifically (Briggs et al. 2012; Gazeley and Aynsley 2012; Harkavy et al. 2013; Hoffman et al. 2008; Iver and Farley 2005; Lawson 2013; Mutemeri and Chetty 2011). The dual enrolment programmes, as well as the Advanced Placement courses that are common in the US, were discussed in Chapter 2 and provide further examples of a form of partnership between school and university, in this case with a clearer emphasis on the transition to university.

Drawing on the research that has been documented in this book, I propose that the capabilities framework for the transition to university provides a productive new entry point for formulating such partnerships. Since the capabilities approach asks what is needed to foster the development of capabilities so as to create meaningful opportunities for learners, the starting point of school-university partnerships would be quite different from typical interventions, many of which are based on deficit understandings such as low aspirations for university, for example. The capabilities approach, and the seven capabilities in the transition to university list, provides a new language for thinking and talking about university readiness, and this, hopefully, will create a space for thinking in new ways about what is needed at the high school level. This study has highlighted the complex and messy interface between school and university as well as the central role that socio-economic context plays. This implies that the nature and focus of partnership interventions with different types of schools is likely to vary depending on the particular strengths and weaknesses of the schools, the partner university and the broader social contexts in which they both function. More practically, the capabilities list could be used as a conceptual tool to guide participatory planning processes (as is emphasised in the capabilities approach) with schools through which specific opportunities and conversion factors faced by learners in the schools are identified. In particular, deliberations would need to explore in detail which capabilities require particular attention for learners at a given school, taking account of different life contexts. Identifying specific conversion factors – both fertile functionings and corrosive disadvantages – that operate within a given school context would help to guide intervention planning. The involvement of learners, as well as teachers and school management in the partnership planning processes from the outset is essential to ensure that the agency of all relevant actors is acknowledged and celebrated as central to the success of partnership initiatives.

Thinking through approaches to university-school partnership possibilities in the South African context specifically must be done against the backdrop of the many difficulties currently being experienced in the schooling sector. It is widely recognised that without major changes and improvements at all levels of the poorly functioning public school system, many learners will exit school without being ready for university and the gap between eligibility and readiness is likely to widen. Hence South African universities need to focus particular attention on what they need to do differently to improve their readiness for the types of learners exiting the school system and for the growing diversity of the student body. Detailed understandings of teaching and learning practices at the school level are essential for universities who wish to understand readiness of students in a contextually relevant and multidimensional way that looks beyond performance in the final school examinations. Forging meaningful, long term partnerships with schools that are typically feeders for the university could provide a basis for understanding student readiness more thoroughly, as well as a platform through which a university and its partner schools could actively seek to improve readiness. The results of this research have indicated a host of areas that could be the focus of such partnerships. Some examples including building stronger learning cultures within schools that include much greater emphasis on written work, integration of ideas and meaningful feedback from teachers; and a clear focus on building in-depth knowledge of key content areas – for teachers and learners. In addition, much greater and more careful attention should be paid to subject choices and the implications that different subject choices have for future study opportunities. Also important are preparation activities that 'offer potential students a real taste of university life' (Briggs et al. 2012, 8); in other words, activities that help to build university knowledge. This is particularly relevant for universities that attract a large body of students who are the first in their families, from their school or community to attend university and thus have little broader support when making the transition.

By way of conclusion: Changing the way we think and talk about access

Perhaps one of the most valuable contributions that the capabilities approach brings to the study of university access and transitions is that it provides us with a new language (Deneulin 2014) for thinking and talking about access and the transition to university. The focus of the capabilities approach on the normative aim of building just societies in which all people have the opportunity to live a flourishing life implies an inherently positive agenda for change. This language can thus help us to move beyond the more common deficit languages in which we refer to the underprepared, at risk and so on. Instead, we can approach issues of university access by exploring who has had the opportunity to develop the seven transition to university capabilities and who has not. We can ask about the conditions – at personal, social, institutional, economic and political levels – that should be in place to enable the development of transition to university capabilities. By focusing on enabling and constraining conditions (conversion factors), the focus shifts quite decisively away from a deficit understanding of the individual student to an analysis of the broader conditions most conducive to fostering well-being and success for diverse students.

A central assumption of the capabilities approach is the recognition and valuing of individual heterogeneity or diversity. Although the focus on the individual within the capabilities approach has been criticised (Carpenter 2009; Dean 2009), my data, as well as many other studies about the first year at university, highlight the importance students accord to being treated as an individual and not only as a member of the student body, or as some students described it being 'just a number'. It was precisely this tendency not to focus on the individual within the domain of access practice, research and statistics measuring access gains that I argued at the start was serving to mask injustices experienced by high school learners and first-year university students during the transition process. With a clear prioritisation of individual well-being and agency, the capabilities approach helps us to overcome this difficulty. The notion of capabilities, and the idea that all high school learners and first-year students should have the opportunity to develop these capabilities – taking into account the personal, social and environmental conversion factors identified – would require that schools and universities put in place integrated support mechanisms. This support should be available to all students, not only those identified as at risk. Students could make use of these support mechanisms, as needed, to foster their realisation of the transition to university capabilities. The starting point would be to identify ways of raising awareness among high school learners and first-year students (as was done on a small scale with the social work students) of the capabilities underpinning a successful transition so that students would be in a position to identify their own strengths and areas needing development. Further, schools and universities, using the capabilities framework proposed here as a starting point, can identify the specific enabling and constraining factors operating within their own contexts, and then use this understanding to work towards creating more enabling environments for their learners and students. Perhaps then we can start moving towards 'the way things ought to be' by breaking down the limiting brick walls, even if only one brick at a time.

References

Briggs, A.R.J., J. Clark and I. Hall. 2012. 'Building Bridges: Understanding Student Transition to University.' *Quality in Higher Education* 18 (1): 3–21. doi:10.1080/13538322. 2011.614468.

Carpenter, Mick. 2009. 'The Capabilities Approach and Critical Social Policy: Lessons from the Majority World?' *Critical Social Policy* 29 (3): 351–373. doi:10.1177/ 0261018309105175.

Dean, Hartley. 2009. 'Critiquing Capabilities: The Distractions of a Beguiling Concept.' *Critical Social Policy* 29 (2): 261–278. doi:10.1177/0261018308101629.

Deneulin, S. 2014. *Wellbeing, Justice and Development Ethics*. Routledge Human Development and Capability Debates Series. Abingdon: Routledge.

Gazeley, L and S Aynsley. 2012. *The Contribution of Pre-entry Interventions to Student Retention and Success. A Literature Synthesis of the Widening Access and Student Retention and Success National Programmes Archive*. York: Higher Education Academy. http://www.heacademy.ac.uk/ assets/documents/WP_syntheses/WASRS_Gazeley.pdf

Harkavy, Ira, Matthew Hartley, Rita Axelroth Hodges and Joann Weeks. 2013. 'The Promise of University-Assisted Community Schools to Transform American Schooling: A Report From the Field, 1985–2012.' *Peabody Journal of Education* 88 (5): 525–540. doi:10.1080/0161956X.2013.834789.

Hoffman, N, J Vargas and J Santos. 2008. 'Blending High School and College.' *New Directions for Higher Education* Winter (144): 15–25.

Iver, Martha Abele Mac, and Elizabeth Farley. 2005. 'Preparing Urban Students for Health Careers A Longitudinal Study of a University-High School Partnership.' *Urban Education* 40 (2): 190–222. doi:10.1177/0042085904272750.

Lawson, Hal A. 2013. 'Third-Generation Partnerships for P-16 Pipelines and Cradle-Through-Career Education Systems.' *Peabody Journal of Education* 88 (5): 637–656. doi:1 0.1080/0161956X.2013.835187.

Mutemeri, Judith and Rajendra Chetty. 2011. 'An Examination of University-school Partnerships in South Africa.' *South African Journal of Education* 31 (4): 505–517.

Sandel, M J. 2010. *Justice. What's the Right Thing to Do?* New York: Penguin Group.

Sen, A. 2009. *The Idea of Justice*. Cambridge, Massachusetts: Harvard University Press.

Index